Auto Industries of Europe, U.S. and Japan

Auto Industries of Europe, U.S. and Japan

by
Richard Phillips, Arthur Way,
A.T. Lowry, Scott Laing, *et al.*

Abt Books
Cambridge, Massachusetts
EIU Special Series 3

338.476292
P56a

Library of Congress Cataloging in Publication Data

Phillips, Richard.
  Auto industries of Europe, U.S., and Japan to 1990.

  (Economist Intelligence Unit special series)
  "Economist Intelligence Unit Ltd."
  1. Automobile industry and trade—Forecasting. I. Way, Arthur. II.
Economist Intelligence Unit Limited. III. Title. IV. Title: Auto industries of
Europe, US, and Japan to 1990. V. Series.
  HD9710.A2P47   1982   338.4'76292   82–13856
  ISBN 0–89011–584–2

Originally published by The Economist Intelligence
Unit as Special Report Nos. 77, 118 and *Motor
Business* No. 107.

© Abt Associates Inc., 1982

Printed in the United States of America

The Authors

Richard Phillips has held a number of positions within the automotive industry, both in the components and vehicle producing sectors. During the course of his work he has traveled extensively in Europe, North America and Japan.

Arthur Way is the Industrial Editor of the Economist Intelligence Unit and responsible for <u>Motor</u> <u>Business</u>, the EIU's quarterly research bulletin on the worldwide automotive industry. He has traveled throughout Europe and North America on automotive research.

A. T. Lowry is a director of M M Corporate Services Ltd, based in London, and specializes in financial and market research. He has traveled widely in North America and the Far East on business, and worked in Japan for two years.

Scott Laing, based in New York, has extensive experience in researching the North American automotive sector. He is the main contributor to the EIU's automotive research bulletin motor business on North American affairs.

Contents

Preface

Part 1: The West European Automotive Industry

Page 3 The Structure and Growth of the West European Automotive Industry: Country Analysis

24 The Companies: Background

88 The Outlook for the 1980s: Structural Developments and Key Issues

94 Production and Sales Forecasts

112 Prospects for the Principal Vehicle Manufacturers

132 Overall Conclusions: Fortune or Failure?

Part 2: Financial Assessment of the U.S. Automotive Industry

136 Background to the U.S. Automotive Industry

170 Current Issues

181 Financial Profiles of the Principal Companies

181 General Motors Corporation

217 Chrysler Corporation

237 American Motors Corporation

251 Volkswagen of America Incorporated

265 Mack Trucks Incorporated

269 Paccar Incorporated

276 Comparative Financial Analysis

300 Conclusions

Part 3: Short Term Prospects for the Japanese Motor Industry

305 Introduction

306 Passenger Cars

313 Commercial Vehicles

List of Tables

Part 1: The West European Automotive Industry

PAGE

5   1.   West European Passenger Car
Production by Major Producing Country, 1970-79

6   2.   West European Commercial Vehicle
Production by Major Producing Country, 1970-79

7   3.   West German Passenger Car
Production by Manufacturer, 1970-79

7   4.   West German Passenger Car
Production by Engine Size, 1970-79

8   5.   West German Commercial Vehicle
Production by Manufacturer, 1970-79

8   6.   West German Commercial
Vehicle Production by Type, 1970-79

9   7.   French Passenger Car
Production by Manufacturer, 1970-79

10   8.   French Passenger Car
Production by Engine Size, 1970-79

11   9.   French Commercial Vehicle
Production by Manufacturer, 1970-79

12   10.   French Commercial Vehicle Production by Type, 1970-79

13   11.   UK Passenger Car Production by Manufacturer, 1970-79

13   12.   UK Passenger Car Production by Engine Size, 1970-79

14   13.   UK Commercial Vehicle Production by Manufacturer, 1970-79

14   14.   UK Commercial Vehicle Production by Type, 1970-79

15   15.   Italian Passenger Car Production by Manufacturer, 1970-79

15   16.   Italian Passenger Car Production by Engine Size, 1970-79

16   17.   Italian Commercial Vehicle
Production by Manufacturer, 1970-79

17   18.   Italian Commercial Vehicle Production by Type, 1970-79

18   19.   Spanish Passenger Car Production by Manufacturer, 1970-79

19   20.   Spanish Commercial Vehicle
Production by Manufacturer, 1970-79

20   21.   Swedish Passenger Car
Production by Manufacturer, 1970-79

20   22.   Swedish Commercial Vehicle
Production by Manufacturer, 1970-79

22   23.   Development of Passenger Car
Demand in Western Europe by Country, 1970-79

23   24.   Development of Commercial Vehicle
Demand in Western Europe by Country, 1970-79

25   25.   The Principal Vehicle Manufacturers of Western Europe

29   26.   Development of Peugeot's Vehicle Production, 1970-79

30   27.   Development of Citroen's Vehicle Production, 1970-79

30   28.   Development of Talbot's
French Vehicle Production, 1970-79

31   29.   Development of Citroen's
Spanish Vehicle Production, 1970-79

32   30.   Development of Talbot's UK Vehicle Production, 1970-79

32   31.   Development of Talbot's
Spanish Vehicle Production, 1970-79

34   32.   Development of Renault's Vehicle Production, 1970-79

35   33.   Development of Fasa
Renault's Vehicle Production, 1970-79

35   34.   Development of Saviem's
Commercial Vehicle Production, 1970-79

36   35.   Development of Berliet's
Commercial Vehicle Production, 1970-79

38   36.   Development of Volkswagen's Vehicle Production, 1970-79

38   37.   Development of Audi
NSU's Passenger Car Production, 1970-79

41   38.   Development of Fiat's Vehicle Production, 1970-79

41   39.   Development of Seat's Vehicle Production, 1970-79

42   40.   Development of Autobianchi's
Passenger Car Production, 1970-79

42   41.   Development of Lancia's
Passenger Car Production, 1970-79

43   42.   Development of Magirus Deutz's
Commercial Vehicle Production, 1970-79

43   43.   Development of Unic Fiat's
Commercial Vehicle Production, 1970-79

44   44.   Development of OM's
Commercial Vehicle Production, 1970-79

46   45.   Development of Ford's UK Vehicle Production, 1970-79

46   46.   Development of Ford's West
German Passenger Car Production, 1970-79

47   47.   Development of Ford's
Spanish Vehicle Production, 1976-79

49   48.   Development of Opel's Vehicle Production, 1970-79

49   49.   Development of Vauxhall's Vehicle Production, 1970-79

52   50.   Development of BL's Vehicle Production, 1970-79

54   51.   Development of Daimier-Benz's Vehicle Production, 1970-79

56   52.   Development of Volvo's Vehicle Production, 1970-79

56   53.   Development of Volvo Car BV's
Passenger Car Production, 1970-79

58   54.   Development of BMW's Passenger Car Production, 1970-79

59   55.   Development of Alfa Romeo's Vehicle Production, 1970-79

60   56.   Development of Saab Scania's Vehicle Production, 1970-79

61   57.   Development of Innocenti's Passenger Car Production, 1970-79

62   58.   Development of Porsche's Passenger Car Production, 1970-79

63   59.   Development of Motor Iberica's
                Commercial Vehicle Production, 1970-79

64   60.   Development of MAN's
                Commercial Vehicle Production, 1970-79

65   61.   Development of Talbot Matra's
                Passenger Car Production, 1970-79

66   62.   Development of Enasa's
                Commercial Vehicle Production, 1970-79

66   63.   Development of DAF Truck's
                Commercial Vehicle Production, 1970-79

79   64.   Forecasts of Economic Growth
                in Western Europe by Country, 1979 & 1980

82   65.   Forecasts of Passenger Car
                Demand in Western Europe by Country, 1980, 1981 & 1985

83   66.   Western Europe's Net
                Exports of Passenger Cars, 1970-85

86   67.   Forecasts of West European Passenger Car
                Production by Major Producing Country, 1980, 1981 & 1985

87   68.   Forecasts of Commercial Vehicle
                Demand in Western Europe by Country, 1980, 1981 & 1985

88   69.   Western Europe's Net
                Exports of Commercial Vehicles, 1970-85

91   70.   Forecasts of West European Commercial Vehicle
                Production by Major Producing Country, 1980, 1981 & 1985

92   71.   Forecasts of UK Commercial
                Vehicle Production by Type, 1980, 1981 & 1985

93   72.   Forecasts of French Commercial
                Vehicle Production by Type, 1980, 1981 & 1985

94   73.   Forecasts of West German Commercial
                Vehicle Production by Type, 1980, 1981 & 1985

95   74.   Forecasts of Italian Commercial
                Vehicle Production by Type, 1980, 1981 & 1985

List of Tables

Part 2: Financial Assessment of the U.S. Automotive Industry

PAGE   TABLE

137   Table 1   Employment, Payrolls and Receipts Related to the Manufacture and Use of Motor Vehicles in the USA in 1977

142   Table 2   US Total Retail Sales of Domestic Type[a] and Imported Passenger Cars and Trucks, 1971–80

143   Table 3   US Total Production and Factory Sales[a] of Passenger Cars and Trucks, 1971–80

144   Table 4   Market Class Comparisons of US Passenger Cars, 1971–80

145   Table 5   US Retail Sales of Passenger Cars, by Manufacturer, 1971–80

146   Table 6   Total US Passenger Car Market Shares by Domestic Manufacturers and Imports, 1971 and 1980

147   Table 7   US Retail Sales by Domestic Manufacturers of New Trucks, Including Their "Captive Imports", by GVW and Type, 1971–80

149   Table 8   US Motor Vehicle Production, by Manufacturer, 1973–80

150   Table 9   US Trade Balance in Motor Vehicles, 1971 and 1980

151   Table 10   Canadian Production of Passenger Cars and Commercial Vehicles by Manufacturer, for Selected Years Between 1971 and 1980

153   Table 11   US Exports of Passenger Cars and Commercial Vehicles, 1971–80

154   Table 12   US New Passenger Car Exports by Country of Destination in 1980

PAGE	TABLE	
155	Table 13	US Imports of Passenger Cars and Commercial Vehicles (Assembled) by Principal Source, 1971-80
154	Table 14	US Imports of Commercial Vehicles (Assembled), Bodies and Chassis, by Country of Origin, 1979-80
157	Table 15	Principal Passenger Car Imports (Other than Canadian), 1971-80
157	Table 16	Sales of Imported Trucks (Other Than Canadian) in the USA, 1975-80
177	Table 17	Sales of Passenger Cars in the USA by Domestic Manufacturers (Excluding Captive Imports), 1980-81
178	Table 18	US Passenger Car Production by Manufacturer, 1980-81
180	Table 19	US Production of Trucks (Including Vans) by Make
183	Table 20	General Motors Corporation: Consolidated Balance Sheet, 1976-81
184	Table 21	General Motors Corporation: Consolidated Assets by Area, 1976-81
184	Table 22	General Motors Corporation: Property, Plant and Equipment (Net of Depreciation), 1976-81
184	Table 23	General Motors Corporation: Current Assets, 1976-81
186	Table 24	General Motors Corporation: Non-Consolidated Subsidiaries and Affiliates, 1976-81
186	Table 25	General Motors Corporation: Stockholders' Equity, 1976-81
188	Table 26	General Motors Corporation: Long Term Debt, 1976-81
189	Table 27	General Motors Corporation: Current Liabilities, 1976-81
189	Table 28	General Motors Corporation: Consolidated Factory Sales, 1976-81

PAGE	TABLE	
190	Table 29	General Motors Corporation: Consolidated Sales by Industry Segment, 1976–81
190	Table 30	General Motors Corporation: Consolidated Sales by Area, 1976–81
192	Table 31	General Motors Corporation: Consolidated Profit and Loss Account, 1976–81
193	Table 32	General Motors Corporation: Consolidated Profit and Loss Account Per Unit Sold, 1976–81
195	Table 33	General Motors Corporation: Gross Profits, 1976–81
195	Table 34	General Motors Corporation: Equity Income of Non-Consolidated Subsidiaries and Affiliates, 1976–81
197	Table 35	General Motors Corporation: Net Income by Area, 1976–81
196	Table 36	General Motors Corporation: Quarterly Dividends, 1976–81
198	Table 37	General Motors Corporation: Source and Application of Funds, 1976–81
199	Table 38	General Motors Corporation: Capital Expenditure on Property, Plant and Equipment by Area, 1976–80
202	Table 39	Ford Motor Company: Consolidated Balance Sheet, 1976–80
203	Table 40	Ford Motor Company: Consolidated Assets by Area, 1976–81
204	Table 41	Ford Motor Company: Current Assets, 1976–81
204	Table 42	Ford Motor Company: Property, Plant and Equipment (Net of Depreciation), 1976–81
205	Table 43	Ford Motor Company: Non-Consolidated Subsidiaries and Affiliates, 1976–81
205	Table 44	Ford Motor Company: Stockholders' Equity, 1976–81
206	Table 45	Ford Motor Company: Long Term Debt, 1976–81

PAGE	TABLE	
207	Table 46	Ford Motor Company: Current Liabilities, 1976–81
207	Table 47	Ford Motor Company: Consolidated Factory Sales, 1976–81
208	Table 48	Ford Motor Company: Consolidated by Industry Segment, 1976–81
209	Table 49	Ford Motor Company: Consolidated Sales by Area, 1976–81
210	Table 50	Ford Motor Company: Consolidated Profit and Loss Account, 1976–81
211	Table 51	Ford Motor Company: Consolidated Profit and Loss Account Per Unit Sold, 1976–81
213	Table 52	Ford Motor Company: Gross Profits, 1976–81
213	Table 53	Ford Motor Company: Equity Income of Non-Consolidated Subsidiaries and Affiliates, 1976–81
212	Table 54	Ford Motor Company: Net Income by Area, 1976–81
214	Table 55	Ford Motor Company: Quarterly Dividends, 1976–81
215	Table 56	Ford Motor Company: Source and Application of Funds, 1976–81
216	Table 57	Ford Motor Company: Capital Expenditure by Area, 1976–81
219	Table 58	Chrysler Corporation: Consolidated Balance Sheet, 1976–81
220	Table 59	Chrysler Corporation: Consolidated Assets by Area, 1976–81
220	Table 60	Chrysler Corporation: Property, Plant and Equipment (Net of Depreciation), 1976–81
221	Table 61	Chrysler Corporation: Current Assets, 1976–81

PAGE   TABLE

222   Table 62   Chrysler Corporation: Non-Consolidated
Subsidiaries and Affiliates, 1976-81

223   Table 63   Chrysler Corporation: Investments at Cost,
1976-80

225   Table 64   Chrysler Corporation: Stockholders' Equity,
1976-81

226   Table 65   Chrysler Corporation: Long Term Debt,
1976-81

227   Table 66   Chrysler Corporation: Current Liabilities,
1976-81

227   Table 67   Chrysler Corporation: Other Liabilities,
1976-80

228   Table 68   Chrysler Corporation: Consolidated Sales,
1976-81

229   Table 69   Chrysler Corporation: Consolidated Sales by
Industry Segment, 1976-81

230   Table 70   Chrysler Corporation: Consolidated Sales by
Area, 1976-81

230   Table 71   Chrysler Corporation: Consolidated Profit and
Loss Account, 1976-81

232   Table 72   Chrysler Corporation: Consolidated Profit
and Loss Account Per Unit Sold, 1976-81

234   Table 73   Chrysler Corporation: Gross Profits, 1976-81

234   Table 74   Chrysler Corporation: Equity Income of
Non-Consolidated Subsidiaries and
Affiliates, 1976-81

236   Table 75   Chrysler Corporation: Net Income by Area,
1976-81

236   Table 76   Chrysler Corporation: Quarterly Dividends on
Common Stock, 1976-81

235   Table 77   Chrysler Corporation: Source and Application
of Funds, 1976-81

239   Table 78   American Motors Corporation: Consolidated
Balance Sheet, 1976-81

241   Table 79   American Motors Corporation: Current Assets,
1976-81

241   Table 80   American Motors Corporation: Non-Consolidated
Subsidiaries, 1976-81

242   Table 81   American Motors Corporation: Stockholders' Equity,
1976-81

242   Table 82   American Motors Corporation: Current Liabilities,
1976-81

244   Table 83   American Motors Corporation: Consolidated
Sales, 1975/76-81

244   Table 84   American Motors Corporation: Consolidated
Sales by Industry Segment, 1975/76-81

245   Table 85   American Motors Corporation: Consolidated
Sales by Area, 1975/76-81

246   Table 86   American Motors Corporation: Consolidated
Profit and Loss Account, 1975/76-81

247   Table 87   American Motors Corporation: Consolidated
Profit and Loss Account Per Unit Sold,
1975/76-81

248   Table 88   American Motors Corporation: Source and
Application of Funds, 1975/76-81

251   Table 89   Volkswagen of America Incorporated:
Consolidated Sales, 1976-80

252   Table 90   Volkswagen of America Incorporated:
Subscriptions to Issued Capital, 1976-80

252   Table 91   Volkswagen of America Incorporated:
Capital Investment, 1976-80

254   Table 92   International Harvester Company:
Consolidated Balance Sheet, 1976-81

255   Table 93   International Harvester Company: Current
Assets, 1976-81

PAGE	TABLE	
256	Table 94	International Harvester Company: Non-Consolidated Subsidiaries, 1976-81
256	Table 95	International Harvester Company: Assets by Product Group, 1978-80
257	Table 96	International Harvester Company: Assets by Area, 1978-80
258	Table 97	International Harvester Company: Stockholders' Equity, 1976-81
258	Table 98	International Harvester Company: Long Term Debt, 1976-81
259	Table 99	International Harvester Company: Current Liabilities, 1976-81
259	Table 100	International Harvester Company: Consolidated Sales, 1975/76-80/81
260	Table 101	International Harvester Company: Consolidated Sales by Product Group, 1975/76-80/81
260	Table 102	International Harvester Company: Consolidated Sales by Area, 1975/76-80/81
261	Table 103	International Harvester Company: Consolidated Profit and Loss Account, 1975/76-80/81
262	Table 104	International Harvester Company: Operating Profits by Product Group, 1977/78-80/81
263	Table 105	International Harvester Company: Operating Profts by Area, 1977/78-80/81
264	Table 106	International Harvester Company: Source and Application of Funds, 1975/76-80/81
266	Table 107	Mack Trucks Inc: Consolidated Balance Sheet, 1976-80
267	Table 108	Mack Trucks Inc: Consolidated Sales, 1976-81
267	Table 109	Mack Trucks Inc: Consolidated Profit and Loss Account, 1976-80

PAGE	TABLE	
268	Table 110	Mack Trucks Inc: Source and Application of Funds, 1978-80
270	Table 111	Paccar Inc: Consolidated Balance Sheet, 1976-81
270	Table 112	Paccar Inc: Consolidated Sales, 1976-81
271	Table 113	Paccar Inc: Consolidated Sales by Segment, 1976-81
271	Table 114	Paccar Inc: Consolidated Sales by Area, 1976-81
272	Table 115	Paccar Inc: Consolidated Profit and Loss Account, 1976-81
273	Table 116	Paccar Inc: Operating Profit by Segment, 1976-80
273	Table 117	Paccar Inc: Operating Profit by Area, 1976-80
274	Table 118	Paccar Inc: Source and Application of Funds, 1976-80
274	Table 119	Paccar Inc: Capital Expenditure by Segment, 1976-80
278	Table 120	US Vehicle Manufacturers' Combined Consolidated Balance Sheet, 1976-81
277	Table 121	US Vehicle Manufacturers' Combined Net Sales, 1976-80
277	Table 122	US Vehicle Manufacturers' Combined Net Sales by Region, 1977-80
279	Table 123	US Vehicle Manufacturers' Combined Gross Margins, 1976-81
281	Table 124	US Vehicle Manufacturers' Combined Consolidated Profit and Loss Account, 1976-81
282	Table 125	US Vehicle Manufacturers' Combined Source and Application of Funds, 1976-81
283	Table 126	US Vehicle Manufacturers' Consolidated Assets, 1976-81
284	Table 127	US Vehicle Manufacturers' Property, Plant and Equipment (Net of Depreciation), 1976-81

PAGE	TABLE	
285	Table 128	US Vehicle Manufacturers' Property, Plant and Equipment (Net of Depreciation) as a Percentage of Total Assets, 1976-81
286	Table 129	US Vehicle Manufacturers' Current Assets, 1976-81
286	Table 130	US Vehicle Manufacturers' Cash, Deposits and Marketable Securities, 1976-81
287	Table 131	US Vehicle Manufacturers' Net Current Assets, 1976-81
287	Table 132	US Vehicle Manufacturers' Stockholders' Equity, 1976-81
289	Table 133	US Vehicle Manufacturers' Loans Payable, 1976-81
289	Table 134	US Vehicle Manufacturers' Long Term Debt, 1976-81
288	Table 135	US Vehicle Manufacturers' Ratio of Long Term Debt to Shareholders' Equity, 1976-81
291	Table 136	US Vehicle Manufacturers' Consolidated Net Sales, 1976-81
292	Table 137	US Vehicle Manufacturers' Percentage of Consolidated Net Sales Outside North America, 1976-80
291	Table 138	US Vehicle Manufacturers' Consolidated Gross Profit[a], 1976-81
293	Table 139	US Vehicle Manufacturers' Consolidated Profit Before Interest Paid[a], 1976-81
293	Table 140	US Vehicle Manufacturers' Consolidated Interest Paid, 1976-81
294	Table 141	US Vehicle Manufacturers' Consolidated Profit Before Tax, 1976-81
294	Table 142	US Vehicle Manufacturers' Consolidated Net Income, 1976-81

PAGE   TABLE

296   Table 144   US Vehicle Manufacturers' Changes in Debt, 1976–81

297   Table 145   US Vehicle Manufacturers' Capital Expenditure, 1976–81

297   Table 146   US Vehicle Manufacturers' Changes in Balances of Cash, Deposits and Marketable Securities, 1976–81

List of Tables

Part 3: Short Term Prospects for the Japanese Motor Industry

Page 306   Table 1   Japanese Production of Passenger Cars by Engine Size Group

307   Table 2   Japanese Passenger Car Production by Manufacturer

307   Table 3   Japanese Production of Non-Countable KD Passenger Car Sets

308   Table 4   New Registrations of Passenger Cars in Japan by Engine Size Group

308   Table 5   New Registrations of Passenger Cars by Make in Japan

309   Table 6   Passenger Car Imports by Make and Size Group

310   Table 7   Japanese Passenger Car Exports by Engine Size Group

311   Table 8   Japanese Passenger Car Exports by Region

311   Table 9   Japanese Exports of Non-Countable KD Passenger Car Sets

312   Table 10   Japanese Passenger Car Exports by Manufacturer

312   Table 11   Japanese Exports of Non-Countable KD Car Sets by Manufacturer

313   Table 12   Forecasts of Passenger Car Sales and Production in Japan

314   Table 13   Japanese Commercial Vehicle Production by Type

315   Table 14   Japanese Goods Vehicle Production by Manufacturer

315   Table 15   Japanese Bus Production by Manufacturer

316   Table 16   Japanese Production of Non-Countable KD Commercial Vehicle Sets by Manufacturer

316   Table 17   New Registrations of Commercial Vehicles by Type in Japan

Page 317   Table 18   New Registrations of Goods Vehicles by Manufacturer in Japan

317   Table 19   New Registrations of Buses by Manufacturer in Japan

318   Table 20   Japanese Commercial Vehicle Exports by Type

318   Table 21   Exports of Japanese Commercial Vehicles by Region

319   Table 22   Japanese Exports of Goods Vehicles by Manufacturer

319   Table 23   Japanese Exports of Buses by Manufacturer

320   Table 24   Forecasts of Japanese Commercial Vehicle Sales and Production

Preface

The U.S.A. currently accounts for approximately 21 percent of global vehicle output, compared with 28 percent in 1970 and 48 percent in 1960. In 1980 and 1981, the U.S.A. was overtaken by Japan as the world's largest vehicle producer. Moreover, foreign competitors have increasingly made their presence felt in the U.S. itself, accounting for a growing proportion of U.S. vehicle sales.

To provide some insights into the future direction of the automotive industries of the U.S., Western Europe and Japan, this volume draws together two reports, first published by the Economist Intelligence Unit and a forecast for the Japanese auto industry published in the third quarter, 1981 issue of Motor Business. The crucial importance of the automotive industry to the well-being of each of the countries involved makes these reports essential reading for all those who are concerned with the economic future.

In Western Europe, individual European governments for some time have understood the need to develop and maintain a substantial automotive industry. The primary motive has apparently been the preservation of employment not only in the direct manufacture of vehicles but also among the many suppliers and support services which feed on the automotive industry. Public financial support for companies in difficulty and inducements for multinational investors were employed in the 1970s in the service of this goal. Nevertheless, competitive pressures from the U.S. and Japan are building remoreselessly. Future industrial challenges will come from countries such as South Korea and Brazil where automotive industries are being established.

Huge capital investment and a dedicated workforce, together with an intensive and aggressive export strategy, has made the Japanese motor industry the most effective and successful in the world. It is possible, though, that the industry has already reached its peak -- at least as far as passenger cars are concerned. The reason for this lies in the depth of feeling in the U.S. and Western Europe about the success of the Japanese. No government -- of whatever political colour -- will remain unmoved for long by the pleadings of its domestic automotive industry in the face of increasing Japanese penetration. Japanese producers who wish further to increase sales to the U.S. and Western Europe will increasingly have to resort to joint ventures, licensing agreements or a local presence. The first moves in this direction have already been made and many more can be expected in the first half of the 1980s. The reports in this volume look at the different but related problems faced by each of these countries in an attempt to predict some of the strategies they will adopt to meet the economic challenges of the 1980s.

Part One:
The West European
Automotive Industry

The Structure and Growth of the West European Automotive Industry

Country Analysis

PRODUCTION

Western Europe accounts for
<u>over 30 per cent of global vehicle output</u>

In 1979 it is estimated that just over 30 per cent of the world's output of motor
vehicles was manufactured in Western Europe. This figure probably rises to more
like 40 per cent if the global production and assembly of West European designed
units is included. Together with their counterparts in North America and Japan,
the major West European vehicle manufacturers dominate the worldwide motor
industry. They provide the engineering, technical and product background to
numerous assembly plants throughout the world, and have developed important
export business. A review of the companies making up the West European automotive sector begins on page 24. This section of the report examines production
and sales by country. A series of 24 tables has been prepared (pages 5 to 23)
aimed at providing the reader with an understanding of the scope and composition
of the industry.

<u>Background to the tables</u>

The first two tables give details of passenger car and commercial vehicle production by country. As with the other 22 tables in this section, a ten year run of
figures is included. Table 1 shows that West Germany is the largest passenger
car producer in Europe, followed by France, Italy, the UK, Spain, Sweden,
Belgium and the Netherlands. It is important to understand the difference between
production and assembly. The dividing line is sometimes rather blurred, but
essentially production takes place where the company itself carries out the design
of the vehicle and the procurement and/or production of the individual components
and subassemblies which go into the finished vehicle. Obviously Renault in France
and Fiat in Italy, for example, fall into this category. Assembly takes place when
the factory in question fits together a kit of parts which is sourced from a parent
or associated company; this kit need not necessarily contain all the parts required
and, as a general rule, a 50 per cent break point is adopted. (The French use a
20 per cent break point, though.) Thus, if the kit contains under 50 per cent of
the parts required (by value) it is usual for the production to be counted at the
assembler, but where the level is above 50 per cent the unit of production is
counted at the source company. This leads to one or two anomalies, and there is
a certain amount of double counting. The most obvious example occurs over BL
and Innocenti; BL exports Mini kits in KD (knocked down) form for Innocenti to
assemble in Italy, but both companies count the output as production. Thus, Table
1 overstates West European passenger car production in 1979 by at least Innocenti's
production of 39,991 units in that year. The true extent of overcounting or, indeed,

undercounting is not known, but even so Tables 1 and 2 give a sufficiently accurate approximation of the position to be worthwhile. All Belgian output is counted as assembly, except for Ford's operation. Hence, although Belgium's output figure per year is typically around the 1 mn mark, actual recorded production is much less. This means that an Opel or a Citroën assembled in Belgium is counted in the West German and French production figures respectively. On the other hand, all Spanish output is regarded as production.

Table 2 provides details of commercial vehicle production by country. Based on 1979 figures, the UK is the largest producer of commercial vehicles in Western Europe, followed by France, West Germany (which is, nevertheless, Europe's largest truck producer), Spain, Italy, Sweden and the Netherlands.

Tables 3-22 provide a further breakdown of the country totals by manufacturer and, for West Germany, France, the UK and Italy, an analysis is given of passenger car production by engine size and commercial vehicle output by weight range. It should be noted that totals do not necessarily add due to rounding.

Table 1

West European Passenger Car Production by Major Producing Country, 1970-79
('000 units)

	1970	1971	1972	1973	1974	1975	1976	1977	1978	1979
West Germany	3,528[a]	3,696	3,522	3,650	2,840	2,908	3,547	3,791	3,890	3,933
France	2,458[a]	2,694[a]	2,719	2,867	2,699	2,546	2,980	3,092	3,111	3,222
Italy	1,720	1,701	1,732	1,823	1,631	1,349	1,471	1,440	1,509	1,481
UK	1,641	1,742	1,921	1,747	1,534	1,268	1,333	1,328	1,223	1,070
Spain	450	453	601	706	705	696	753	989	986	966
Sweden	279	287	318	342	327	316	317	235	254	297
Belgium	234	279	233	241	139	182	285	286	265	257
Netherlands	67	78	87	95	69	61	74	53	65	90
Total	10,377	10,930	11,133	11,471	9,944	9,326	10,760	11,214	11,303	11,316

a French figures for 1970 and 1971 are not strictly comparable with subsequent years due to the inclusion of non-countable CKD kits; see footnote to Table 7 on page 9.

Source: Various national authorities.

Table 2

West European Commercial Vehicle Production by Major Producing Country, 1970-79
('000 units)

	1970	1971	1972	1973	1974	1975	1976	1977	1978	1979
UK	458	456	408	417	403	381	372	386	385	408
France	292[a]	316[a]	298	351	376	315	423	415	397	392
West Germany	314	286	294	299	260	278	321	314	296	317
Spain	89	79	95	116	133	118	113	141	158	157
Italy	135	116	107	135	142	110	119	143	148	151
Sweden	31	30	33	37	42	50	51	52	51	58
Netherlands	12	13	12	13	12	10	11	13	13	15
Total	1,331	1,296	1,247	1,368	1,368	1,262	1,410	1,464	1,448	1,498

a French figures for 1970 and 1971 are not strictly comparable with subsequent years due to the inclusion of non-countable CKD kits; see footnote to Table 9 on page 11.

Source: Various national authorities.

Table 3

West German Passenger Car Production by Manufacturer, 1970–79
('000 units)

	1970	1971	1972	1973	1974	1975	1976	1977	1978	1979
Volkswagen	1,518	1,622	1,373	1,364	1,170	1,050	1,221	1,278	1,346	1,304
Opel	812	832	871	868	578	656	919	922	953	960
Ford	409	479	436	456	286	413	487	543	544	547
Daimler–Benz	280	284	324	332	340	350	378	409	404	433
BMW	159	164	182	196	185	217	268	285	312	328
Audi NSU	317	282	299	410	266	205	242	318	295	323
Porsche	17	11	15	15	10	9	33	36	37	36
Others	16	23	21	9	5	6	–	–	–	–
Total	3,528	3,696	3,522	3,650	2,840	2,908	3,547	3,791	3,890	3,933

Source: VDA.

Table 4

West German Passenger Car Production by Engine Size, 1970–79
('000 units)

cc rating Cars	1970	1971	1972	1973	1974	1975	1976	1977	1978	1979
500–1,000	108	96	47	35	43	123	230	173	156	160
1,001–2,000	2,675	2,879	2,656	2,836	2,105	2,157	2,608	2,841	2,759	2,744
2,001–3,000	333	283	416	432	387	377	425	504	654	693
over 3,000	12	30	47	56	36	29	38	50	56	60
Estate cars	399	407	356	291	269	221	246	223	265	275
Total	3,528	3,696	3,522	3,650	2,840	2,908	3,547	3,791	3,890	3,933

Source: VDA.

Table 5

West German Commercial Vehicle Production by Manufacturer, 1970–79
('000 units)

	1970	1971	1972	1973	1974	1975	1976	1977	1978	1979
Daimler–Benz	106	98	103	117	125	145	180	174	157	172
Volkswagen	103	93	104	99	70	72	94	94	93	92
MAN	14	15	14	16	16	16	19	21	20	21
Magirus–Deutz	19	14	12	11	14	18	23	18	19	20
Opel	9	7	6	6	5	2	3	3	4	8
Others	63	58	56	50	30	26	2	3	3	3
Total	314	286	294	299	260	278	321	314	296	317

Source: VDA

Table 6

West German Commercial Vehicle Production by Type, 1970–79
('000 units)

	1970	1971	1972	1973	1974	1975	1976	1977	1978	1979
Rigid goods vehicles										
up to 2 tons gvw	9	10	6	3	3	2	3	3	4	8
2–6 tons gvw	185	157	179	177	128	123	163	160	156	162
6–16 tons gvw	69	72	63	66	59	65	60	56	59	55
over 16 tons gvw	22	20	19	23	31	50	58	55	47	56
Articulated units	14	14	12	14	20	19	18	20	16	20
Buses	15	12	15	16	18	19	20	18	15	15
Total	314	286	294	299	260	278	321	314	296	317

Source: VDA.

Table 7

French Passenger Car Production by Manufacturer, 1970-79

('000 units)

	1970[a]	1971[a]	1972	1973	1974	1975	1976	1977	1978	1979
Renault	1,056	1,069	1,050	1,101	1,174	1,042	1,218	1,259	1,241	1,404
Peugeot	525	559	573	656	596	564	656	676	742	756
Citroën	471	578	602	607	531	548	614	667	679	679
Talbot	403	484	491	498	385	383	483	477	431	365
Others	3	3	4	6	12	8	8	13	18	18
Total	2,458	2,694	2,719	2,867	2,699	2,546	2,980	3,092	3,111	3,222

a Figures for 1970 and 1971 are not strictly comparable with subsequent years due to the inclusion of non-countable CKD kits; this has the effect of inflating the 1970 and 1971 totals by about 310,000 units in each year. For the effect on individual companies see footnotes to Tables 26, 27, 28 and 32.

Source: Chambre Syndicale des Constructeurs Automobiles.

10

Table 8

French Passenger Car Production by Engine Size, 1970–79
('000 units)

	1970[a]	1971[a]	1972	1973	1974	1975	1976	1977	1978	1979
Up to 1,000 cc	921	790	817	875	1,089	920	846	873	709	597
1,000–1,500 cc	1,047	1,295	1,301	1,369	1,126	1,083	1,447	1,555	1,695	1,817
Over 1,500 cc	490	609	602	623	484	543	686	664	707	807
Total	2,458	2,694	2,719	2,867	2,699	2,546	2,980	3,092	3,111	3,222

a Figures for 1970 and 1971 are not strictly comparable with subsequent years due to the inclusion of non-countable CKD kits; this has the effect of inflating the 1970 and 1971 totals by about 310,000 units in each year. For the effect on individual companies see footnotes to Tables 26, 27, 28 and 32.

Source: Chambre Syndicale des Constructeurs Automobiles.

Table 9

French Commercial Vehicle Production by Manufacturer, 1970-79
('000 units)

	1970[a]	1971[a]	1972	1973	1974	1975	1976	1977	1978	1979
Renault	104	105	106	108	118	87	147	140	131	141
Peugeot	51	62	66	77	93	80	103	106	120	110
Citroën	69	85	62	67	66	50	65	69	55	48
Saviem	36	33	33	37	40	35	41	35	31	29
Talbot	-	-	-	28	24	25	28	29	25	27
Unic	8	7	9	10	10	14	16	17	17	19
Berliet	23	23	22	23	25	24	24	20	18	17
Others	1	-	-	-	-	-	-	-	-	1
Total	292	316	298	351	376	315	423	415	397	392

a Figures for 1970 and 1971 are not strictly comparable with subsequent years due to the inclusion of non-countable CKD kits; this has the effect of inflating the 1970 and 1971 totals by about 40,000 units in each year. For the effect on individual companies see footnotes to Tables 26, 27 and 32.

Source: Chambre Syndicale des Constructeurs Automobiles.

11

12

Table 10

French Commercial Vehicle Production by Type, 1970–79
('000 units)

	1970[a]	1971[a]	1972	1973	1974	1975	1976	1977	1978	1979
Rigid goods vehicles										
up to 2.5 tons gvw	187	211	190	231	250	204	287	291	275	275
2.5–6 tons gvw	60	63	65	75	76	62	83	75	73	63
6–15 tons gvw	17	15	17	15	16	22	24	23	27	32
over 15 tons gvw	18	17	15	15	18	17	15	13	10	10
Articulated units	7	8	9	12	12	7	10	10	9	8
Buses	3	4	3	4	4	3	4	3	4	3
Total	292	316	298	351	376	315	423	415	397	392

a Figures for 1970 and 1971 are not strictly comparable with subsequent years due to the inclusion of non-countable CKD kits; this has the effect of inflating the 1970 and 1971 totals by about 40,000 units in each year. For the effect on individual companies see footnotes to Tables 26, 27 and 32.

Source: Chambre Syndicale des Constructeurs Automobiles.

Table 11

UK Passenger Car Production by Manufacturer, 1970-79
('000 units)

	1970	1971	1972	1973	1974	1975	1976	1977	1978	1979
BL	789	887	916	876	739	605	688	651	612	504
Ford	448	367	547	453	384	330	383	407	324	399
Talbot	217	282	264	265	262	227	145	169	196	103
Vauxhall	178	199	184	138	137	99	109	93	84	59
Others	9	8	11	14	13	8	9	7	6	6
Total	1,641	1,742	1,921	1,747	1,534	1,268	1,333	1,328	1,223	1,070

Source: SMMT.

Table 12

UK Passenger Car Production by Engine Size, 1970-79
('000 units)

	1970	1971	1972	1973	1974	1975	1976	1977	1978	1979
Up to 1,000 cc	245	272	245	234	205	165	135	147	145	127
1,001-1,600 cc	993	973	1,026	908	784	649	736	725	697	616
1,601-2,800 cc	324	425	573	523	467	404	405	391	314	277
Over 2,800 cc	79	72	77	82	78	50	58	64	67	50
Total	1,641	1,742	1,921	1,747	1,534	1,268	1,333	1,328	1,223	1,070

Source: Department of Industry.

Table 13

UK Commercial Vehicle Production by Manufacturer, 1970-79

('000 units)

	1970	1971	1972	1973	1974	1975	1976	1977	1978	1979
Ford	141	121	144	137	131	129	142	148	106	167
BL	173	174	140	137	125	133	120	120	131	125
Vauxhall	102	126	91	107	112	91	86	92	117	88
Talbot	32	26	24	26	25	19	14	16	18	18
Others	10	9	9	9	9	8	10	10	12	11
Total	458	456	408	417	403	381	372	386	385	408

Source: SMMT.

Table 14

UK Commercial Vehicle Production by Type, 1970-79

('000 units)

	1970	1971	1972	1973	1974	1975	1976	1977	1978	1979
Rigid goods vehicles										
car derived vans ⎱	243[a]	255[a]	247[a]	101	93	81	82	86	82	93
others up to 3.5 tons gvw ⎰				152	145	121	139	153	165	173
3.5-14 tons gvw	142[b]	134[b]	103[b]	96	96	111	88	87	78	82
over 14 tons gvw	31	25	18	25	23	23	21	21	24	25
Articulated units	18	15	10	12	12	9	9	12	12	10
Buses	23	27	30	30	34	36	33	28	23	26
Total	458	456	408	417	403	381	372	386	385	408

a Up to 3 tons.   b 3-14 tons.

Source: Department of Industry.

Table 15

Italian Passenger Car Production by Manufacturer, 1970-79

('000 units)

	1970	1971	1972	1973	1974	1975	1976	1977	1978	1979
Fiat Auto	1,560	1,514	1,525	1,559	1,360	1,125	1,256	1,201	1,247	1,232
of which:										
Fiat	1,419	1,372	1,368	1,390	1,206	1,007	1,098	1,057	1,104	1,081
Autobianchi	95	88	113	114	108	71	94	73	89	89
Lancia	45	53	42	53	45	46	63	69	52	60
Ferrari	1	1	2	2	1	1	1	2	2	2
Alfa Romeo	108	123	141	205	208	190	201	201	219	208
Innocenti	51	62	63	58	61	33	13	38	41	40
Others	1	2	4	1	1	1	1	1	1	1
Total	1,720	1,701	1,732	1,823	1,631	1,349	1,471	1,440	1,509	1,481

Source: ANFIA.

Table 16

Italian Passenger Car Production by Engine Size, 1970-79

('000 units)

	1970	1971	1972	1973	1974	1975	1976	1977	1978	1979
Up to 500 cc	447	366	206	73	9	4	7	3	-	-
501-1,000 cc	400	376	532	766	772	586	575	550	496	400
1,001-1,500 cc	648	722	795	759	587	477	565	565	627	708
1,501-2,000 cc	219	229	185	218	259	277	321	319	372	332
Over 2,000 cc	6	8	13	7	5	4	3	4	13	41
Total	1,720	1,701	1,732	1,823	1,631	1,349	1,471	1,440	1,509	1,481

Source: ANFIA.

15

Table 17

Italian Commercial Vehicle Production by Manufacturer, 1970-79
('000 units)

	1970	1971	1972	1973	1974	1975	1976	1977	1978	1979
Fiat group	132[a]	112[a]	105[a]	132[a]	139[a]	108[a]	117[a]	141[a]	145	149
of which:										
Fiat	105	90	85	104	108	83	94	116	128	131
OM	23	21	18	26	30	24	21	22	13	14
Magirus	-	-	-	-	-	-	1	2	4	4
Alfa Romeo	3	4	3	3	3	2	2	2	3	2
Others[b]	-	-	-	-	-	-	-	-	-	-
Total	135	116	107	135	142	110	119	143	148	151

a Includes output from Autobianchi and Lancia which are currently not producers of commercial vehicles. b Throughout the period production of other manufacturers has not exceeded 500 units per year.

Source: ANFIA.

Table 18

Italian Commercial Vehicle Production by Type, 1970-79

('000 units)

	1970	1971	1972	1973	1974	1975	1976	1977	1978	1979
Rigid goods vehicles										
up to 2 tons gvw	25	26	22	22	21	13	19	22	29	38
2-6 tons gvw	62	51	49	64	64	58	62	77	85	83
6-12 tons gvw	19	18	17	22	18	10	11	13	9	8
over 12 tons gvw	22	15	13	19	23	19	17	19	12	12
Articulated units	4	3	2	4	6	4	6	9	8	5
Buses	3	4	4	5	8	6	5	5	6	6
Total	135	116	107	135	142	110	119	143	148	151

Source: ANFIA.

17

Table 19

Spanish Passenger Car Production by Manufacturer, 1970-79
('000 units)

	1970	1971	1972	1973	1974	1975	1976	1977	1978	1979
Seat	280	254	335	359	361	329	343	347	284	295
Fasa Renault	88	101	126	166	167	193	202	224	235	261
Ford	-	-	-	-	-	-	18	213	261	227
Citroen	27	37	42	52	70	93	109	108	106	109
Talbot	37	29	63	87	76	67	82	96	99	73
Authi	19	31	34	43	31	15	-	-	-	-
Total	450	453	601	706	705	696	753	989	986	966

Source: Agrupación Nacional de Fabricantes de Automoviles y Camiones.

Table 20

Spanish Commercial Vehicle Production by Manufacturer, 1970-79
('000 units)

	1970	1971	1972	1973	1974	1975	1976	1977	1978	1979
Citroën	14	15	16	21	22	18	23	33	46	52
Motor Ibérica	6	6	7	9	13	11	16	29	30	27
Metalurgica de Santa Ana	8	8	8	9	10	12	13	13	16	17
Enasa	13	14	18	23	27	25	20	21	18	15
Mevosa	8	8	11	12	14	14	10	15	14	15
Fasa Renault	11	9	12	16	17	13	11	13	13	14
Ford	-	-	-	-	-	-	-	1	7	5
Talbot	5	4	5	7	9	7	5	5	5	5
CAF	3	2	2	2	3	2	3	5	5	4
Seat	3	1	3	3	3	3	4	6	4	4
Others	15	12	12	14	17	14	7	-	-	-
Total	89	79	95	116	133	118	113	141	158	157

Source: Agrupación Nacional de Fabricantes de Automoviles y Camiones.

Table 21

Swedish Passenger Car Production by Manufacturer, 1970-79
('000 units)

	1970	1971	1972	1973	1974	1975	1976	1977	1978	1979
Volvo	205	214	234	252	234	225	221	159	182	213
Saab Scania	74	73	84	89	93	91	96	76	73	84
Total	279	287	318	342	327	316	317	235	254	297

Source: Association of Swedish Automotive Manufacturers and Wholesalers.

Table 22

Swedish Commercial Vehicle Production by Manufacturer, 1970-79
('000 units)

	1970	1971	1972	1973	1974	1975	1976	1977	1978	1979
Volvo	17	17	18	21	23	31	30	30	30	33
Saab Scania	14	13	15	16	18	19	21	22	21	25
Total	31	30	33	37	42	50	51	52	51	58

Source: Association of Swedish Automotive Manufacturers and Wholesalers.

DEMAND

1979 was a record year for sales of passenger cars -

Tables 23 and 24 provide details of West European demand during the 1970s for
passenger cars and commercial vehicles respectively.

In the passenger car sector demand in 1979 amounted to a new high of almost 10.5
mn units, 3.1 per cent above 1978's level. Of the major markets, France and the UK
have exhibited the strongest growth during the decade while the Italian market,
after a firm performance in the first half of the 1970s, was relatively weak in the
second half. All other markets, except Portugal, show gains over the ten year
period.

The impact of the 1974/75 recession is clearly evident from Table 23. In 1974
passenger car demand fell by 13.4 per cent, with individual country performances
ranging from a 35.2 per cent decline in Denmark to a 15.0 per cent increase in
Sweden. However, it is noteworthy that since 1974 passenger car demand rose
every year up to 1979.

- and commercial vehicles

1979 was also a peak year for commercial vehicle sales in Western Europe. An
estimated 1.24 mn units were sold, 9.2 per cent above the previous year's total.
As with passenger cars the market was seriously affected in 1974/75, but whereas
the overall demand for cars staged a minor recovery in 1975, commercial vehicle
sales continued to fall quite dramatically. Thus, after an 11.9 per cent drop in
1974 a further fall of 10.2 per cent was experienced in 1975, to make a cumulative
decline of 20.9 per cent between the top of the previous cycle and the low of the
downturn. Nevertheless, higher sales have been recorded each year since 1975,
although 1973's peak was not breached until 1978.

France and the UK are easily the largest markets, followed by West Germany,
Italy and Spain. On a ten year view all markets show an increase except Denmark
and Norway, which held steady, and Switzerland and Finland, where recorded
statistics show a fall.

Table 23

Development of Passenger Car Demand in Western Europe by Country, 1970-79
('000 units)

	1970	1971	1972	1973	1974	1975	1976	1977	1978	1979
West Germany	2,107	2,152	2,143	2,031	1,693	2,106	2,312	2,561	2,664	2,623
France	1,297	1,469	1,638	1,746	1,525	1,482	1,858	1,907	1,945	1,976
UK	1,077	1,286	1,638	1,661	1,269	1,194	1,286	1,324	1,592	1,716
Italy	1,364	1,435	1,470	1,449	1,281	1,055	1,188	1,219	1,216	1,350[a]
Spain	399	433	506	595	576	572	620	663	654	621
Netherlands	432	403	432	430	404	450	508	552	585	569
Belgium	301	266	336	341	336	365	421	429	424	424[a]
Switzerland	211	235	259	239	202	190	204	234	272	296[a]
Sweden	203	198	221	226	260	285	313	241	201	215
Austria	127	195	222	187	167	185	225	296	158	220[a]
Denmark	108	104	92	122	79	116	152	141	133	130[a]
Republic of Ireland	54	52	64	74	61	52	70	82	106	96[a]
Finland	92	75	101	118	96	117	92	90	81	100
Norway	70	81	75	89	90	103	127	145	78	89
Portugal	60	73	78	79	88	84	98	76	53	50[a]
Total	7,902	8,457	9,275	9,387	8,127	8,356	9,474	9,960	10,162	10,475[a]

a Estimated.

Source: Various national authorities.

Table 24

Development of Commercial Vehicle Demand in Western Europe by Country, 1970-79
('000 units)

	1970	1971	1972	1973	1974	1975	1976	1977	1978	1979
France	208	227	249	270	253	206	293	298	300	315
UK	257	257	...[b]	300[a]	237[a]	225	215	231	262	306
West Germany	165	163	149	138	108	109	137	138	156	170
Spain	78	75	87	101	101	94	93	101	104	106
Italy	85	79	81	83	101	76	95	110	98	108[d]
Netherlands	47	43	40	43	40	37	42	43	47	48
Belgium	25	24	24	26	23	21	24	26	29	36
Portugal	16	15	20	25	21	18	21	33	29	31[d]
Denmark	25	25	32	49	24	30	45	35	23	25[d]
Austria	16	16	20	15	14	12	18	19	19	20[d]
Sweden	19	17	16	17	17	17	19	20	17	17
Norway	16	20	22	12	11	12	14	17	14	16
Switzerland	13	14	17	18	15	8	8	11	14	17[d]
Republic of Ireland	10	9	9	10	8	7	8	10	13	13[d]
Finland	23	21	12	13	14	14	14	13	12	14
Total	1,003	1,005	778[c]	1,120	987	886	1,046	1,105	1,137	1,242[d]

a Excludes buses and coaches. b No details of commercial vehicle registrations are available for the UK in 1972. c Excludes UK. d Estimated.

Source: Various national authorities.

23

The Companies

A fragmented industrial structure still exists -

Compared with North America, Western Europe has a multitude of independent
vehicle producing companies. Although it is becoming increasingly valid to refer
to a West European motor industry - as opposed, for example, to a separate
British or West German industry - it is still the case that the European based
companies are heavily bound by national loyalties. Governments are keen to keep
at least a part of a country's vehicle manufacturing capability under domestic
ownership and control, and hence in many cases solutions to company problems
have been national in character. In this the French government has probably
demonstrated the most nationalistic approach, and has successfully fended off
most foreign intervention. For example, Fiat's part ownership of Citroën came to
nothing, and when the French company required help in the mid 1970s a "French
solution" was provided through a merger with Peugeot. Strong support has been
provided to the British motor industry by the UK government. The most visible
evidence of this is seen in the rescue of British Leyland (now officially known as
BL) in 1975, and subsequent extensive financial support. Had BL collapsed or
passed into foreign ownership the British motor industry would have effectively
passed into the hands of non-national interests. The desire of a country to retain
ownership and control explains the continuation of a larger number of companies
manufacturing vehicles in Western Europe than economic analysis would suggest is
logical. It is possible that there has been at some time a weakening of European
companies' competitive position vis-à-vis their global competitors because of this
factor, but as the need to compete effectively became the paramount consideration
for managements other methods of securing economies of scale have been developed.
One of the most promising has been through joint ventures; vehicle manufacturing
companies throughout Western Europe have established extensive links involving
cooperation in the fields of research and development, production, exchange of
components and subassemblies, and distribution. Sometimes cooperation has
resulted in setting up a new jointly owned facility, and in a number of instances a
company has taken a (minority) equity holding in another. And whereas joint ventures have traditionally been on a European scale, companies are now increasingly
finding partners from elsewhere - especially in North America and Japan.

In contrast, the US owned companies have had the major advantage of being able
to regard Western Europe as one market, and have organised their output accordingly. The best example is provided by Ford which has rationalised its vehicle
production facilities in the UK, West Germany and Spain on a European basis.
General Motors was rather slow in recognising the advantage of being a US producer in Europe, but is now acting to remedy the position. Chrysler, on the other
hand, withdrew from Europe in 1978 and sold its operation to Peugeot Citroën -
thereby affording the French company the unique opportunity to become a European
based "European" company.

– despite extensive rationalisation

Nevertheless, during the past 20 years there has been considerable rationalisation within the West European motor industry. The result is that the sector is dominated by a few giant companies which have their base in West Germany, France, Italy or the UK. On the basis of 1979 production figures, five companies achieved vehicle output in excess of 1.5 mn units. The leader – by a substantial margin – is the French PSA (Peugeot Citroën Talbot) group with production of over 2.3 mn units; the majority of this output consisted of passenger cars and light commercial vehicles produced in facilities in France, Spain and the UK. Europe's second largest vehicle manufacturer in 1979 is state owned Renault, thereby giving France the top two positions. In third place comes Volkswagen/Audi NSU with output concentrated in passenger cars and light commercial vehicles; all of the group's European output of 1.72 mn units was produced in West Germany, making Volkswagen the most "national" of European companies – notwithstanding its sizeable interests in North and South America. Fiat is in fourth place, just fractionally behind Volkswagen with 1.72 mn units. However, unlike the PSA group and Volkswagen, Fiat has extensive and important activities in the commercial vehicle sector – through Iveco. Although Fiat is heavily concentrated in Italy, the company has sizeable production facilities in West Germany, Spain and (to a lesser extent) France. Western Europe's fifth largest producer is Ford which has major operations in the UK, West Germany, Belgium and Spain. Following these five there is quite a gap to General Motors, which is the only other company to have breached the 1 mn unit level in 1979.

The leading 19 producers

Table 25 indicates the leading 19 producers in Western Europe's automotive sector, based on 1979 production details. The 19 companies are ranked in descending order of total vehicle output and, where appropriate, an analysis is provided of production by major facility or subsidiary. Company profiles are given for these 19 manufacturers after Table 25, and Part 1 of this report concludes with an examination of Western Europe's smaller vehicle producers.

Table 25

The Principal Vehicle Manufacturers of Western Europe

	Production in 1979		
	Passenger cars	Commercial vehicles	Total
1. PSA group			
Peugeot (France)	755,593	109,872	865,465
Citroën (France)	679,327	48,251	727,578
Talbot (France)	364,799	27,369	392,168
Citroën (Spain)	109,130	51,600	160,730
Talbot (UK)	102,960	17,576	120,536
Talbot (Spain)	72,891	4,477	77,368
Total	2,084,700	259,145	2,343,845
1978	(2,253,795)	(267,973)	(2,521,768)

(continued)

Table 25 (continued)

The Principal Vehicle Manufacturers of Western Europe

		Production in 1979		
		Passenger cars	Commercial vehicles	Total
2.	Renault			
	Renault (France)	1,403,949	141,046	1,544,995
	Fasa Renault (Spain)	261,430	13,892	275,322
	Saviem (France)	-	28,926	28,926
	Berliet (France)	-	16,718	16,718
	Total	1,665,379	200,582	1,865,961
	1978	(1,476,270)	(193,430)	(1,669,700)
3.	Volkswagen/Audi NSU			
	Volkswagen (West Germany)	1,304,466	92,450	1,396,916
	Audi NSU (West Germany)	323,395	-	323,395
	Total	1,627,861	92,450	1,720,311
	1978	(1,640,981)	(93,067)	(1,734,048)
4.	Fiat			
	Fiat (Italy)	1,081,473	130,854	1,212,327
	Seat (Spain)	294,865	3,994	298,859
	Autobianchi (Italy)	88,734	-	88,734
	Lancia (Italy)	60,459	-	60,459
	Magirus Deutz (West Germany)	-	20,184	20,184
	Unic Fiat (France)	-	18,646	18,646
	OM (Italy)	-	13,713	13,713
	Magirus (Italy)	-	4,263	4,263
	Ferrari (Italy)	2,308	-	2,308
	Total	1,527,839	191,654	1,719,493
	1978	(1,532,343)	(183,384)	(1,715,727)
5.	Ford			
	Ford (UK)	398,684	167,232	565,916
	Ford (West Germany)	546,957	-	546,957
	Ford (Belgium)	256,884	-	256,884
	Ford (Spain)	227,493	4,939	232,432
	Total	1,430,018	172,171	1,602,189
	1978	(1,394,280)	(113,503)	(1,507,783)
6.	General Motors			
	Opel (West Germany)	960,243	8,223	968,466
	Vauxhall (UK)	58,760	87,672	146,432
	Total	1,019,003	95,895	1,114,898
	1978	(1,036,697)	(121,242)	(1,157,939)

(continued)

Table 25 (continued)

The Principal Vehicle Manufacturers of Western Europe

		Production in 1979		
		Passenger cars	Commercial vehicles	Total
7.	BL	503,776	124,644	628,420
	1978	(611,625)	(131,478)	(743,103)
8.	Daimler-Benz	433,203	171,656	604,859
	1978	(403,707)	(157,026)	(560,733)
9.	Volvo			
	Volvo (Sweden)	212,782	33,499	246,281
	Volvo Car BV (Netherlands)	89,700	–	89,700
	Total	302,482	33,499	335,981
	1978	(246,621)	(29,944)	(276,565)
10.	BMW	328,281	–	328,281
	1978	(311,793)	–	(311,793)
11.	Alfa Romeo	207,514	2,036	209,550
	1978	(219,499)	(3,098)	(222,597)
12.	Saab	83,758	24,781	108,539
	1978	(72,516)	(21,334)	(93,850)
13.	Innocenti	39,991	–	39,991
	1978	(40,719)	–	(40,719)
14.	Porsche	36,011	–	36,011
	1978	(36,879)	–	(36,879)
15.	Motor Ibérica	–	27,278	27,278
	1978	–	(29,553)	(29,553)
16.	MAN	–	21,225	21,225
	1978	–	(20,364)	(20,364)
17.	Talbot Matra	16,638	–	16,638
	1978	(17,277)	–	(17,277)
18.	Enasa	–	15,052	15,052
	1978	–	(18,009)	(18,009)
19.	DAF Truck	–	14,982	14,982
	1978	–	(10,646)	(10,646)

PSA GROUP (PEUGEOT CITROEN TALBOT)

Peugeot is Europe's number one following the takeover of Citroën –

If one had suggested in 1970 that Western Europe's largest vehicle producer by the end of the decade would be the Peugeot group, the reaction would have been one of utter disbelief. Peugeot's development in the 1970s from a middle ranking, rather provincial, French company to Europe's number one (and the world's number four) has been accomplished by two major takeovers/mergers – with Citroën in 1974 and Chrysler Europe in 1978. Peugeot was initially a reluctant partner to Citroën when the latter faced severe financial problems as a result of the 1974/75 recession, but was persuaded by the French government to take Citroën on board. Despite fundamental differences in each company's approach which suggested that the merger would be a disaster, the alliance has proved remarkably fruitful. The injection of sound business and financial sense from Peugeot to curb some of the excesses of Citroën's brilliant (but expensive) engineering and design talent has had a significant impact on Citroën's fortunes. Although the two marques continue to produce recognisably different ranges of passenger cars – Peugeot utilising traditional engineering in a model lineup noted for reliability and durability, Citroën employing advanced engineering, especially with regard to suspension systems – there have been moves to rationalise the group's sourcing of major subassemblies (such as engines and transmissions) and other components.

– and Chrysler Europe

Following the successful absorption of Citroën into the group it is probable that Peugeot became aware of its latent managerial and organisational abilities. With a young and dynamic chief in the form of Mr Jean-Paul Parayre, the idea of further expansion became attractive and, in one of the motor industry's best kept secrets, negotiations started with the US Chrysler Corporation. These discussions led to an announcement in August 1978 that Peugeot Citroën had reached an agreement with the US company to acquire Chrysler Europe. Thus, overnight, Peugeot became the largest vehicle producer in Europe, although since that time questions have been raised over the wisdom of the move. Chrysler's European operations had not been notably successful either in product or financial terms. A loss of FFr100 mn was reported in 1978 and it seems inevitable that losses have grown significantly in 1979; stocks of finished vehicles have built up, labour disputes have occurred in the UK and Spanish factories, and to cap it all shipments of CKD car kits from the UK to Iran (a major part of the UK company's activity) have fallen dramatically. Nevertheless, Peugeot has demonstrated its confidence in Talbot's (the new name for Chrysler Europe) future by announcing an important $100 mn expansion to the Spanish facilities; interestingly, Chrysler Spain was the only part of what is now Talbot to make a profit in 1978.

PSA is heavily dependent on Europe –

Peugeot Citroën Talbot differs from the other leading automotive companies by being principally a European, rather than a world, company. Whereas Fiat, Volkswagen and Renault are currently expanding their sphere of influence on a global basis, Peugeot Citroën Talbot is mainly a supplier to Europe. A number of non-European ventures exist – for example, in Nigeria – and discussions are taking place which may result in the establishment of new operations – for example, in Egypt – but the group remains heavily dependent on market conditions in Europe.

– and the passenger car sector

Another, perhaps more serious, weakness arises over its dependence on the passenger car sector. When Citroën merged with Peugeot the former's commercial vehicle subsidiary – Berliet – was hived off and merged with Renault's Saviem. With the takeover of Chrysler Europe, Peugeot Citroën once more acquired a truck producer in the shape of Dodge (of the UK) and Barreiros (of Spain). Whether these two will be able to withstand the growing competition in the West European commercial vehicle sector remains to be seen, but Peugeot has stated its intention to develop them rather than try to find a buyer. Agreement has been reached with DAF Trucks to examine possible areas of technical and manufacturing cooperation.

Details of production from 1970 to 1979

Tables 26-31 present details of passenger car and commercial vehicle output for the six principal subsidiaries which make up Peugeot Citroën Talbot's European operations.

Table 26 clearly shows the underlying strength of Peugeot during the 1970s. Apart from declines in the recessionary years of 1974 and 1975, output of passenger cars increased every year to reach a level around 50 per cent higher in 1979 than in 1970. In the case of commercial vehicles (all under 4 tons gross vehicle weight) output more than doubled.

Table 26

Development of Peugeot's Vehicle Production, 1970-79

	Passenger cars		Commercial vehicles	
	Units	% change over previous year	Units	% change over previous year
1970[a]	525,201	19.2	51,451	6.4
1971[a]	559,480	6.5	61,513	19.6
1972	572,845	2.4	66,458	8.0
1973	655,690	14.5	77,264	16.3
1974	596,163	-9.1	92,786	20.1
1975	563,821	-5.4	80,164	-13.6
1976	655,760	16.3	102,810	28.2
1977	676,109	3.1	105,786	2.9
1978	742,303	9.8	119,500	13.0
1979	755,593	1.8	109,872	-8.1

a Figures for 1970 and 1971 are not strictly comparable with subsequent years due to the inclusion of non-countable CKD kits; in Peugeot's case this has the effect of inflating the 1970 and 1971 totals by approximately 30,000 passenger cars and 3,000 commercial vehicles in each year.

Source: Chambre Syndicale des Constructeurs d'Automobiles.

The pattern of Citroën's output during the 1970s has been almost as impressive as Peugeot's - at least as far as passenger cars are concerned. Output between 1970 and 1979 rose by 44.2 per cent, with a decline recorded in only one year - 1974. But Citroën's performance in the commercial vehicle sector has been far less consistent. Production has been extremely cyclical with, if anything, a downward tendency. It should be noted that the figures in Table 27 exclude Berliet's output, and refer to light goods vehicles of up to 4 tons gross vehicle weight which are marketed under the Citroën marque.

Table 27

Development of Citroën's Vehicle Production, 1970-79

| | Passenger cars | | Commercial vehicles | |
	Units	% change over previous year	Units	% change over previous year
1970[a]	471,078	10.7	69,079	-14.2
1971[a]	578,328	22.8	85,297	23.5
1972	601,918	4.1	61,540	-27.9
1973	606,674	0.8	67,338	9.4
1974	531,136	-12.5	66,026	-1.9
1975	548,451	3.3	50,377	-23.7
1976	614,321	12.0	64,928	28.9
1977	667,280	8.6	68,779	5.9
1978	678,949	1.7	55,497	-19.3
1979	679,327	0.1	48,251	-13.1

a Figures for 1970 and 1971 are not strictly comparable with
subsequent years due to the inclusion of non-countable CKD kits;
in Citroën's case this has the effect of inflating the 1970 and
1971 totals by approximately 50,000 passenger cars and
25,000 commercial vehicles in each year.

Source: Chambre Syndicale des Constructeurs d'Automobiles.

From Table 28 it is possible to see the distinctly mediocre showing of Chrysler's
French operations during the past ten years. The opening years of the decade
were bright enough and 1973's output of passenger cars almost reached the 0.5
mn level. But the company suffered badly in 1974/75 and, despite a reasonable
recovery in 1976, somehow failed to regain its momentum. By the time the
Chrysler Corporation sold out in 1978 the production base was on the decline
once again and there was a particularly serious dip in 1979 - despite buoyant
market conditions and inclusion of the attractive Horizon model in the company's
range.   Output of light vans (up to 2.5 tons gross vehicle weight) commenced in
1973, since when output has been consistently around 26,000 units per year.

Table 28

Development of Talbot's French Vehicle Production, 1970-79

| | Passenger cars | | Commercial vehicles | |
	Units	% change over previous year	Units	% change over previous year
1970[a]	402,870	3.8	-	-
1971[a]	484,267	20.2	-	-
1972	491,340	1.5	32	
1973	497,858	1.3	27,641	x863.8
1974	384,844	-22.7	24,362	-11.9
1975	383,169	-0.4	24,783	1.7

(continued)

Table 28 (continued)

Development of Talbot's French Vehicle Production, 1970-79

| | Passenger cars | | Commercial vehicles | |
	Units	% change over previous year	Units	% change over previous year
1976	482,696	26.0	27,957	12.8
1977	476,565	-1.3	28,533	2.1
1978	430,694	-9.6	24,574	-13.9
1979	364,799	-15.3	27,369	11.4

a Figures for 1970 and 1971 are not strictly comparable with subsequent years due to the inclusion of non-countable CKD kits; in Talbot's case this has the effect of inflating the 1970 and 1971 totals by approximately 50,000 passenger cars in each year.

Source: Chambre Syndicale des Constructeurs d'Automobiles.

Citroën's build up of its Spanish operations during the 1970s has been impressive. Production of passenger cars has expanded from 26,981 units in 1970 to a level in excess of 100,000 during the second half of the decade. Commercial vehicle output has also shown a significant - albeit less spectacular - advance.

Table 29

Development of Citroën's Spanish Vehicle Production, 1970-79

| | Passenger cars | | Commercial vehicles | |
	Units	% change over previous year	Units	% change over previous year
1970	26,981	13.0	14,247	13.4
1971	36,923	36.8	14,955	5.0
1972	41,567	12.6	16,269	8.8
1973	52,098	25.3	20,837	28.1
1974	69,671	33.7	21,707	4.2
1975	92,783	33.2	18,167	-16.3
1976	108,721	17.2	22,958	26.4
1977	108,368	-0.3	33,191	44.6
1978	106,434	-1.8	45,558	37.3
1979	109,130	2.5	51,600	13.3

Source: Agrupación Nacional de Fabricantes de Automoviles y Camiones.

Chrysler's deteriorating position in the UK is clearly evident from the following table. Peak output for passenger cars and commercial vehicles was recorded in 1971 and 1970 respectively. In the passenger car sector production levels remained at a respectable level until 1975 when unit output was almost halved within two years. This led to the severe financial difficulties which resulted in the UK government mounting a £162 mn rescue operation. Production recovered in 1977/78, but following the revolution in Iran the company's important export business with that country was badly disrupted in 1979. Together with an ageing model range, it is hardly surprising that output fell by almost 50 per cent. Conditions have been better in the commercial vehicle sector.

Table 30

Development of Talbot's UK Vehicle Production, 1970-79

	Passenger cars		Commercial vehicles	
	Units	% change over previous year	Units	% change over previous year
1970	216,995	24.8	31,972	0.2
1971	281,538	29.7	26,027	-18.6
1972	263,893	-6.3	24,419	-6.2
1973	265,413	0.6	26,100	6.9
1974	261,801	-1.4	25,004	-4.2
1975	226,612	-13.4	19,211	-23.2
1976	144,586	-36.2	14,360	-25.3
1977	169,492	17.2	15,645	8.9
1978	196,481	15.9	17,617	12.6
1979[a]	102,960	-47.6	17,576	-0.2

a 1979 figures are based on weekly average production.

Source: SMMT.

Chrysler España's passenger car output during the 1970s has been somewhat erratic. but nevertheless increased markedly from 36,979 units in 1970 to around 100,000 in 1977/78. Commercial vehicle output, on the other hand, has not been a significant part of the company's Spanish presence and has tended to fluctuate around the 5,000 units per year level. It is interesting to note, though, that Spain has become the centre for Talbot's heavy truck production.

Table 31

Development of Talbot's Spanish Vehicle Production, 1970-79

	Passenger cars		Commercial vehicles	
	Units	% change over previous year	Units	% change over previous year
1970	36,979	1.0	5,190	-21.8
1971	29,352	-20.6	3,638	-29.9
1972	62,962	114.5	5,026	38.2
1973	86,510	37.4	7,181	42.9
1974	76,097	-12.0	8,671	20.7
1975	66,655	-12.4	6,679	-23.0
1976	82,453	23.7	4,589	-31.3
1977	96,435	17.0	5,294	15.4
1978	98,934	2.6	5,227	-1.3
1979	72,891	-26.3	4,477	-14.3

Source: Agrupación Nacional de Fabricantes de Automoviles y Camiones.

RENAULT

A successful state owned group –

Renault made excellent progress in 1979 to become Western Europe's second largest vehicle producer, moving up from fourth place in 1978 and overtaking Volkswagen and Fiat. Although state owned, Renault prefers to think of itself as a private company with a single shareholder rather than as a nationalised organisation. The extent of the French government's support is unknown, but Renault has demonstrated that it is quite capable of holding its own in the commercial world. At the same time, though, few doubt that the French government would fail to provide whatever support might become necessary to support Renault's position, and the company's current expansionist moves find favour in official circles.

– strong in passenger cars –

One of the peculiarities of Renault's product planning is that the introduction of a new model has not necessarily resulted in the apparently superseded model being deleted; for example, the R14 did not immediately replace the R12, nor the R18 the R16. The result is that Renault has an extensive lineup of passenger cars ranging in size from the supermini R5 and utilitarian R4 to the large hatchback R20/30 range. The mid range models have been successfully updated, and although the smaller models are largely based on ageing designs they continue to find a ready market. The most recent model introduction, the Fuego sporting coupé, looks like being a strong contender in that specialist market niche, but Renault still has no effective challenger for the top end of the market.

– and determined to play a world role –

More recently, there have been strong indications that Renault intends to become a world force in the automotive sector. In Europe, a major project, valued at $400 mn, has been agreed with Portugal involving the construction of a facility capable of producing 55,000 passenger cars and 220,000 engines per year by the second half of the 1980s. Also in Europe, agreement has been reached with Volvo whereby Renault is to acquire a 20 per cent holding in Volvo's passenger car operations. The two sides plan to cooperate in the design, development and manufacture of a range of subassemblies.

However, it is the USA where Renault has made potentially the most significant moves with two important linkups. The first was an agreement with American Motors in early 1979 under which the French company has acquired a 22.5 per cent interest in the US company with a view to cooperating in a number of ventures. Initially the deal centres on expanding marketing opportunities for both companies, American Motors benefiting from higher Jeep sales through Renault's distribution network in developing countries, while Renault gains access to American Motors' 2,400 North American dealers. Eventually it is planned that Renault designed cars will be assembled by American Motors in the USA. Already the deal has shown up other opportunities, and it is reported that Renault is to produce cars in Mexico as a result of the American Motors connection.

- but weak in commercial vehicles

In the second move, Renault has purchased 20 per cent of the US truck producer, Mack. Again this provides further marketing opportunities because Renault is exporting (Club of Four based) trucks of 9-16 tons gvw for class 6 usage to the USA for distribution through Mack's dealers. This is a useful development because Renault's RVI (Renault Industrial Vehicles) operation - essentially Saviem and Berliet - represents a weak area of the group's overall activities. RVI has incurred heavy financial losses since its formation and is still not functioning as an effective integrated organisation, largely as a result of fundamental clashes in Saviem's and Berliet's approach; this suggests that whatever integration is achieved will be by a slow and painful process. RVI is primarily a supplier to the French market and there is no real EEC presence beyond limited sales of trucks in Belgium and the UK. Furthermore, its role elsewhere remains in the development stage with progress slower than expected.

Production details

Tables 32 to 35 provide details of output by Renault and its main European subsidiaries between 1970 and 1979.

Table 32

Development of Renault's Vehicle Production, 1970-79

	Passenger cars		Commercial vehicles	
	Units	% change over previous year	Units	% change over previous year
1970[a]	1,055,803	15.9	103,942	5.9
1971[a]	1,069,070	1.3	105,244	1.3
1972	1,049,658	-1.8	105,849	0.6
1973	1,100,971	4.9	108,371	2.4
1974	1,174,409	6.7	117,787	8.7
1975	1,042,261	-11.3	86,711	-26.4
1976	1,218,358	16.9	147,084	69.6
1977	1,259,038	3.3	139,512	-5.1
1978	1,240,941	-1.4	131,143	-6.0
1979	1,403,949	13.1	141,046	7.6

a Figures for 1970 and 1971 are not strictly comparable with subsequent years due to the inclusion of non-countable CKD kits; in Renault's case this has the effect of inflating the 1970 and 1971 totals by approximately 180,000 passenger cars and 12,000 commercial vehicles in each year.

Source: Chambre Syndicale des Constructeurs d'Automobiles.

34

Table 33

Development of Fasa Renault's Vehicle Production, 1970-79

	Passenger cars		Commercial vehicles	
	Units	% change over previous year	Units	% change over previous year
1970	87,612	16.7	11,108	13.7
1971	100,923	15.2	9,330	-16.0
1972	126,491	25.3	12,250	31.3
1973	166,003	31.2	15,671	27.9
1974	166,771	0.5	16,637	6.2
1975	192,759	15.6	13,225	-20.5
1976	201,557	4.6	11,134	-15.8
1977	224,358	11.3	13,144	18.1
1978	235,329	4.9	13,339	1.5
1979	261,430	11.1	13,892	4.1

Source: Agrupación Nacional de Fabricantes de Automoviles y Camiones.

In contrast to Renault's success in passenger car manufacturing, Tables 34 and 35 demonstrate the weakness of the group's commercial vehicle operations. In particular, Berliet's production base has been shrinking since the mid 1970s.

Table 34

Development of Saviem's Commercial Vehicle Production, 1970-79

	Units	% change over previous year
1970	36,321	4.9
1971	33,212	-8.6
1972	32,984	-0.7
1973	36,971	12.1
1974	39,561	7.0
1975	35,339	-10.7
1976	40,676	15.1
1977	35,059	-13.8
1978	30,733	-12.3
1979	28,926	-5.9

Source: Chambre Syndicale des Constructeurs d'Automobiles.

Table 35

Development of Berliet's Commercial Vehicle Production, 1970-79

	Units	% change over previous year
1970	22,677	13.4
1971	23,305	2.8
1972	21,672	-7.0
1973	23,244	7.3
1974	25,181	8.3
1975	23,975	-4.8
1976	23,799	-0.7
1977	20,455	-14.1
1978	18,215	-11.0
1979	16,718	-8.2

Source: Chambre Syndicale des Constructeurs d'Automobiles.

VOLKSWAGEN/AUDI NSU

A return from the brink of disaster -

Volkswagen's history during the past ten years proves that it is still possible to
recover from a seemingly irretrievable situation and prosper. The company found
itself in desperate trouble in the early 1970s as a result of becoming overdependent
on a single model - the legendary Beetle. Moreover, a hefty percentage of sales
were accounted for in the USA, and when the company lost its competitive edge in
that market there was a dramatic slump in output. This coincided with the 1973 oil
crisis with the result that output plummeted from over 1.6 mn passenger cars in
1971 to little more than 1 mn in 1975. Enormous financial losses were recorded at
this time and the workforce was cut back.

- by means of a three pronged programme

In order to recover its poise Volkswagen directed its attention towards three key
priorities - replacing the model range, regaining competitiveness in the US market,
and reducing the labour force. In all three objectives the company has achieved
a high measure of success. The current model lineup - Polo, Derby, Golf, Jetta,
Passat, Scirocco - represents a highly relevant European range. The company
has achieved satisfactory production runs to take advantage of economies of scale,
and has been clever in adapting its hatchback models - Polo and Golf - into notchback (three box) versions in the form of the Derby and Jetta.

Meanwhile, Volkswagen's presence in the US market has recently gone from
strength to strength - thanks to the US consumer's current interest in downsized
cars. The company's assembly facility for the Rabbit (the US name for the Golf)
in Pennsylvania has built up to full capacity working and is expected to produce
about 200,000 units in 1980. Indeed, Volkswagen's success in the USA has prompted
it to search for a suitable location for a second assembly plant.

In its West German factories Volkswagen was able to reduce the labour force by around 25,000 in the mid 1970s, and the company was helped in its recovery programme by being allowed to offset its huge losses of 1974 and 1975 against subsequent profits for tax purposes.

Expansion on an international scale –

Volkswagen has important operations in South America, especially in Brazil where Volkswagen do Brazil is responsible for all of Volkswagen's interests in South America. In 1979 Volkswagen acquired a controlling interest in Chrysler do Brazil. Thus, although in Europe Volkswagen is concentrated in West Germany, it is developing into a world company. It remains internationally minded and, for example, is examining the possibility of establishing a passenger car assembly operation in South Korea with Hyundai.

– and diversification at home –

There seems little doubt that the events of the early 1970s have had a lasting effect on the company's philosophy. Diversification has taken place on three fronts. First, as already noted, Volkswagen has moved from being essentially a one model company to a position where it has a well balanced model range. Secondly, it has placed increasing emphasis on commercial vehicles. Apart from making light vans it had kept clear of the commercial vehicle sector until its agreement with MAN to design, develop and produce a range of goods vehicles in the 6-9 ton gross vehicle weight class. And thirdly, it has diversified out of the automotive industry through acquisition of other companies. The proposed purchase of the West German computer company Nixdorf fell through, but this was followed up by the purchase of the Triumph typewriter company. In view of Volkswagen's healthy liquidity position, other acquisitions are possible.

– but the mainstream activity remains the main area for attention

On the question of Volkswagen's mainstream business, passenger car manufacturing, the company has made strenuous attempts to move upmarket with the Audi range. In this there has been only partial success, and Audi's products are still some way from being equated with those of Mercedes-Benz and BMW. Nevertheless, there have been a number of interesting technical developments, notably the use of a five cylinder engine in the Audi 100 model – and, more recently, the announcement of a four wheel drive Quattro model which appears to have radically altered previous assumptions about the suitability of four wheel drive for everyday road vehicles. It is noteworthy, though, that the wankel rotary engine as fitted to the troublesome NSU Ro80 model has been dropped. On the technical front Volkswagen's main claim to fame (and fortune) has been the development of a small diesel engine for passenger cars. The diesel version of the Golf has found a ready market, especially in North America where it is estimated that almost 50 per cent of Rabbit production will be diesel engined in 1980.

Production details

Tables 36 and 37 provide details of Volkswagen's and Audi NSU's vehicle production during the 1970s. The serious slide in Volkswagen's passenger car output in the first half of the decade is clearly evident and, despite a recovery in the second half. production has yet to match 1970/71 levels. Meanwhile commercial vehicle output has remained fairly static following a slump in 1974/75.

Table 36

Development of Volkswagen's Vehicle Production, 1970-79

| | Passenger cars | | Commercial vehicles | |
	Units	% change over previous year	Units	% change over previous year
1970	1,518,365	-0.9	102,832	-4.8
1971	1,622,490	6.9	93,415	-9.2
1972	1,373,183	-15.4	104,160	11.5
1973	1,364,154	-0.7	99,335	-4.6
1974	1,169,980	-14.2	69,718	-29.8
1975	1,050,286	-10.2	71,651	2.8
1976	1,220,943	16.2	93,920	31.1
1977	1,277,571	4.6	93,882	-
1978	1,345,981	5.4	93,067	-0.9
1979	1,304,466	-3.1	92,450	-0.7

Source: VDA.

Audi NSU also experienced a sharp fall in output during 1974/75. In the latter year production was almost 50 per cent below the peak 1973 year, but by 1979 there had been a good recovery.

Table 37

Development of Audi NSU's Passenger Car Production, 1970-79

	Units	% change over previous year
1970	316,539	19.7
1971	282,200	-10.8
1972	299,484	6.1
1973	409,793	36.8
1974	266,420	-35.0
1975	205,162	-23.0
1976	242,081	18.0
1977	317,928	31.3
1978	295,000	-7.2
1979	323,395	9.6

Source: VDA.

FIAT

The 1974/75 recession brought a policy of diversification –

The Fiat group – the largest private sector company in Italy – occupies a special
role in the Italian economy. As with Volkswagen, the 1974/75 recession gave
Fiat quite a fright. The company's initial reaction was to adopt a policy of
diversification in order to reduce its dependence on the passenger car sector.
Now, after a series of structural changes, Fiat has split itself into eleven operating
divisions of which two major ones are Fiat Auto (passenger cars) and Iveco
(commercial vehicles). Over the years Fiat has absorbed a number of other
vehicle producing interests. Thus, Fiat Auto comprises the Fiat, Autobianchi,
Lancia, and Ferrari marques, while Iveco includes the Fiat, OM, Unic and
Magirus marques.

– but Fiat is now investing heavily in its passenger car interests

After several years of low investment in its passenger car activities Fiat has
recently changed its approach and has begun to invest heavily. In Italy this
renewed interest is taking two main forms: the introduction of new technology to
increase productivity (for example, an extensive use of robots and the development of the unique Robogate production system); and an extensive new model programme of which the Ritmo (Strada) and Panda are only the beginning. A series
of new model introductions is planned for the early 1980s aimed at revamping
almost the entire range.

But despite Fiat's confidence – as expressed in this investment programme – the
company is vulnerable to the difficult economic, social and political conditions of
Italy. In particular, the labour relations climate leaves much to be desired; the
company has publicly stated that 1979's outturn was unsatisfactory with an estimated output of 200,000 cars lost through labour disputes, and there is recognition
that productivity increases are vital if competitiveness is to be maintained. Fiat
has taken a hard line during 1979 in an attempt to rid itself of troublemakers within
its factories, but a quick solution to this perennial problem does not seem likely.

In the passenger car markets of Western Europe Fiat has achieved a fair measure
of success with its model range. The 127 model, in particular, has proved to be
a worthy contender in the supermini class, and the company has demonstrated the
ability to respond to developing market needs quickly – for example, by introducing
a diesel engined version of the Ritmo. Autobianchi is essentially a supplier to the
local market (which accounts for about 75 per cent of the division's output), while
Lancia probably needs further investment and development if the company is to
reach its underlying potential. Problems with the Lancia Monte Carlo (a small
volume, two seater, sports car) which led to the model's temporary withdrawal
have not helped, but perhaps the introduction of the Delta (winner of the European
car of the year award), which shares a number of subassemblies with the Strada,
will herald better times for Lancia. Fiat's prime market weakness is its failure
to secure higher sales in North America. The company suffers from a poor image
in that market, and it is significant that Iveco's commercial vehicles are marketed
in the USA under the Magirus marque.

Iveco represents Fiat's ambitions in the commercial vehicle sector

Iveco represents Fiat's attempt to become number one in the European commercial
vehicle sector. It is still some way behind Daimler-Benz, but with production
facilities in Italy (Fiat and OM), France (Unic) and West Germany (Magirus
Deutz), the basis for a comprehensive attack on European markets is there.
Iveco, with headquarters in the Netherlands, is a shining example of a pan European
organisation which works. Impressive progress has been made in the areas of
product and production rationalisation and market development, and in an important
move in 1979 Fiat bought out its previous partner in Iveco (KHD) to become sole
owner.

World company status is Fiat's aim -

Fiat is developing into a world company. It has major interests outside Europe,
notably in South America. Like Volkswagen, Fiat is using its Brazilian facilities
as a source of subassemblies for its European factories and is already importing
assembled engines. In Eastern Europe the company has extensive links, and
there are plans to use Poland as a source for a new Fiat model, the Zero. In
Western Europe, though, as far as passenger cars are concerned Fiat appears to
be preoccupied with sorting itself out in Italy. The company was invited by the
Spanish government to become more deeply involved in Seat, but this offer has
not been taken up. Fiat apparently cannot justify the investment required to put
Seat on a firmer footing and is to withdraw completely, thereby allowing the
Spanish operation to link up with another major vehicle manufacturer - probably
from Japan; it is understood that both Toyota and Nissan have expressed interest.

- and there is recognition of the value of joint ventures

Despite these developments, though, Fiat recognises the desirability of entering
into joint ventures with other companies. A cooperative agreement has been signed
with Peugeot for the production of a light van and there is a possibility that
Peugeot's and Fiat's South American interests will join forces. Fiat is a member
of the Sofim (small diesel engine) venture, along with Alfa Romeo and Renault.
And it appears that other collaborative agreements are being actively sought.

Production details

Tables 38 to 44 indicate passenger car and commercial vehicle output of Fiat and
its six principal subsidiaries from 1970 to 1979. Fiat itself has witnessed a
general decline in its production base for passenger cars throughout the 1970s,
with quite severe damage done in 1974/75. Despite the buoyancy of European
markets generally in 1978/79, this has failed to be reflected in production terms -
although the "lost" 200,000 units would obviously have made quite a difference.
In commercial vehicles Fiat's performance has been far brighter, probably as a
result of enhanced marketing opportunities through Iveco's distribution network.

Although Fiat and Seat are now severing connections, Seat's production figures
are included in this section of the report.

Table 42

Development of Magirus Deutz's Commercial Vehicle Production, 1970-79

	Units	% change over previous year
1970	19,428	34.8
1971	14,362	-26.1
1972	11,766	-18.1
1973	11,291	-4.0
1974	14,040	24.3
1975	17,852	27.2
1976	23,071	29.2
1977	18,461	-20.0
1978	18,685	1.2
1979	20,184	8.0

Source: VDA.

Fiat's commercial vehicle facility in France, Unic, has benefited from its association with Iveco. Investment in new production facilities has had a marked impact on production performance in the second half of the 1970s.

Table 43

Development of Unic Fiat's Commercial Vehicle Production, 1970-79

	Units	% change over previous year
1970	8,066	-1.8
1971	7,293	-9.6
1972	9,174	25.8
1973	10,018	9.2
1974	10,343	3.2
1975	13,573	31.2
1976	15,674	15.5
1977	17,110	9.2
1978	16,658	-2.6
1979	18,646	11.9

Source: Chambre Syndicale des Constructeurs d'Automobiles.

Despite membership of Iveco, OM's output record in the second half of the 1970s has been dismal, with 1978/79 being particularly depressed years.

Table 44

Development of OM's Commercial Vehicle Production, 1970-79

	Units	% change over previous year
1970	22,702	18.3
1971	20,866	-8.1
1972	18,043	-13.5
1973	25,824	43.1
1974	29,588	14.6
1975	23,716	-19.8
1976	20,940	-11.7
1977	21,567	3.0
1978	12,662	-41.3
1979	13,713	8.3

Source: ANFIA.

FORD

An integrated European operation

Since Ford integrated its European facilities into Ford of Europe there has been significant expansion of the US company's operations. Based on 1979 output figures, Ford has built up a big lead in Europe over its principal US rival, General Motors. There is a widespread network of component and subassembly producing facilities throughout Europe, but passenger car production is centred on West Germany, the UK and Spain. In addition, there are several assembly locations, notably in Belgium where the Taunus/Cortina model is assembled. (Since this assembled output is not included elsewhere in Ford's production statistics it is counted as production in the official statistics.) Commercial vehicle production is concentrated almost exclusively in the UK.

Passenger cars: an attractive five model lineup

On the passenger car front the company has developed an attractive and relevant five model European range - Fiesta, Escort, Taunus/Cortina, Capri and Granada. Interest in the marketplace has been sustained by the introduction of facelifts and new models on a regular basis. Ford's greatest success is its position in the UK where it has taken over as the natural market leader from BL; all five models are consistently the best sellers in their respective classes. But in other major European markets the same kind of success has eluded Ford.

The process of production rationalisation is at an advanced stage. Ford's policy has been to secure economies of scale in component and subassembly manufacturing by concentrating output in factories where long runs can be achieved, and which can then supply factories of final assembly. For example, the Bridgend engine plant in South Wales - scheduled to come on stream in 1980 - will supply engines for the European output of Ford's Erika (the new Escort) which will be produced in the UK and West Germany. Thus, Ford operates on a true pan European basis and is able to regard Western Europe as one nation when it comes to investment and product sourcing. This allows a good deal of flexibility which enables Ford to "top up" supply in a market whenever local producing facilities are unable to meet demand. In practice this has been of greatest benefit to Ford's marketing thrust in the UK which has received cars from West Germany, Belgium, Spain and the Republic of Ireland. But in cases where a model has a limited level of output, Ford concentrates production in a single facility. Thus, all Capris and Granadas are produced in West Germany.

It was widely thought that Ford took a gamble over the introduction of the super-mini Fiesta model, which involved utilising front wheel drive - for which the company had no previous production experience - in a ferociously competitive market sector. Moreover, the choice of a greenfield site in Valencia, Spain, for the majority of the Fiesta's output could have caused formidable problems. In the event, though, the gamble has paid off handsomely. Not only is the Fiesta an outstanding success in its class but it has provided Ford with a contender in a market niche which can only become more important in the fuel conscious 1980s. Also, Ford has proved its competence in front wheel drive engineering, which will be incorporated in the Erika.

However, not everything has been plain sailing. Labour unrest remains a problem in the UK and Spain, and attempts to set up a component manufacturing plant in the Lorraine district of France foundered when PSA and Renault attacked the French government's plan to offer financial incentives.

Commercial vehicles: strong and successful UK base

As already noted, Ford's commercial vehicle operations are primarily located in the UK. However, for its heavy duty Transcontinental truck the Netherlands was chosen as the assembly point - even though many of the parts (including engines from Cummins) are sourced from the UK.

Ford has in general achieved good success in the commercial vehicle sector, but the impact of current individual models is mixed. For example, whereas the Transit van has been a phenomenal success and, indeed, the inspiration of a whole generation of "copies" from other manufacturers, the Transcontinental is far less of a hit. In addition, the long serving 'D' series truck is beginning to show its age and will be replaced before long. Recognising the need to do more, Ford launched a five year, £400 mn investment programme in 1977 aimed at narrowing the gap between itself and Europe's pacemakers - Daimler-Benz and Iveco. As part of this plan, Ford Trucks Europe, with headquarters at Basildon in the UK, has been set up.

European operations a major prop to Ford's worldwide position

There is no doubt that the buoyancy of Ford's European business is currently a major prop to the US company's overall position. Huge losses were chalked up by Ford's US operations in 1979 - reportedly around the $1 bn level. Whether this was a factor in Ford's decision to postpone the proposed additional European car producing facility is uncertain. But despite this setback in the USA, Ford is expected to spend around $5.5 bn in Europe between 1979 and 1985 - excluding whatever might be required if additional car manufacturing capacity is installed.

Production details

Tables 45–47 provide details of Ford's vehicle production during the 1970s in the UK, West Germany and Spain. An indication of Ford's output in Belgium is provided in Table 1 since it is the only producer (as opposed to assembler) in Belgium.

During the past ten years passenger car output in the UK has declined, while commercial vehicle output increased. To a certain extent this masks Ford's commitment to the UK, which has increasingly become an important source of subassemblies for continental factories. The inconsistency of output levels in the UK is partly explained by the periodic occurrence of lengthy strikes; thus, Ford's nine week stoppage in the UK in 1978 is clearly reflected in the figures.

Table 45

Development of Ford's UK Vehicle Production, 1970-79

	Passenger cars		Commercial vehicles	
	Units	% change over previous year	Units	% change over previous year
1970	448,422	-15.7	140,848	2.8
1971	366,602	-18.2	120,661	-14.3
1972	546,722	49.1	143,519	18.9
1973	453,448	-17.1	137,217	-4.4
1974	383,724	-15.4	131,268	-4.3
1975	329,648	-14.1	129,111	-1.6
1976	383,220	16.3	141,628	9.7
1977	406,633	6.1	148,369	4.8
1978	324,407	-20.2	106,472	-28.2
1979[a]	398,684	22.9	167,232	57.1

a 1979 figures are based on weekly average production.

Source: SMMT.

Following a sharp downturn in 1974, passenger car output in the West German facilities improved usefully between 1975 and 1977. However, 1978 and 1979 were years of consolidation.

Table 46

Development of Ford's West German Passenger Car Production, 1970-79

	Units	% change over previous year
1970	409,409	36.1
1971	478,556	16.9
1972	435,966	-8.9
1973	456,022	4.6
1974	285,545	-37.4

(continued)

Table 46 (continued)

Development of Ford's West
German Passenger Car Production, 1970-79

	Units	% change over previous year
1975	413,135	44.7
1976	486,607	17.8
1977	542,750	11.5
1978	544,160	0.3
1979	546,957	0.5

Source: VDA.

Ford's ambitious project in Spain to produce the Fiesta commenced production in 1976. Output built up in 1977 and 1978, and in the latter year Ford overtook Fasa Renault to become Spain's second largest passenger car producer. However, Ford was pushed into third place again in 1979 when labour problems at Valencia caused a loss of output. A van version of the Fiesta was introduced in 1977.

Table 47

Development of Ford's Spanish Vehicle Production, 1976-79

	Passenger cars		Commercial vehicles	
	Units	% change over previous year	Units	% change over previous year
1976	17,508		–	
1977	213,268	x12.2	629	
1978	260,939	22.4	7,031	x 11.2
1979	227,493	-12.8	4,939	-29.8

Source: Agrupación Nacional de Fabricantes de Automoviles y Camiones.

GENERAL MOTORS

Contrasting fortunes at Opel and Vauxhall

When General Motors' executives in Detroit sit down to consider their European operations it must seem as though they have, in Opel and Vauxhall, the automotive equivalent to the beauty and the beast. Opel, nicknamed the "money machine" and with a production level in 1979 of almost 1 mn vehicles, is in a different league from Vauxhall whose passenger car operations during the 1970s have undergone an almost total eclipse. Vauxhall never recovered from a series of disastrous mistakes beginning in the 1960s when its individual and rather successful model range began to be replaced by models which incorporated heavy and, for the UK market, unsuitable American styling overtones. This, coupled with a level of output which could no longer continue to justify a model range in its own right, caused Vauxhall to move closer to Opel - to the point where it is increasingly an assembly satellite of GM's West German subsidiary as far as passenger cars are concerned. Already Vauxhall is assembling Opel kits. and built up units bearing a Vauxhall badge - such as the Astra and Royale models - are imported from West Germany.

Opel is responsible for GM's
<u>European passenger car development -</u>

Meanwhile Opel has taken over full responsibility for developing General Motors' European passenger car range and has evolved an extremely attractive lineup - Kadett (Astra). Ascona/Manta (Cavalier), Rekord (Carlton). Commodore, and Senator/Monza (Royale). Special mention should be made of the models which occupy the two ends of the range's spectrum. The new Kadett, announced in August 1979. represents a significant advance in GM's small car credentials. Attractively styled in the modern European idiom. the Kadett is available in hatch-back. notchback (three box) and estate car form. and manages to provide good interior space in overall compact dimensions. At the top end of the range the Senator saloon and Monza coupé models have at last provided GM with worthy contenders in the large. executive car category after the disappointing Diplomat and Admiral models.

<u>- while Vauxhall (Bedford) handles commercial vehicles</u>

In the commercial vehicle sector Vauxhall (Bedford) plays the dominant role in GM's European operations. A full range of goods vehicles is produced from the Chevanne car derived van to the heavy duty TM articulated unit. As well as being an important supplier to the UK market. Bedford has had notable success in continental European markets which take around 30 per cent of the company's output.

<u>Massive expansion of GM's operations planned</u>

However, despite the strength of Opel in cars and Vauxhall in commercial vehicles. General Motors in Western Europe has found itself in the uncharacteristic position of trailing Ford in a major market. In order to close this gap GM recently announced major expansion projects for Europe which will increase the company's output by 300,000 passenger cars per year. The main plank of this investment programme. valued at $2 bn. involves the construction of a new car assembly plant in Spain but. in addition. component and subassembly operations are to be established in several locations, including the UK. Spain and Austria - the last country being chosen for engine and transmission production.

<u>Production details</u>

Although Opel produces nearly 1 mn passenger cars per year, its role as a commercial vehicle producer is minimal. In the second half of the 1970s Opel made a good recovery from the 1974/75 recession, and 1979's outturn represented a new record.

Table 48

Development of Opel's Vehicle Production, 1970-79

	Passenger cars		Commercial vehicles	
	Units	% change over previous year	Units	% change over previous year
1970	811,640	3.0	9,212	-29.1
1971	831,872	2.5	6,846	-25.7
1972	871,364	4.7	6,117	-10.6
1973	868,182	-0.4	6,173	0.9
1974	578,264	-33.4	5,381	-12.8
1975	655,877	13.4	1,662	-69.1
1976	918,856	40.1	2,840	70.9
1977	922,304	0.4	2,863	0.8
1978	952,656	3.3	3,799	32.7
1979	960,243	0.8	8,223	116.5

Source: VDA.

Table 49 reveals the patchy performance of Vauxhall during the 1970s, with 1979 car production barely more than a quarter that of the peak year in 1971. It is important to remember, though, that these figures do not include car assembly; in 1979 Vauxhall assembled an estimated 40,000 units from Opel kits - 30,000 Cavaliers and 10,000 Carltons. On present trends Vauxhall will cease car production altogether within the next couple of years. The company currently produces only the Chevette model, which is likely to see its prospects badly dented by the imported Vauxhall Astra. In contrast, Vauxhall's commercial vehicle output has remained reasonably - albeit erratically - steady over the ten year period.

Table 49

Development of Vauxhall's Vehicle Production, 1970-79

	Passenger cars		Commercial vehicles	
	Units	% change over previous year	Units	% change over previous year
1970	178,089	3.7	101,660	-0.8
1971	199,092	11.8	126,394	24.3
1972	183,957	-7.6	90,813	-28.2
1973	138,353	-24.8	107,257	18.1
1974	136,903	-1.0	112,151	4.6
1975	98,621	-28.0	91,421	-18.5
1976	109,118	10.6	86,389	-5.5
1977	93,237	-14.6	91,747	6.2
1978	84,041	-9.9	117,443	28.0
1979[a]	58,760	-30.1	87,672	-25.3

a 1979 figures are based on weekly average production.

Source: SMMT.

BL

<u>Deteriorating conditions led to state takeover in 1975</u>

BL (more commonly, if unofficially, known as British Leyland) was formed from
the 1968 merger between the Leyland Motor Corporation and British Motor
Holdings. Although the group contains many famous passenger car and commercial vehicle marques - Austin, Morris, MG, Jaguar, Rover, Triumph, Vanden
Plas, Leyland, Scammell, etc - BL has had a distinctly chequered career since
the merger. Indeed, BL's example shows how difficult it is to bring together into
a coherent whole a collection of formerly independent and proud vehicle manufacturing companies. The failure to rationalise sufficiently quickly, coupled with
falling sales in the period following the 1973 oil crisis, led to a financial crisis
in 1975 - at a time, moreover, when massive capital funds were required to finance the investment for the company's survival and future prosperity. Unable to
obtain the finance required from private sector sources, the UK government
stepped in with a major support programme and became the company's majority
shareholder. However, the government's original rescue proposals were soon
overtaken by events and, in another shakeup, a new executive chairman was
appointed in November 1977 in the form of Sir Michael Edwardes.

The present policy at BL favours a decentralised approach. The main operating
divisions have been split into independent units, but are supported by a central
organisation. However, BL's problems are far from over and the company is
dependent on further government aid (about £950 mn had been provided since
1975 at the last count) for its survival. As recently as December 1979 the
government allocated another £300 mn tranche of public funds for BL's recovery
programme.

The urgent need for a new mid
<u>range car paves way for Honda's Bounty</u>

With regard to passenger cars, BL urgently needs new models to replace its
existing lineup - particularly in the mid range category. In order to plug this
gap sooner rather than later, BL began searching for a partner and eventually
concluded an agreement with Honda, whereby the British company will assemble
a new Honda design from the middle of 1981. This significant move indicates
BL's desire to become involved in the kind of joint ventures which are increasingly
used by vehicle manufacturing companies as a way of benefiting from economies of
scale without losing independence. It is clear from statements made by BL's
management that further joint ventures are being sought as a matter of urgency,
and there is speculation that the ties between BL and Honda will become stronger
and closer.

<u>Much depends on the Mini Metro</u>

Another important milestone will be the launch of the Mini Metro, BL's offering
in the supermini class, which is expected to be unveiled in September/October
1980. Heavy investment has gone into all aspects of this project, including the
extensive use of industrial robots on the production line. There has been evidence

lately of the management adopting a firm line on industrial relations in order to forestall potential trouble closer to the Mini Metro's introduction date.

Although BL has not been without success in recent years with its passenger cars - the Rover SD1 (2300/2600/3500 range) was voted car of the year for 1976, and the TR7, despite teething troubles, has matured into a strong challenger in the sports car market - aspects of the product planning process have been rather strange. New models have frequently not adequately replaced superseded ones, the most notable example being the Allegro which was meant to replace the best selling 1100/1300 range.

Problems with cars have spilt over into commercial vehicles

The problems of the car divisions have had a serious impact on BL's commercial vehicle operations. The once dynamic truck and bus producing activities of the Leyland Motor Corporation have been severely affected as a result of being starved for so long of the financial and managerial resources necessary for them to meet the challenges of the continental producers. A disproportionate amount of attention was directed towards the main problem area - Austin Morris - with consequences for the truck division which have only become apparent in the past two or three years. The failure to capitalise on the underlying strength of what is now Leyland Vehicles is probably the single biggest mistake made by British Leyland's management in the early 1970s, but since 1975 - and especially since Edwardes - much has been done to make up this deficiency. Indeed, some encouraging signs are emerging that Leyland Vehicles' fortunes are beginning to turn round, and the arrival of two critical new models - the T43 Landtrain (normal control truck for developing country markets) and T45 Roadtrain (heavy duty truck for UK and European markets) - is a good start. A new, modern truck assembly hall has commenced operations at Leyland (in Lancashire).

On a less bright note, though, BL has problems with its light/medium commercial vehicle operation at Bathgate, Scotland, and with certain of its bus producing plants; Park Royal, where the Titan double deck bus is produced, is scheduled to close in 1980.

Expansion of four wheel drive output

Perhaps BL's greatest success is the Land Rover division whose products continue to find a ready market throughout the world - despite growing competition from newer designs of other manufacturers. In response to this success a £280 mn investment programme was commissioned aimed at doubling output to 150,000 units per year by the mid 1980s.

On the international scene there has been both expansion and contraction

Looking at the international scene BL's policy appears confused and inconsistent. At a time when most other manufacturers have understood the overriding need to operate on a European basis, BL has withdrawn on a wide front. Interests in Spain were sold and the Innocenti operation in Italy was seemingly abandoned - although Nuova Innocenti continues to source kits for Minis from the UK. Moreover, there now appears to be a question mark over BL's continued presence in

Belgium where Minis and Allegros are assembled at Seneffe. More seriously, there is little evidence that BL's dealer network on the continent is sufficiently developed to secure a worthwhile market presence for the new models which will be coming along.

Meanwhile, BL is developing its links quite strongly in other areas - notably Africa and India. In Nigeria BL has a 40 per cent interest in, and a management contract to run, what is probably the most advanced truck plant in any developing country. And in India BL has invested £27 mn in Ashok Leyland.

Production details

BL's disastrous production record is highlighted in Table 50. Apart from a recovery in 1976. passenger car output has fallen every year since 1972. 1979's car output probably represents around 45 per cent of the company's output capability. The decline in commercial vehicle output is also serious, albeit less marked.

Table 50

Development of BL's Vehicle Production, 1970-79

	Passenger cars		Commercial vehicles	
	Units	% change over previous year	Units	% change over previous year
1970	788,737	-5.1	172,968	-6.7
1971	886,721	12.4	174,235	0.7
1972	916,218	3.3	140,097	-19.6
1973	875,839	-4.4	136,649	-2.5
1974	738,503	-15.7	124,658	-8.8
1975	605,141	-18.1	133,099	6.8
1976	687,875	13.7	120,174	-9.7
1977	651,069	-5.4	120,271	0.1
1978	611,625	-6.1	131,478	9.3
1979[a]	503,776	-17.6	124,644	-5.2

a 1979 figures are based on weekly average production.

Source: SMMT.

DAIMLER-BENZ

Output is concentrated in high value products

Although Daimler-Benz is ranked only eighth in Europe in terms of vehicle output, the company comes near the top if value turnover is used as the measuring rod. There are two reasons for this: first, its position as the largest truck producer in Western Europe; and, secondly, its output of large, mainly luxurious (and therefore high priced) passenger cars. The company enjoys a solid reputation for building a high level of technical and engineering excellence into its products which, in turn, are noted for their quality, reliability and durability.

A solid performance in passenger cars –

Daimler-Benz achieved great success during the 1970s in the passenger car
sector. Output has been firm throughout the period, falling in only one year,
1978 – and then as a result of industrial action rather than a weakening of demand.
Indeed, the company benefits from a strong order book and is able to plan for
expansion with confidence.

The image of a Mercedes-Benz car (the marque name of Daimler-Benz) varies
subtly from market to market. In its native West Germany and several other
continental markets the marque is not especially endowed with an upmarket image.
Diesel engines are fitted to a high proportion of output (about 49 per cent in 1979),
and certain models – admittedly mainly the base ones – are utilised for taxi work.
In contrast, in North America and the UK Daimler-Benz deliberately fosters an
upmarket image and its models compete with Cadillac, Jaguar and even Rolls-
Royce at the top end of the scale.

As well as making saloon cars, Daimler-Benz is famous for a series of sporting
coupés which perhaps are best described as grand touring cars. In 1978 an estate
car range was added to the lineup.

– and commercial vehicles

The commercial vehicle operations are a major source of strength. A comprehensive range of rigid and articulated goods vehicles and buses are produced in
West Germany, and there is a sizeable manufacturing facility in Brazil which is
used to supply the US market. In view of the growing acceptance of diesel powered
trucks in North America in the context of high fuel prices, Daimler-Benz is establishing a truck assembly plant at Hampton, Virginia.

There are other signs too that Daimler-Benz is spreading its wings. It has
entered into a joint venture with Steyr, in Austria, for the production of light 4x4
vehicles, and it is reported that discussions have taken place with Chinese officials
concerning the possibility of setting up truck manufacturing operations in that
country.

Production details

From Table 51 it is possible to see Daimler-Benz's remarkably consistent output
performance in the 1970s. Despite being a producer of essentially large, and
therefore thirsty, cars, the company managed to ride the 1974/75 recession without
witnessing a production decline. Over the 1970-79 period passenger car output
advanced by an average of 5 per cent per year. On the face of it commercial
vehicle output increased even more firmly – by an average of 5.5 per cent per
year. However, from 1976 onwards Daimler-Benz's commercial vehicle production
figures include those of Hanomag-Henschel, a subsidiary company which was
acquired in the late 1960s.

Table 51

Development of Daimler-Benz's Vehicle Production, 1970-79

| | Passenger cars | | Commercial vehicles | |
	Units	% change over previous year	Units	% change over previous year
1970	280,419	9.2	106,258	16.1
1971	284,230	1.4	98,280	-7.5
1972	323.878	13.9	102,513	4.3
1973	331,682	2.4	116,554	13.7
1974	340.006	2.5	125,239	7.5
1975	350,098	3.0	145,256	16.0
1976	378.241	8.0	180,244	24.1
1977	409.090	8.2	174,091	-3.4
1978	403.707	-1.3	157,026	-9.8
1979	433.203	7.3	171,656	9.3

Source: VDA.

VOLVO

A vital plank in Sweden's economy

As Sweden's largest industrial enterprise Volvo occupies a special place in that country's economy. In addition to producing a range of large cars, medium and heavy duty trucks. and buses in Sweden, Volvo has a passenger car producing facility in the Netherlands (Volvo Car BV) and various assembly locations else-where - of which probably the most important is the truck operation in Brazil which is scheduled to come on stream in 1980.

The company's products have traditionally been well engineered and are noted for their safety. durability and reliability - qualities which have enabled Volvo to command a strong and loyal market following.

Recent difficulties with passenger cars -

On the passenger car side Volvo produces two distinct ranges, the 2 series in Sweden and the 3 series in the Netherlands. The 2 series has been a success, but is now urgently in need of updating. For 1980 tastes, its styling is rather heavy and outmoded. and Volvo can no longer claim to have a near monopoly when it comes to building safety into cars.

In the mid 1970s, following the 1973 oil crisis, Volvo made a move into small cars through acquiring DAF's ailing passenger car business. This diversification. though. was ill timed and has resulted in serious and protracted problems. Growing financial strains caused Volvo to seek help from the Dutch government and at the start of 1978 a rescue package was announced. Since that time con-ditions seem to have improved and output of 89.000 units in 1979 was a considerable improvement on 1978's outturn - albeit some way off the 100,000 breakeven target. Furthermore. there are indications that the 3 series. after a shaky start. is attracting a greater market following, particularly in its latest manual gear-box and five door versions.

– but commercial vehicles are benefiting from high investment

In the commercial vehicle sector Volvo is benefiting from the fruits of a heavy investment programme, valued at Skr1 bn, which has effectively updated its entire model range since the mid 1970s. Further investment of up to Skr3 bn is envisaged which suggests that Volvo does not intend to lose the initiative in this vital area of its business. In both passenger cars and commercial vehicles Volvo is heavily dependent on export sales and, in an attempt to improve sales to North America, an agreement has been reached with Freightliner to distribute Volvo trucks.

Volvo has been active in joint ventures –

Volvo has been one of the most active companies in the search for joint ventures. The company suffers from the twin effects of producing at low volumes in an environment of high manufacturing costs. This means that Volvo has been unable to earn sufficient profits to finance the new products necessary to retain, let alone expand, its position in the marketplace. The company has entered into a number of joint ventures – for example, the V6 petrol engine project with Renault and Peugeot on cars, and the Club of Four with Magirus Deutz, DAF and Saviem on trucks – but these have not provided a long term solution to Volvo's funda-mental requirement.

– and the search for a partner

The attempt to find a partner has been long and tortuous. Initially a merger with Saab Scania was proposed, but was called off. Then an arrangement whereby the Norwegian government would have acquired a 40 per cent holding in the Swedish company was worked out, but was scuppered by protests from shareholders. More recently a tieup with Renault has been announced whereby the French company will eventually acquire a 20 per cent holding in Volvo's passenger car operations in return for cooperation on component and subassembly manufacturing.

Production details

Table 52 provides details of Volvo's passenger car and commercial vehicle output in Sweden, while Table 53 gives Volvo Car BV's production. In the case of Swedish output it is noticeable how Volvo's commercial vehicle interests have performed much more strongly than the passenger car operations during the past ten years.

Table 52

Development of Volvo's Vehicle Production, 1970-79

| | Passenger cars | | Commercial vehicles | |
	Units	% change over previous year	Units	% change over previous year
1970	204,991	...	17,397	...
1971	214,438	4.6	16,913	-2.8
1972	233,965	9.1	18,448	9.1
1973	252,036	7.7	20,596	11.6
1974	234,189	-7.1	23,291	13.1
1975	225,424	-3.7	30,989	33.1
1976	221,453	-1.8	29,858	-3.6
1977	158,885	-28.3	29,866	-
1978	181,740	14.4	29,944	0.3
1979	212,782	17.1	33,499	11.9

Source: Association of Swedish Automotive Manufacturers and Wholesalers.

Table 53

Development of Volvo Car BV's
Passenger Car Production, 1970-79

	Units	% change over previous year
1970[a]	67,262	10.8
1971[a]	78,087	16.1
1972[a]	87,396	11.9
1973[a]	94,906	8.6
1974[a]	69,234	-27.0
1975	60,528	-12.6
1976	74,223	22.6
1977	53,368	-28.1
1978	64,881	21.6
1979	89,700	38.3

a DAF's output; Volvo took over in 1975.

Source: CBS.

BMW

An enviable reputation enhanced by new models

BMW (Bayerische Motoren Werke or, in English, Bavarian Motor Works) has won an enviable reputation as a producer of high quality, high performance sporting saloons and coupés. It is noticeable, though, that increasing emphasis of late has been placed on the luxury and economy aspects of the company's model range.

BMW's image has been considerably enhanced over the past four years with the introduction of two new model series. The first, the 6 series, is a high performance, luxuriously equipped, well styled, two door coupé, while the second, the 7 series, provides BMW's answer to Mercedes-Benz in the large luxury saloon category. These newer models have joined the 3 series and (now rather ancient) 5 series to provide BMW with an extremely competitive lineup.

Growing interest in motor sport –

BMW is the smallest of the major West German vehicle producers and as such has worked hard at promoting itself. Like Porsche, BMW has chosen to become more closely involved in motor racing and in 1979 sponsored the Procar programme at grand prix meetings. BMW's sporting credentials were furthered by the introduction in 1978 of the M1 model – a mid engined and exotic looking sports car.

– and diesel engines

The current interest in diesel engined cars on the continent has caused BMW to examine closely this power form, and agreement has been reached with Steyr to construct a factory in Austria which will eventually be producing diesel engines at the rate of 100,000–150,000 per year.

Motorcycle operations face stiff competition –

BMW differs from most of the other principal West European vehicle manufacturers in two interesting ways. First, it has no interests in commercial vehicle manufacturing. And, secondly, there is a sizeable facility for the production of motorcycles. This operation, however, has found it difficult to compete effectively against the Japanese in world markets at a time when the Deutschmark has been strong and the yen has shown considerable weakness.

– but the future is faced with confidence

As a small company in automotive terms BMW should perhaps be more vulnerable than its larger counterparts. Nevertheless, since the mid 1970s the company's production and financial performance has been highly creditable and BMW has more than held its own. BMW has found and successfully exploited a worthwhile market niche and has had the courage to spend a relatively high proportion of turnover on research and development. The future is faced with confidence, even though substantial funds will be required to maintain the investment programme.

Production details

BMW suffered only a minor setback in 1974 and has moved forward strongly ever since. The introduction of the 6 series in 1976, which extended BMW's range, coincided with a notable boost in output.

Table 54

Development of BMW's
Passenger Car Production, 1970-79

	Units	% change over previous year
1970	158,618	13.6
1971	163,832	3.3
1972	181,964	11.1
1973	196,075	7.8
1974	184,681	-5.8
1975	217,458	17.7
1976	267,618	23.1
1977	284,771	6.4
1978	311,793	9.5
1979	328,281	5.3

Source: VDA.

ALFA ROMEO

A loss making state owned company –

Alfa Romeo, Italy's second largest vehicle producer, is a subsidiary of the state
owned IRI organisation. During the past few years Alfa Romeo has recorded huge
losses and has therefore become heavily dependent on outside (i e state) sources
of finance.

There are two main centres for passenger car production – Milan and Naples
(where the Alfasud plant is located). To a certain extent the company is an
instrument of government policy, and it seems probable that it would not have
chosen Naples for a major new production facility had it been given a free hand.

– with an interesting range of cars

Alfa Romeo is one of the more glamorous names in the automotive industry. It
has a well deserved reputation for high performance, and attractively (and distinctively) styled products which have a sporting flavour. The current range
upholds this tradition, but it is now obvious that the company is no longer generating the finance to continue along these lines independently. Discussions are
understood to have taken place with several potential partners, with Nissan
emerging as favourite. It seems probable therefore that Alfa Romeo and Nissan
will cooperate in a joint venture to produce a passenger car model in southern
Italy, at a completely new facility near to the Alfasud works. Details are scanty,
but Nissan is likely to supply perhaps up to 25-30 per cent of the required parts
from Japan – including body stampings. This development has prompted Fiat to
hold its own discussions with Alfa Romeo, but nothing concrete seems to have
transpired.

CHART 1

WESTERN EUROPE

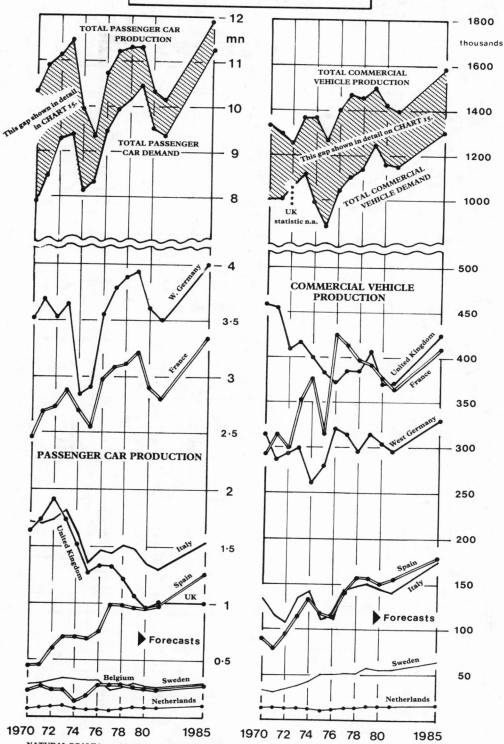

TOTAL PASSENGER CAR PRODUCTION

This gap shown in detail in CHART 15.

TOTAL PASSENGER CAR DEMAND

W. Germany

France

PASSENGER CAR PRODUCTION

United Kingdom

Italy

Spain

UK

Forecasts

Belgium

Sweden

Netherlands

TOTAL COMMERCIAL VEHICLE PRODUCTION

This gap shown in detail on CHART 15.

TOTAL COMMERCIAL VEHICLE DEMAND

UK statistic n.a.

COMMERCIAL VEHICLE PRODUCTION

United Kingdom

France

West Germany

Spain

Italy

Forecasts

Sweden

Netherlands

NATURAL SCALE is used for this summary chart. The same data are shown again in CHART 2 using LOGARITHMIC SCALE.
The same scale is then used through the subsequent 11 charts.

This allows the performance of any line plotted to be compared with any other line that is plotted in the set of 12 charts.

Sources: Tables 1, 2, 67 and 70.
Demand figures from Tables 65 and 68.

Footnotes and sources accompany the relevant Tables in the text

59

CHART 2

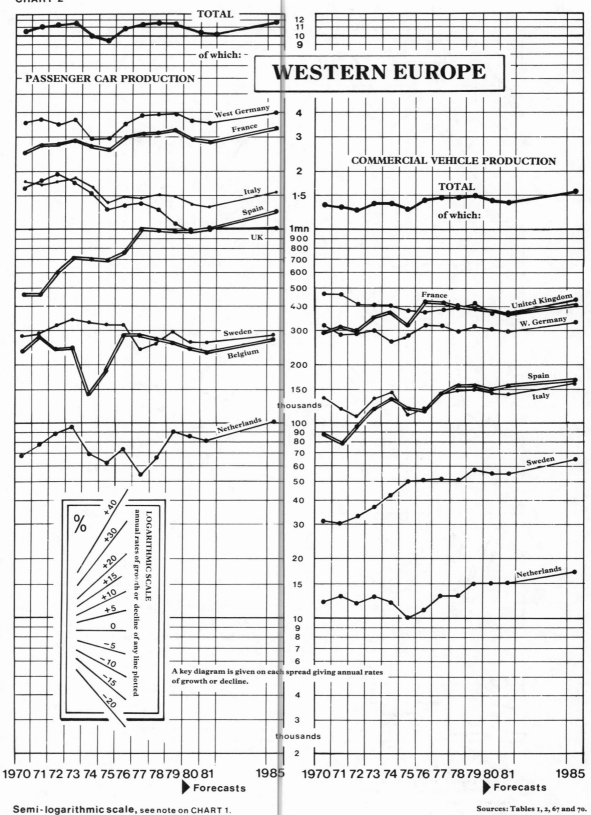

TOTAL

of which:

PASSENGER CAR PRODUCTION

WESTERN EUROPE

West Germany

France

Italy

Spain

UK

COMMERCIAL VEHICLE PRODUCTION

TOTAL

of which:

France

United Kingdom

W. Germany

Sweden

Belgium

Spain

Italy

thousands

Netherlands

Sweden

Netherlands

%

LOGARITHMIC SCALE
annual rates of growth or decline of any line plotted

+40
+30
+20
+15
+10
+5
0
−5
−10
−15
−20

A key diagram is given on each spread giving annual rates
of growth or decline.

thousands

1970 71 72 73 74 75 76 77 78 79 80 81   1985
▶ Forecasts

1970 71 72 73 74 75 76 77 78 79 80 81   1985
▶ Forecasts

Semi-logarithmic scale, see note on CHART 1.

Sources: Tables 1, 2, 67 and 70.

CHART 3

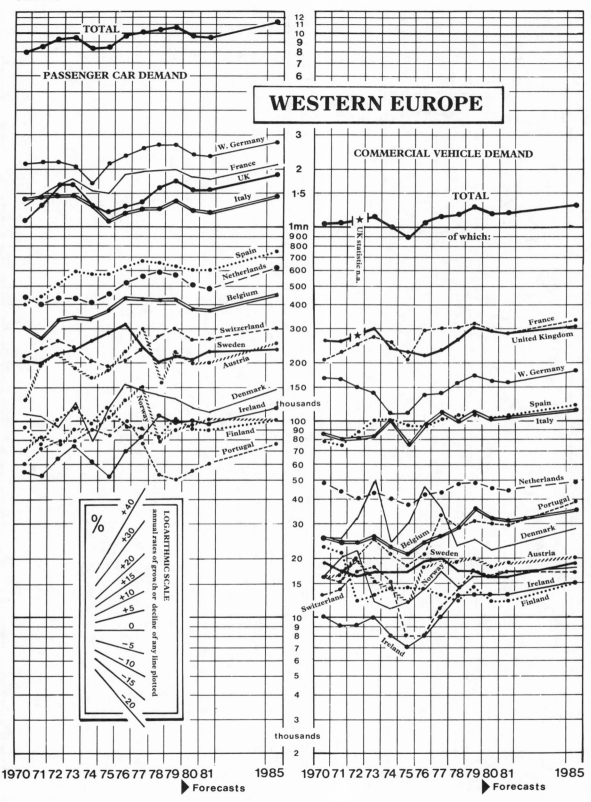

TOTAL

PASSENGER CAR DEMAND

W. Germany

France

UK

Italy

WESTERN EUROPE

COMMERCIAL VEHICLE DEMAND

TOTAL

of which:

UK statistic n.a.

Spain

Netherlands

Belgium

Switzerland

Sweden

Austria

Denmark

Norway

Ireland

Finland

Portugal

France

United Kingdom

W. Germany

Spain

Italy

thousands

Netherlands

Portugal

Denmark

Belgium

Sweden

Austria

Norway

Ireland

Finland

Switzerland

Ireland

% LOGARITHMIC SCALE
annual rates of growth or decline of any line plotted

+40
+30
+20
+15
+10
+5
0
−5
−10
−15
−20

12
11
10
9
8
7
6

3

2

1·5

1mn
900
800
700
600
500

400

300

200

150

thousands

100
90
80
70
60
50
40

30

20

15

10
9
8
7
6
5
4

3

thousands

2

1970 71 72 73 74 75 76 77 78 79 80 81   1985   1970 71 72 73 74 75 76 77 78 79 80 81   1985

▶ Forecasts   ▶ Forecasts

Semi-logarithmic scale, see note on CHART 1.

Sources: Tables 23, 24, 65 and 68.

CHART 4

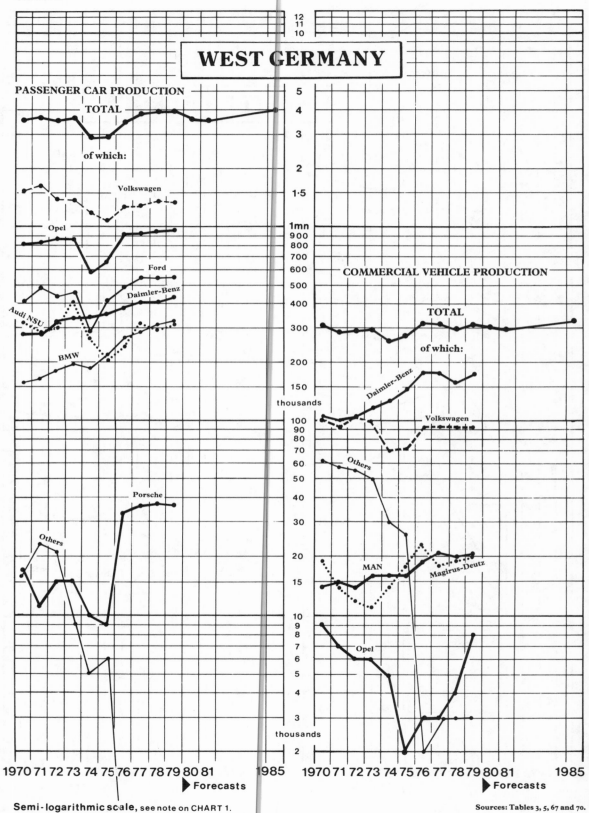

WEST GERMANY

PASSENGER CAR PRODUCTION

TOTAL

of which:

Volkswagen

Opel

Ford

Daimler-Benz

Audi NSU

BMW

Porsche

Others

COMMERCIAL VEHICLE PRODUCTION

TOTAL

of which:

Daimler-Benz

Volkswagen

Others

MAN

Magirus-Deutz

Opel

thousands

thousands

1970 71 72 73 74 75 76 77 78 79 80 81   1985

▶ Forecasts

1970 71 72 73 74 75 76 77 78 79 80 81   1985

▶ Forecasts

Semi-logarithmic scale, see note on CHART 1.

Sources: Tables 3, 5, 67 and 70.

CHART 5

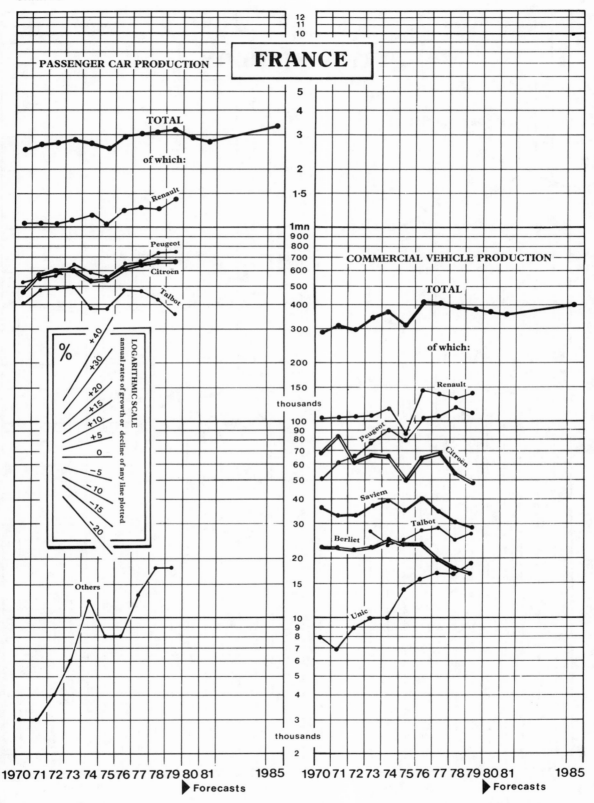

FRANCE

PASSENGER CAR PRODUCTION

TOTAL

of which:

Renault

Peugeot

Citroën

Talbot

% LOGARITHMIC SCALE
annual rates of growth or decline of any line plotted

+40
+30
+20
+15
+10
+5
0
−5
−10
−15
−20

Others

COMMERCIAL VEHICLE PRODUCTION

TOTAL

of which:

Renault

Peugeot

Citroën

Saviem

Talbot

Berliet

Unic

1970 71 72 73 74 75 76 77 78 79 80 81 — 1985

1970 71 72 73 74 75 76 77 78 79 80 81 — 1985

▶ Forecasts

▶ Forecasts

Semi-logarithmic scale, see note on CHART 1.

Sources: Tables 7, 9, 67 and 70.

CHART 6

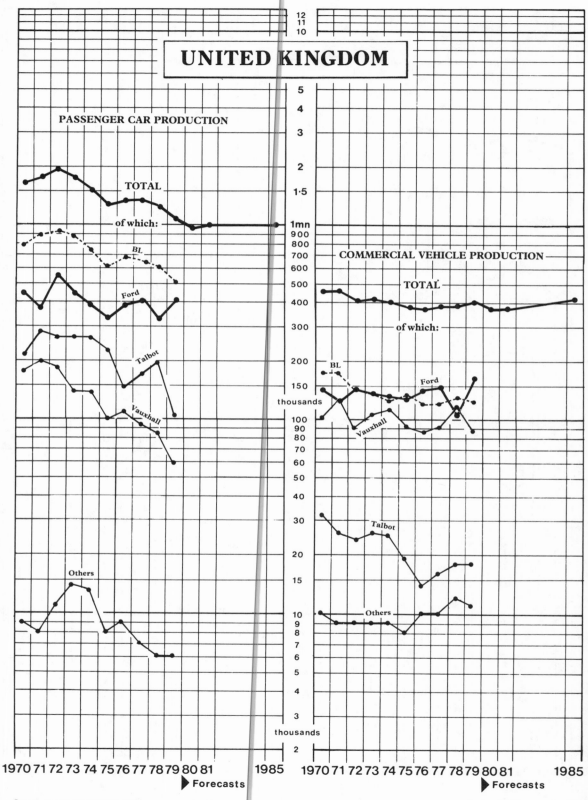

UNITED KINGDOM

PASSENGER CAR PRODUCTION

TOTAL

of which:

BL

Ford

Talbot

Vauxhall

Others

COMMERCIAL VEHICLE PRODUCTION

TOTAL

of which:

BL

Ford

Vauxhall

Talbot

Others

thousands

thousands

12
11
10

5
4
3

2

1·5

1mn
900
800
700
600

500

400

300

200

150

100
90
80
70
60
50

40

30

20

15

10
9
8
7
6

5

4

3

2

1970 71 72 73 74 75 76 77 78 79 80 81   1985

▶ Forecasts

1970 71 72 73 74 75 76 77 78 79 80 81   1985

▶ Forecasts

Semi-logarithmic scale, see note on CHART 1.

Sources: Tables 11, 13, 67 and 70.

64

CHART 7

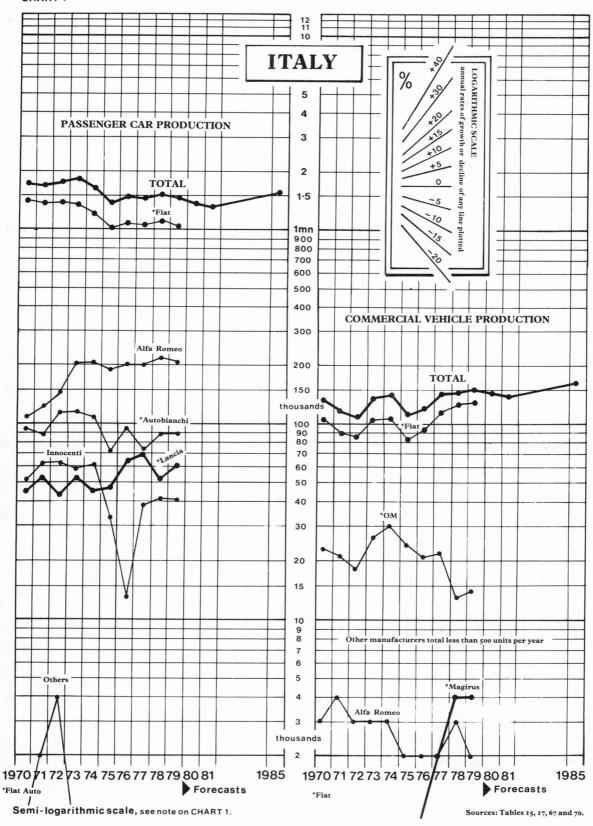

ITALY

PASSENGER CAR PRODUCTION

LOGARITHMIC SCALE
annual rates of growth or decline of any line plotted

%
+40
+30
+20
+15
+10
+5
0
−5
−10
−15
−20

TOTAL

*Fiat

Alfa Romeo

*Autobianchi

Innocenti

*Lancia

Others

COMMERCIAL VEHICLE PRODUCTION

TOTAL

*Fiat

*OM

Other manufacturers total less than 500 units per year

*Magirus

Alfa Romeo

1970 71 72 73 74 75 76 77 78 79 80 81   1985

*Fiat Auto   ▶ Forecasts

Semi-logarithmic scale, see note on CHART 1.

1970 71 72 73 74 75 76 77 78 79 80 81   1985

*Fiat   ▶ Forecasts

Sources: Tables 15, 17, 67 and 70.

65

CHART 8

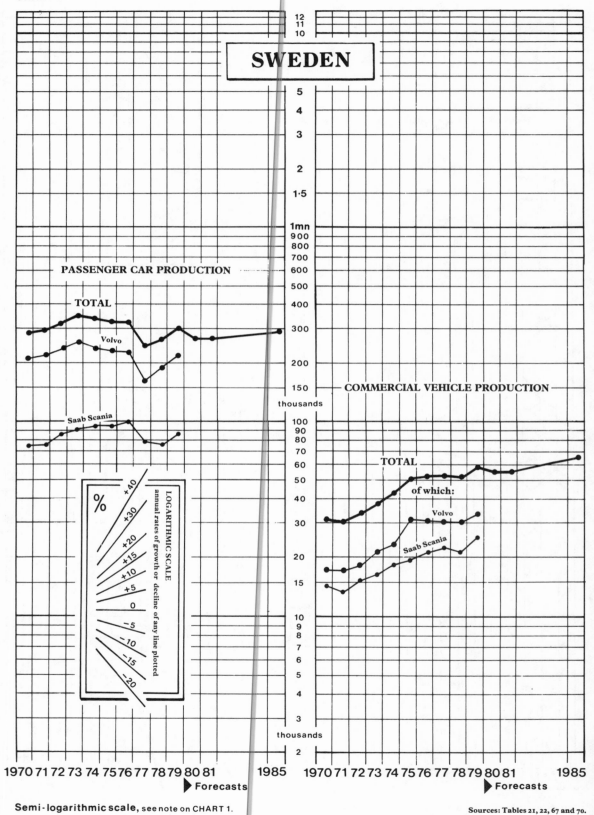

SWEDEN

PASSENGER CAR PRODUCTION

TOTAL

Volvo

Saab Scania

thousands

COMMERCIAL VEHICLE PRODUCTION

TOTAL

of which:

Volvo

Saab Scania

thousands

%
LOGARITHMIC SCALE
annual rates of growth or decline of any line plotted

+40
+30
+20
+15
+10
+5
0
−5
−10
−15
−20

1970 71 72 73 74 75 76 77 78 79 80 81   1985
► Forecasts

1970 71 72 73 74 75 76 77 78 79 80 81   1985
► Forecasts

Semi-logarithmic scale, see note on CHART 1.

Sources: Tables 21, 22, 67 and 70.

CHART 9

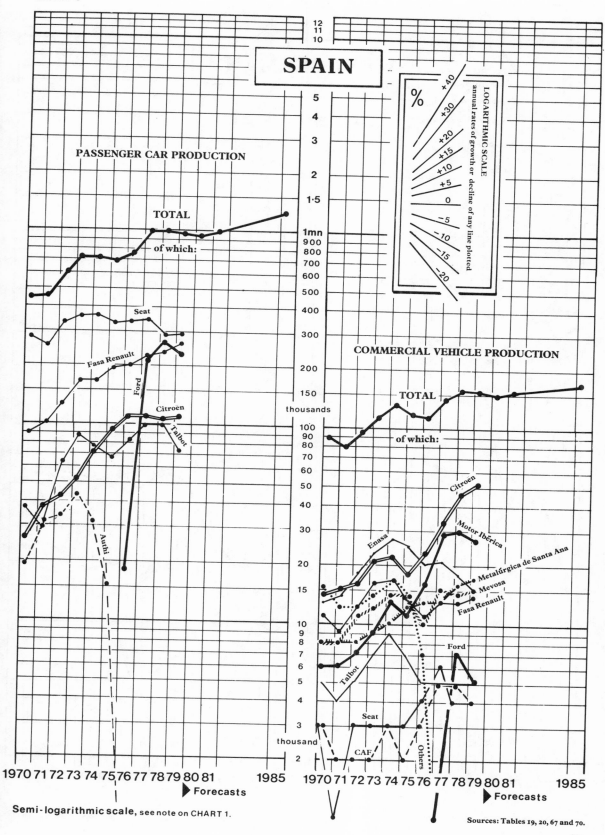

SPAIN

LOGARITHMIC SCALE
annual rates of growth or decline of any line plotted

%
+40
+30
+20
+15
+10
+5
0
−5
−10
−15
−20

PASSENGER CAR PRODUCTION

TOTAL
of which:

Seat

Fasa Renault

Ford

Citroën

Talbot

Authi

COMMERCIAL VEHICLE PRODUCTION

TOTAL
of which:

Citroën

Motor Ibérica

Enasa

Metalúrgica de Santa Ana

Mevosa

Fasa Renault

Talbot

Ford

Seat

CAF

Others

12
11
10

5
4
3

2

1·5

1mn
900
800
700
600
500

400

300

200

150

thousands

100
90
80
70
60

50

40

30

20

15

10
9
8
7
6
5

4

3

thousand

2

1970 71 72 73 74 75 76 77 78 79 80 81   1985
► Forecasts

Semi-logarithmic scale, see note on CHART 1.

1970 71 72 73 74 75 76 77 78 79 80 81   1985
► Forecasts

Sources: Tables 19, 20, 67 and 70.

67

CHART 10

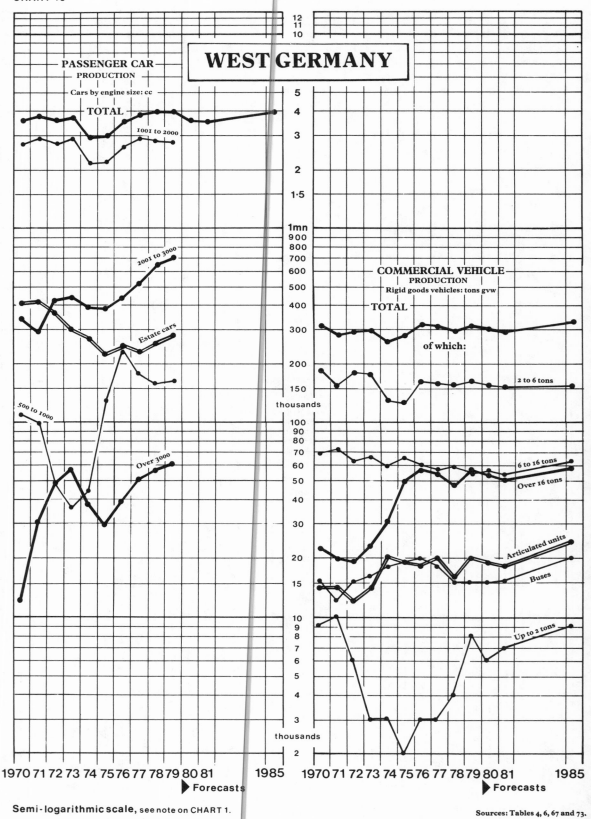

WEST GERMANY

PASSENGER CAR PRODUCTION
Cars by engine size: cc

TOTAL

1001 to 2000

2001 to 3000

Estate cars

500 to 1000

Over 3000

COMMERCIAL VEHICLE PRODUCTION
Rigid goods vehicles: tons gvw

TOTAL

of which:

2 to 6 tons

6 to 16 tons

Over 16 tons

Articulated units

Buses

Up to 2 tons

1970 71 72 73 74 75 76 77 78 79 80 81   1985

1970 71 72 73 74 75 76 77 78 79 80 81   1985

▶ Forecasts   ▶ Forecasts

Semi-logarithmic scale, see note on CHART 1.

Sources: Tables 4, 6, 67 and 73.

CHART 11

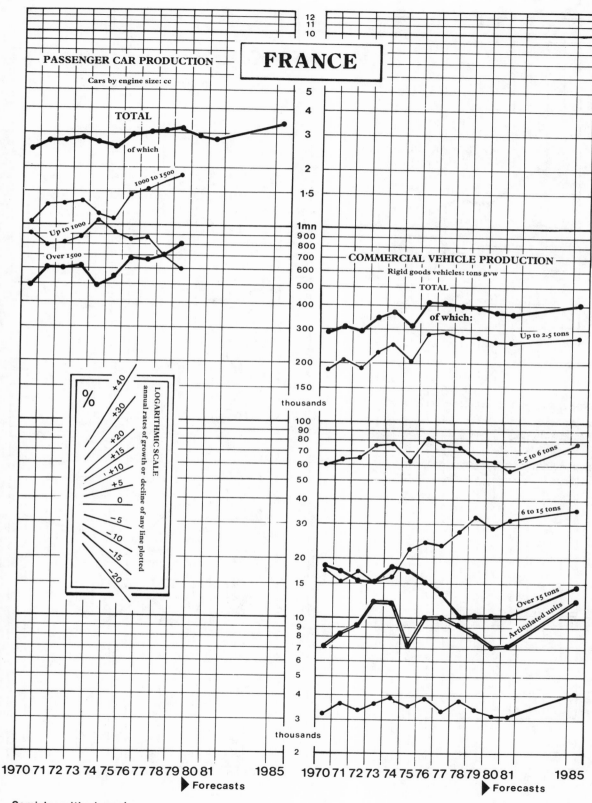

PASSENGER CAR PRODUCTION

Cars by engine size: cc

FRANCE

TOTAL

of which

1000 to 1500

Up to 1000

Over 1500

LOGARITHMIC SCALE
annual rates of growth or decline of any line plotted

%
+40
+30
+20
+15
+10
+5
0
−5
−10
−15
−20

12
11
10

5
4
3

2

1·5

1mn
900
800
700
600
500
400
300
200
150

thousands

COMMERCIAL VEHICLE PRODUCTION

Rigid goods vehicles: tons gvw

TOTAL

of which:

Up to 2.5 tons

100
90
80
70
60
50
40
30
20
15
10
9
8
7
6
5
4
3
2

2.5 to 6 tons

6 to 15 tons

Over 15 tons

Articulated units

thousands

1970 71 72 73 74 75 76 77 78 79 80 81   1985
▶ Forecasts

1970 71 72 73 74 75 76 77 78 79 80 81   1985
▶ Forecasts

Semi-logarithmic scale, see note on CHART 1.

Sources: Tables 8, 10, 67 and 72.

69

CHART 12

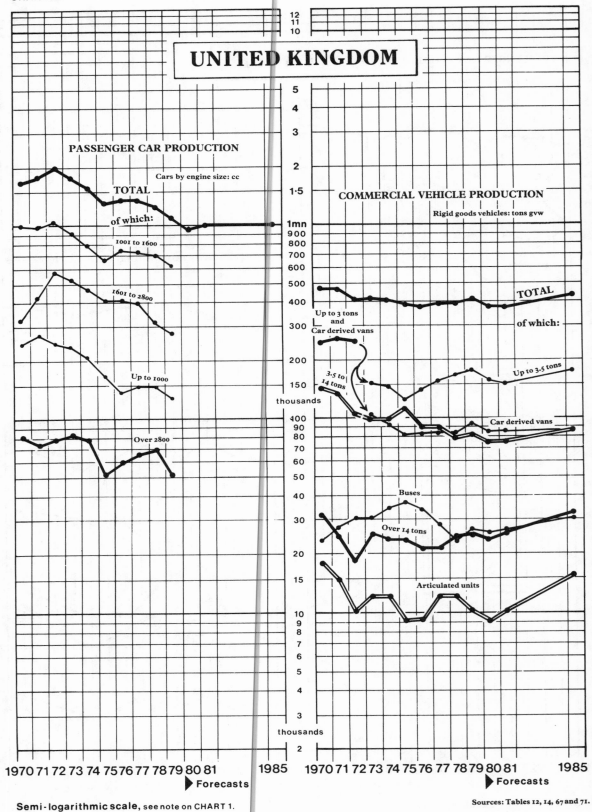

UNITED KINGDOM

PASSENGER CAR PRODUCTION

Cars by engine size: cc

TOTAL

of which:

1001 to 1600

1601 to 2800

Up to 1000

Over 2800

COMMERCIAL VEHICLE PRODUCTION

Rigid goods vehicles: tons gvw

TOTAL

of which:

Up to 3 tons and Car derived vans

3.5 to 14 tons

Up to 3.5 tons

Car derived vans

Buses

Over 14 tons

Articulated units

thousands

thousands

1970 71 72 73 74 75 76 77 78 79 80 81   1985

▶ Forecasts

1970 71 72 73 74 75 76 77 78 79 80 81   1985

▶ Forecasts

Semi-logarithmic scale, see note on CHART 1.

Sources: Tables 12, 14, 67 and 71.

CHART 13

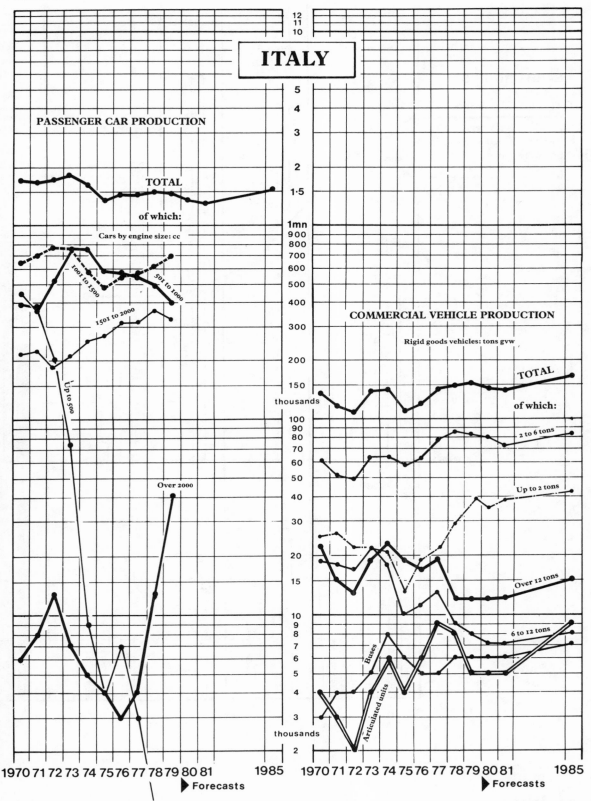

ITALY

PASSENGER CAR PRODUCTION

TOTAL

of which:

Cars by engine size: cc

1001 to 1500

501 to 1000

1501 to 2000

Up to 500

Over 2000

COMMERCIAL VEHICLE PRODUCTION

Rigid goods vehicles: tons gvw

TOTAL

of which:

2 to 6 tons

Up to 2 tons

Over 12 tons

6 to 12 tons

Buses

Articulated units

thousands

thousands

12
11
10

5
4
3

2

1·5

1mn
900
800
700
600
500

400

300

200

150

100
90
80
70
60
50

40

30

20

15

10
9
8
7
6
5

4

3

2

1970 71 72 73 74 75 76 77 78 80 81   1985
▶ Forecasts

1970 71 72 73 74 75 76 77 78 79 80 81   1985
▶ Forecasts

Semi-logarithmic scale, see note on CHART 1.

Sources: Tables 16, 18, 67 and 74.

CHART 14

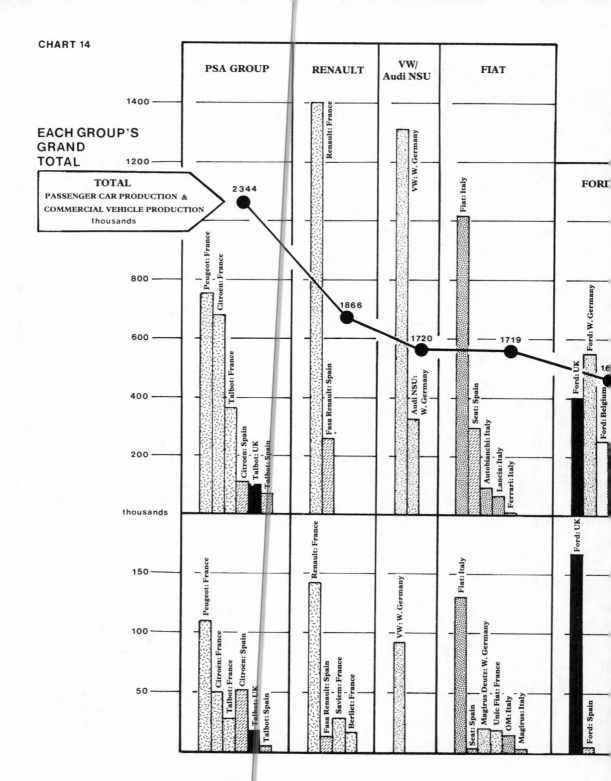

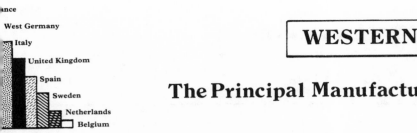

WESTERN EUROPE

The Principal Manufacturers in 1979

Source: Table 25.

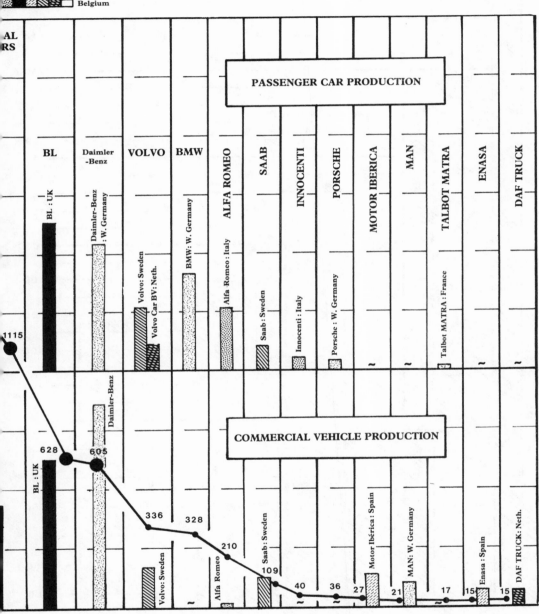

73

CHART 15

WESTERN EUROPE

NET EXPORTS

thousand units

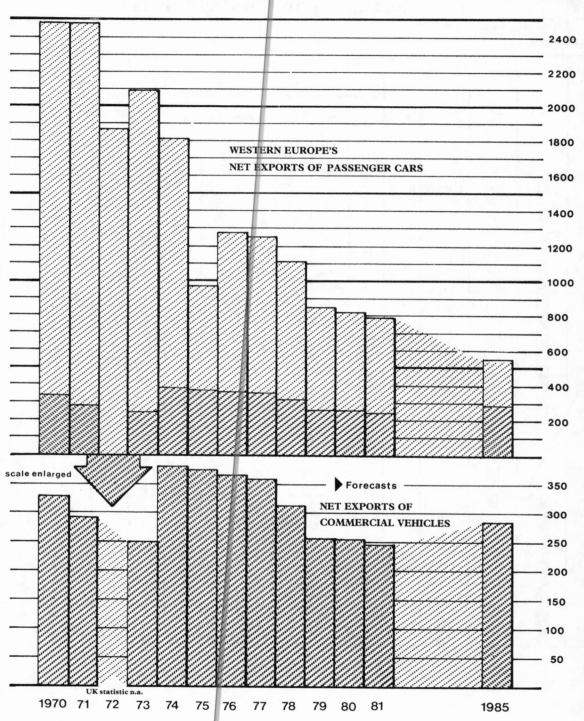

WESTERN EUROPE'S
NET EXPORTS OF PASSENGER CARS

2400

2200

2000

1800

1600

1400

1200

1000

800

600

400

200

scale enlarged

► Forecasts

NET EXPORTS OF
COMMERCIAL VEHICLES

350

300

250

200

150

100

50

UK statistic n.a.

1970 71 72 73 74 75 76 77 78 79 80 81 1985

This chart is derived from the gap between demand and production in
Western Europe shown on CHART 1.

Sources: Tables 66 and 69.

Alfasud has been a successful product, but heavy financial loser

The Alfasud operation extends Alfa Romeo's reputation into the small car category, but in financial terms the venture is a disaster. A substantial part of the problem is the impossibility of making a rural and industrially inexperienced workforce assume the work ethic appropriate for a West German car factory, and continued high levels of absenteeism remain a big headache. Moreover, despite new variants and an excellent reputation for being a "driver's" car, the Alfasud is in need of a revamp to update its image.

Production details

Thanks to the Alfasud operation Alfa Romeo's output of passenger cars has almost doubled in the ten years 1970-79.

Table 55

Development of Alfa Romeo's Vehicle Production, 1970-79

| | Passenger cars | | Commercial vehicles | |
	Units	% change over previous year	Units	% change over previous year
1970	107,989	3.5	3,315	22.9
1971	123,309	14.2	3,708	11.9
1972	140,595	14.0	2,814	-24.1
1973	204,902	45.7	3,081	9.5
1974	208,386	1.7	2,609	-15.3
1975	189,682	-9.0	2,128	-18.4
1976	201,145	6.0	2,031	-4.6
1977	201,118	-	2,057	1.3
1978	219,499	9.1	3,098	50.6
1979	207,514	-5.5	2,036	-34.3

Source: ANFIA.

SAAB SCANIA

A small scale producer -

With an annual output of just over 108,000 vehicles in 1979, Saab Scania is small in automotive terms - although the vehicle producing interests are but a part of a fairly sizeable Swedish industrial group with quite a wide range of interests. The company produces passenger cars and commercial vehicles and, like its compatriot Volvo, suffers from producing at low volume in a high production cost location. Also like Volvo, Saab Scania has a well deserved reputation for producing rugged, dependable vehicles with a high degree of built in safety.

<u>- which emphasises advanced technology</u>

In order to survive in an industrial sector where being big helps, Saab Scania deliberately stresses advanced technology. Unable to afford frequent body changes, Saab favours timeless, if unexciting, styling, but this is peppered with technical excellence. For example, much attention is currently directed towards turbo-charging, and so successful is this application in Saab's models that about 25 per cent of the company's car output in 1980 will be equipped with a turbocharger. Another innovation - to be incorporated in 1981 models - is the APC turbocharging system which allows the vehicle to operate on varying grades of fuel without the need to adjust engine settings.

<u>Agreement with Lancia opens up opportunities on a wide front</u>

An important development for Saab is its agreement with Lancia to explore areas of mutual interest. There are several facets to this tieup and benefits are expected in the fields of marketing, product design and development, and pro-duction. An extremely crucial aspect arises over marketing; Saab recognises that its limited model lineup is unable to provide the dealers with a range suffi-ciently wide to ensure viability, but with Lancia's complementary models dis-tributed through Saab's dealers the problem is solved. This is a good example of how two smaller companies (notwithstanding Lancia's parentage) can come together for the benefit of both.

<u>Specialisation in heavy duty trucks</u>

With regard to commercial vehicles, Scania again follows the same basic philo-sophy of specialisation - in this case in heavy duty trucks. In addition to the Swedish base there are plants in Latin America (Brazil and Argentina) and the Netherlands. The truck range is essentially sound and profitable, but Scania will need a new cab design soon. The company is showing increased interest in developing bus production.

Table 56

<u>Development of Saab Scania's Vehicle Production, 1970-79</u>

	Passenger cars		Commercial vehicles	
	Units	% change over previous year	Units	% change over previous year
1970	73,980	...	13,773	...
1971	72,960	-1.4	12,757	-7.4
1972	83,997	15.1	14,585	14.3
1973	89,467	6.5	15,943	9.3
1974	92,554	3.5	18,325	14.9
1975	90,962	-1.7	19,414	5.9
1976	95,927	5.5	20,796	7.1
1977	76,498	-20.3	21,652	4.1
1978	72,516	-5.2	21,334	-1.5
1979	83,758	15.5	24,781	16.2

Source: Association of Swedish Automotive Manufacturers and Wholesalers.

INNOCENTI

A reasonable recovery following BL's withdrawal

Until 1976 Innocenti was the Italian subsidiary of BL. A version of the Mini was (and is) produced from KD kits sourced from the UK. However, mounting losses at a time when BL could ill afford financial liabilities in foreign lands caused the British company to withdraw. Eventually a new consortium picked up the pieces and Nuova Innocenti was born. As can be seen from Table 57 output has recovered impressively during the past three years. As noted above, KD kits are still received from BL, and currently Innocenti is totally dependent on this supply line. It seems clear that contingency plans for an alternative model may well be needed some day, although BL has no intention of phasing out the current Mini when the Mini Metro is launched later in 1980. Another weakness of Innocenti is its heavy reliance on the Italian market for sales. In 1978, for example, Innocenti sold just over 5,000 units in other EEC countries - a mere 13 per cent of output.

It should be noted that all Innocenti production is double counted since BL includes the KD kits in its own output figures.

Table 57

Development of Innocenti's
Passenger Car Production, 1970-79

	Units	% change over previous year
1970	50,630	6.0
1971	61,950	22.4
1972	62,834	1.4
1973	58,471	-6.9
1974	60,711	3.8
1975	33,061	-45.5
1976	12,789	-61.3
1977	38,120	198.1
1978	40,719	6.8
1979	39,991	-1.8

Source: ANFIA.

PORSCHE

Production has been boosted by the 924/928 models

In line with the traditions of West German vehicle manufacturers in general, Porsche has earned a well deserved reputation for sheer engineering integrity. A range of exotic - yet practical - high performance, high specification sports cars is produced consisting of two basic types: the old, but evergreen, 911 series; and the newer 924/928 models. The 924 and 928 share a number of features, including the basic body shape, but differ in their mechanical specification. The former was initially compared rather unfavourably with previous Porsche offerings

when it was introduced in 1975, but the 928 which followed just over a year later
has restored Porsche's position as maker of some of the world's most exciting
roadgoing machinery. Moreover, the 924/928 series has provided the West
German company with a much higher production base, as shown in Table 58.

Apart from producing cars, there is a well known and well respected engineering
consultancy, and Porsche has been to the fore in technical developments. Much
work has been carried out in such areas as aerodynamics and turbocharging, and
knowledge gained has been incorporated in the company's road cars. Many
developments have been tried and proven on the world's racing circuits (including
Le Mans where Porsche has chalked up a string of successes).

Porsche is a classic example of a small European vehicle manufacturer which has
managed to find a small, yet profitable and worthwhile, market niche. Apart
from its domestic market, Porsche has important business in the US and UK
markets.

Table 58

Development of Porsche's
Passenger Car Production, 1970-79

	Units	% change over previous year
1970	16,757	9.6
1971	10,905	-34.9
1972	14,503	33.0
1973	15,415	6.3
1974	9,915	-35.7
1975	9,424	-5.0
1976	32,554	245.4
1977	36,130	11.0
1978	36,879	2.1
1979	36,011	-2.4

Source: VDA.

MOTOR IBERICA

Recent difficulties –

This Spanish manufacturer, noted for its expansionist minded management,
produces a range of agricultural and construction equipment as well as vans,
light trucks and buses under the Ebro marque. The company's position has
weakened recently as a result of falling domestic demand and growing problems
over competing effectively in export markets. Nevertheless, as can be seen
from Table 59, Motor Ibérica has achieved an impressive production record
during the 1970s with quite an increase in its scale of operations.

Despite this expansion, though, it had been an open secret for some time that the Canadian Massey Ferguson group - itself not in the best of financial health - was attempting to sell its 36 per cent holding in Motor Ibérica. Discussions are understood to have been held with a number of interested parties but, in January 1980, it was announced that Massey Ferguson's stake is to be acquired by Nissan for around $40 mn. It is still too early to assess the precise implications of this potentially far reaching deal, but clearly Motor Ibérica could provide a useful base for Nissan's European ambitions.

Table 59

Development of Motor Ibérica's
Commercial Vehicle Production, 1970-79

	Units	% change over previous year
1970	6,408	1.7
1971	6,113	-4.6
1972	7,187	17.6
1973	9,011	25.4
1974	12,657	40.5
1975	10,821	-14.5
1976	16,304	50.7
1977	28,642	75.7
1978	29,553	3.2
1979	27,278	-7.7

Source: Agrupación Nacional de
Fabricantes de Automoviles y Camiones.

MAN

A heavy commercial vehicle producer -

MAN is an important and powerful West German based engineering company which has interests in commercial vehicle manufacturing in West Germany as well as owning ÖAF (a truck producer) in Austria. Production is concentrated in the heavy end of the truck weight classes and there is also a certain amount of bus output.

- with objectives to move down the weight range -

Recognising the need to lessen its dependence on heavy commercial vehicles, MAN has made moves to diversify down the weight range and to develop its non-automotive activities such as printing machinery manufacture. In order to achieve the former objective the company entered into an alliance with Volkswagen to design, develop and produce a new range of trucks in the 6-9 tons gvw class; these were launched on to the market in the second half of 1979. Under the agreement both sides are carrying out assembly, with Volkswagen supplying cabs, rear axles and gearboxes, while MAN supplies the engines, frames and front axles. This deal has prompted speculation that there could be much closer cooperation between Volkswagen and MAN in the future.

- and expand internationally

MAN has international ambitions too, but these were badly thwarted when a proposed deal with White Motor of the USA was called off. Under this MAN would have acquired a 12.6 per cent interest in White, together with access to the all important US market. As it is, MAN appears to have been left behind in the race for a US presence by its European counterparts, Daimler-Benz, Iveco, Volvo and Renault. Nevertheless, MAN already has factories in several key markets including Australia and South Africa.

Table 60 provides details of MAN's output between 1970-79.

Table 60

Development of MAN's
Commercial Vehicle Production, 1970-79

	Units	% change over previous year
1970	13,954	11.1
1971	14,622	4.8
1972	13,668	-6.5
1973	15,639	14.4
1974	16,296	4.2
1975	15,706	-3.6
1976	18,667	18.9
1977	21,337	14.3
1978	20,364	-4.6
1979	21,225	4.2

Source: VDA.

TALBOT MATRA

Two models are produced for Talbot

Originally known as Matra Sports, this small French company was formed through the merger between René Bonnet and Engins Matra SA in 1968. Although independent, the company had a long association with Simca (Chrysler France) and current activities involve the production of the Talbot Matra Bagheera, a mid engined sports coupé, and Talbot Matra Rancho, a distinctively styled three door estate car. These are distributed through the Talbot dealer network.

Table 61

Development of Talbot Matra's
Passenger Car Production, 1970-79

	Units	% change over previous year
1970	2.053	7.2
1971	1.703	-17.0
1972	2.159	26.8
1973	4.228	95.8
1974	11.264	166.4
1975	7.338	-34.9
1976	7.376	0.5
1977	12.094	64.0
1978	17,277	42.9
1979	16.638	-3.7

Source: Chambre Syndicale des
Constructeurs Automobiles.

ENASA

The need to regain competitiveness -

Enasa (Empresa Nacional de Autocamiones, SA). a Spanish company producing Pegaso trucks and buses and Sava vans, has found conditions increasingly tough in the second half of the 1970s. In 1979 production slumped to 15,052 units, 16.4 per cent down on 1978's level, and another hefty loss, possibly approaching $100 mn, was incurred. Like Motor Ibérica, Enasa has been hit on two fronts: one of the main problems has been the generally dull condition of the Spanish economy which has resulted in falling truck sales. And, secondly, the recovery of the peseta after 1977's devaluation has led to a decline in export competitiveness.

- results in a US partner

Concern over the medium term prospects for Enasa resulted in discussions taking place with several international truck manufacturing groups, and at the beginning of 1980 it was announced that International Harvester (the largest US truck producer) is to acquire 35 per cent of the company. This means that the grand design of the 1970s which aimed at developing Enasa into a viable and independent Spanish owned commercial vehicle manufacturer is now at an end.

Table 62

Development of Enasa's
Commercial Vehicle Production, 1970-79

	Units	% change over previous year
1970	12,839	18.0
1971	14,469	12.7
1972	17,690	22.3
1973	23,136	30.8
1974	26,517	14.6
1975	24,559	-7.4
1976	20,309	-17.3
1977	20,554	1.2
1978	18,009	-12.4
1979	15,052	-16.4

Source: Agrupación Nacional de Fabricantes de Automoviles y Camiones.

DAF TRUCK

Liaison with International Harvester has failed

Originally associated with what is now Volvo Car BV, DAF Truck of the Netherlands currently stands as an independent company. Ownership is divided between
three parties, the Van Doorne family, state owned Dutch State Mines, and International Harvester (the largest US heavy truck producer). Following DAF's
breakup in the mid 1970s the truck division's search for a partner led it to the
US group, but the relationship never really blossomed and contacts between the
two sides are reported to be cool. More recently, discussions have started with
the PSA group which, through Talbot, now has an interest in the truck and bus
business. It is understood that both sides are examining areas of potential
cooperation on technical and manufacturing affairs. During the past few years
DAF Truck has not found the going easy, but the company is believed to have
regained profitability in 1979 after a sustained period of losses.

Table 63

Development of DAF Truck's
Commercial Vehicle Production, 1970-79

	Units	% change over previous year
1970	11,191	2.4
1971	12,341	10.3
1972	11,994	-2.8
1973	12,546	4.6
1974	12,230	-2.5

(continued)

Table 63 (continued)

Development of DAF Truck's
Commercial Vehicle Production, 1970-79

	Units	% change over previous year
1975	10,250	-16.2
1976	11,352	10.8
1977	12,481	9.9
1978	10,646	-14.7
1979	14,982	40.7

Source: CBS.

OTHER COMPANIES PRODUCING OVER 10,000 UNITS ANNUALLY

Apart from the 19 companies described above, only two others produced in excess of 10,000 vehicles in 1979. These were Metalúrgica de Santa Ana and Mevosa – both Spanish based.

Metalúrgica de Santa Ana –

This company produces Land Rovers under licence from BL. In 1979 output totalled 17,150 units – a creditable 8.9 per cent improvement over 1978.

– and Mevosa

Mevosa produces trucks and a few buses based on Volkswagen and Daimler-Benz designs. Output in 1979 amounted to 14,982 units (14,861 trucks and 121 buses), a 3.4 per cent advance over 1978.

COMPANIES PRODUCING BETWEEN 1,000 AND 10,000 UNITS ANNUALLY

A further nine companies in the UK, France, West Germany and Spain have been identified as producing between 1,000 and 10,000 units per year. In order of volume they are: Seddon Atkinson, CAF, Rolls-Royce Motors, ERF, Kässbohrer, Foden, Alpine, Auwärter and Lotus.

Seddon Atkinson

This UK company manufactures a range of heavy duty rigid and articulated trucks (16 tons gvw plus). Formerly an independent company, Seddon Atkinson is now a wholly owned subsidiary of International Harvester – the USA's biggest truck producer. IH is looking to become a significant force in the West European truck business and is reportedly delighted with its association with Seddon Atkinson. In 1979 output amounted to 4,732 units.

CAF

Sometimes referred to as Viasa, CAF is a Spanish company which holds a licence from American Motors to produce Jeeps. These are marketed by Motor Ibérica. Production in 1979 totalled 4,499 units - 12.4 per cent lower than 1978's outturn of 5,135 units.

Rolls-Royce Motors

This company has done extremely well since being hived off as a separate enterprise when the original Rolls-Royce group went into receivership in 1970. As well as producing its famous line of passenger cars under the Rolls-Royce and Bentley marques, the company has important diesel engine manufacturing facilities. Rolls-Royce Motors' financial performance has been impressive during the 1970s, but latest figures (for 1979) indicate a setback. The main problem area is the diesel engine division, where a number of traditional markets - for example, the generating set sector - declined markedly; also a big order for tank engines for Iran was cancelled. But cars, too, have turned in results below expectations, largely as a consequence of sterling's strength which has reduced margins on Rolls-Royce Motors' sizeable export business.

In 1979 the company produced 3,343 cars, of which an estimated 2,000 were for export; in addition, automotive diesel engine sales increased.

In June 1980 it was announced that Rolls-Royce Motors and Vickers (a major UK engineering group) were to merge, a move aimed at lessening RRM's vulnerability to the varying fortunes of the motor industry. Certainly the company has faced a difficult period recently as a result of economic recession and the need to maintain capital spending at a high level (to bring the Silver Spirit into production). However, the introduction of a new model is an important development and, with the added security of the Vickers connection, the company is expected to ride out the current recession quite comfortably.

ERF

Founded by a branch of the Foden family, ERF produces a range of specialist and heavy duty (16 tons gvw plus) goods vehicles. The company's main production facility is at Sandbach (Cheshire), but a new factory is planned for Wrexham, North Wales, which is aimed at increasing ERF's position in the medium truck market; this development, however, has been suspended for the moment in the light of the difficult conditions currently evident in the UK truck market.

Production in 1979 amounted to 3,172 units.

Kässbohrer

Based in West Germany, Kässbohrer produces bus chassis and bodies. Output in 1979 totalled 2,008 units.

Foden (Sandbach Engineering Company)

Based (like ERF) at Sandbach, Foden produces heavy duty commercial and specialist vehicles above 24 tons gvw. During 1979 (when the company produced 1,664 vehicles) and up to the middle of 1980, Foden underwent intensive rationalisation and streamlining in an effort to recover its market and financial position. New vehicles were successfully introduced and market share increased, but the company's inherently weak financial position began to tell as the economic recession developed. Receivers and managers were appointed by the company's bankers in July 1980, and in October 1980 the company's assets were acquired by Paccar of the USA (the manufacturer of Kenworth and Peterbilt trucks).

Alpine

This is a French company producing sports cars. Output in 1979 totalled 1,381 units.

Auwärter

This is another West German company producing bus chassis and bodies. In 1979 production reached 1,092 units.

Lotus

Well known for its successes in Formula 1 motor racing - the company won the prestigious world champion car constructors cup in 1963, 1965, 1968, 1970, 1972, 1973 and 1978 - Lotus's road going passenger car range currently consists of the Esprit, Eclat and Elite models. Apart from the Esprit - now available in turbo-charged form - which is an out and out sports car with two seats and a mid engined configuration, Lotus's models are best described as high performance grand touring cars. Founded by a brilliant engineer, Colin Chapman, who is now the company's chairman, Lotus has gradually moved upmarket from the days when it sold the famous Elan in kit form to enthusiasts. However, this move was accompanied by a somewhat shaky financial position - a situation alleviated with support from American Express.

Production in 1979 amounted to 1,031 units, of which an estimated 300 were exported. This is a low export ratio compared with past trends and is explained by difficulties in the US market. However, Lotus's fortunes in the USA should be considerably improved now that Rolls-Royce Motors has agreed to distribute Lotus cars through its own network.

COMPANIES PRODUCING BELOW 1,000 UNITS ANNUALLY

A surprisingly large number of companies, in both the passenger car and commercial vehicle sectors, produce below 1,000 vehicles per year in Western Europe. They include the following 28 manufacturers:

-   AC, a UK based company, produces mid engined sports cars;

- Aston Martin Lagonda, a UK company producing high performance grand touring and luxury cars;

- Bristol, also UK based, produces exclusive grand touring cars;

- CBM Verney, a specialist French commercial vehicle company;

- De Tomaso, an Italian producer of high performance cars;

- Dennis, part of the UK Hestair group, produces municipal vehicles, fire engines and buses. The company is becoming a significant supplier of buses for the UK and certain export markets, and has recently launched a 16 ton gvw truck for general haulage;

- Dennison is based in the Republic of Ireland and produces commercial goods vehicles of over 16 tons gvw, utilising cabs imported from Sisu of Finland;

- FBW, a specialist truck and bus manufacturer in Switzerland;

- FTF, a Dutch producer of heavy duty trucks;

- Faun, a producer of specialist and military vehicles in West Germany;

- Ginaf, a Dutch specialist commercial vehicle producer;

- Ginetta, a UK producer of sports cars;

- Lamborghini, Italian based company manufacturing high performance, exotic sporting cars;

- Maserati, another Italian producer of high performance sports and grand touring cars;

- MOL, a Belgian producer of specialist heavy duty chassis, with strong interests in the mobile crane sector;

- Monteverdi, a Swiss based producer of grand touring cars;

- Morgan, a British company manufacturing sports cars in the traditional style;

- Mowag, a specialist truck producer based in Switzerland;

- Panther, a UK company producing a variety of exotic cars ranging in design from the traditional to the futuristic;

- Reliant, a manufacturer of small economy cars and the grand touring Scimitar model; also produces three wheelers;

- Reynolds Boughton, a UK manufacturer of specialist units, particularly strong in fire fighting vehicles;

- Saurer, a Swiss commercial vehicle producer;

- Shelvoke and Drewry, a UK company manufacturing municipal vehicles;

- Sisu, Finnish based, produces commercial vehicles;

- Sovam, a French manufacturer of specialist commercial vehicles;

- Steyr, an Austrian based company specialising in four wheel drive units; a new venture with Daimler-Benz will increase output markedly;

- TVR, a British producer of sports and grand touring cars; and, finally,

- Terberg, a Dutch producer of specialist commercial vehicles.

The Outlook for the 1980s

Structural Developments and Key Issues

<u>Change has been a constant feature of the automotive industry in the postwar period</u>

The postwar growth of the motor industries of individual countries in Western Europe has been a powerful - indeed, vital - force in the region's economic development and prosperity. Immense change has taken place during the past 30 years, both in terms of product specification and the industry's structure. In particular, the increasingly competitive nature of vehicle markets, associated mainly with the reduction of tariff barriers, has had a profound impact. Whereas during the 1950s and early 1960s domestic vehicle manufacturers essentially supplied their local markets with distinctively styled and tailored products, the 1970s witnessed a gradual convergence of consumer tastes and vehicle designs in Europe - a development which led to the emergence of a recognisably European flavour to the motor industries of West Germany, France, the UK, Italy etc. In reviewing change over the past three decades, however, two significant factors are evident which are important to keep in mind when assessing future prospects. The first is that change has been a constant characteristic of the motor industry's development; the need to respond to external circumstances, coupled with the inherent innovative tendencies of the vehicle manufacturing companies, ensures that this is so. And secondly, change has been evolutionary rather than revolutionary; this, in part, reflects the necessarily lengthy lead time of even the simplest innovation, as well as the sheer cost and complexity.

This being the case, the blueprint for the West European motor industry's development in the 1980s, in terms of the likely structural changes, is already laid out. Events since the mid 1970s provide powerful clues as to the sector's probable evolvement during the next five to ten years. Thus, this opening section of Part 2 examines the more crucial developments which are identified as having a bearing on the automotive industry's current structure, and suggests how these may continue to influence events in the future.

<u>The role of government has increased -</u>

One of the most significant developments is the increasing involvement of government in the affairs of the automotive industry. As a prime economic activity it is natural for individual governments to take a deep interest in the vehicle manufacturing sector. Not only is the automotive industry an important employer in its own right but it also provides widespread employment opportunities among a whole network of direct and indirect supporting activities. The Western world's lifestyle is heavily dependent on motorised road transport for the movement of people and goods, and hence the presence of a wide ranging and successful motor industry within a country is important from the standpoint of keeping down vehicle imports and, frequently, building up exports. Volkswagen in West Germany and Renault in France are two examples of vehicle manufacturing companies acting as dynamic economic powerhouses in their respective countries.

During the past decade – and especially since 1974/75 – the role of government in the affairs of the West European automotive sector has undergone a subtle, yet significant, change. Today, governments are much more involved in the industry as sponsors and providers of finance, thereby implying a measure of ownership and control. This changed stance can be directly traced to the difficult conditions faced by vehicle manufacturers in the wake of the 1973 oil crisis – difficulties which caused a number of them to seek urgent financial assistance. In virtually all cases the response of government was to provide the necessary finance for survival and development, either through preferential tax treatment or direct injection of funds.

– and is aimed at preserving employment –

Although public ownership of vehicle manufacturers is now more common in Western Europe than ten years ago, there is little evidence to suggest that this is due to doctrinal factors. Indeed, governments have become owners usually as a last resort and have in many cases attempted to find other solutions. Thus, the French government persuaded private sector Peugeot to take over Citroën when the latter experienced financial difficulties – although Citroën's commercial vehicle subsidiary (Berliet) was hived off and merged with state owned Renault's Saviem. Similarly, the UK government sponsored a rescue of Chrysler UK – involving £162 mn of public funds – which still left ownership totally with the US corporation. More recently, the Dutch government organised a rescue of Volvo Car BV in the hope that viability will be reached within a few years, and thereby encourage the Swedish parent to increase its equity holding. It would appear that the motive, in all cases, is preservation of employment. The rescue of BL in the UK provides as good an example as any. Had BL collapsed it was estimated that up to 1 mn jobs would have been at risk – 200,000 in the company itself and the remainder in BL's suppliers. Faced with consequences such as these the UK government clearly had no alternative other than provide whatever finance was required to maintain operations.

– or expanding it

With the recovery of demand in the latter part of the 1970s, governments have continued to exercise influence over the vehicle manufacturing sector. But whereas the original motive for state intervention was survival, the emphasis now is on expansion, and this is likely to set the tone for government involvement in the 1980s. The forceful realisation of the crucial status of the automotive sector in a country's economic framework has caused a scramble among governments to attract foreign investment. This has traditionally meant encouraging Ford and General Motors, but opportunities are now widening. There is currently a greater willingness on the part of the principal European companies to become more heavily committed in important markets (for example, through setting up component manufacturing facilities) and, as the 1980s progress, Japanese companies are expected to enter the European arena with assembly operations; indeed, the early moves in this potentially far reaching development have already been made. It is important to determine the response of government to the likelihood of substantial investment opportunities over the next few years. Based on recent events, it seems reasonable to assume that European governments will be increasingly competing with each other in offering ever more attractive financial packages to multinational vehicle manufacturers. Most of the running so far has been made by the less developed countries, such as Spain and Portugal, which are in the process of building up their motor industries, but intense competition can be expected from other countries which are either eager to establish a greater presence in the motor sector (for example, Austria and Norway), or keen to maintain a high and growing level of commitment (for example, Italy and the UK). The UK, in particular, has succeeded in attracting various significant deals lately, including the Ford engine plant at Bridgend (South Wales) and DeLorean's assembly plant at Belfast (Northern Ireland). Those who say that these ventures have been achieved only in the context of hefty financial assistance are probably right, but the point is that the provision of government finance and inducements will continue to be a strong - perhaps decisive - factor in determining the location of new motor industry investment throughout the 1980s. It is understandable that vehicle producers wishing to invest in Western Europe should take full advantage of these incentives, which from the position of individual governments are entirely consistent with their objective of preserving and expanding employment opportunities.

There has been extensive rationalisation and integration on national lines

As far as the automotive industry is concerned, the past twenty years have seen extensive moves towards rationalisation and integration. Mergers and takeovers have been a common feature, but it is interesting that these have taken place primarily on national, rather than European, lines. Over the years Fiat, for example, has absorbed a number of smaller Italian companies such as Ferrari and Lancia, while BL is basically the end result of a whole series of mergers and takeovers within the British motor industry. Attempts at forming pan European groupings have not been conspicuously successful, although Fiat's Iveco provides a shining exception.

Although companies now need to adopt a European and, indeed, global outlook, it is unlikely that major mergers involving cross frontier associations will be a feature of the 1980s. The pressures which have so far prevailed - and notably the desire to keep ownership, and hence control, within a nation state - are forecast to remain paramount.

Companies have established joint ventures as a means of maintaining independence

In order to retain their independence, yet at the same time benefit from economies of scale in component and subassembly manufacturing, the small and middle rank companies have vigorously adopted the joint venture concept. A good example of the potential breadth of a cooperative understanding between partners is provided by the agreement with Saab and Lancia. These companies are (or plan to be) collaborating in the fields of sales and marketing, technical development and production. For a smaller company it is quite feasible to survive and prosper on a limited production base, provided that there is a relationship with suppliers or partners which affords cost effective components and subassemblies to be procured. Interestingly, the larger manufacturers have also entered into joint ventures as a means of establishing a worthwhile and cost effective entry into specific market segments. Thus, Europe's two largest manufacturers - PSA (through Peugeot) and Renault - joined together with Volvo in a venture (to produce V6 petrol engines) which independently none of the partners could have justified.

The West European automotive sector is a maze of joint ventures and many more are expected to surface during the 1980s. An interesting development, though, arises over the changing scope of these agreements. Initially, they were typically between West European companies - as, for example, in the case of the V6 engine venture or the Club of Four (an agreement between Volvo, DAF Truck, Magirus Deutz and Saviem to produce a medium weight truck range). More recently, however, an increasingly global dimension has been evident. In particular, the Japanese are flexing their muscles in Europe, as indicated by BL's deal with Honda and the possibility of Nissan's venture with Alfa Romeo. Moreover, the geographical spread of joint ventures is widening, with European companies taking the lead in a number of instances, especially in North America; the proposal whereby American Motors plans to assemble Renault car designs is an example of this.

The emergence of a Western market

The end result will be the formation of a Western market with the products of Western Europe, North America and Japan showing a high degree of commonality in both passenger cars and trucks. This inevitably leads to the question of market shares. It will be seen in the following section (on production and sales forecasts for 1985) that Western Europe's net exports of passenger cars have been declining, and are expected to continue sliding up to 1985. As the 1980s progress it is forecast that exporting built up vehicles from Western Europe will become increasingly tougher. Many developing countries, especially those with high vehicle demand, are establishing their own motor industries which are usually provided with protection from outside competition. Furthermore, it is unlikely that the Japanese market will provide much in the way of greater marketing opportunities for West European companies in the 1980s. The one exception is the USA, which currently presents a golden opportunity for European suppliers in view of the demand for downsized cars and medium range diesel engined goods vehicles. It is probable that the already great interest shown by European companies in the USA will grow even stronger, so that by the mid 1980s there will be a heavy European influence in the North American market. But unlike the Japanese, who have shown reluctance in establishing assembly operations, the Europeans are likely to favour a local presence. Volkswagen has led the way with its plant in Pennsylvania, to be followed by another - probably near Detroit. Renault's moves have involved American Motors and Mack, while the possibility of a PSA/Chrysler collaboration cannot yet be ruled out. Both MAN and Daimler-Benz plan to begin commercial vehicle assembly. Obviously the inherent strength of the US automotive industry should not be minimised, but as the US manufacturers' models are downsized and more consumers choose a smaller car, this can only enhance the marketing opportunities of European (and Japanese) designed units. Thus, the average US motorist, who has traditionally favoured a large US model, is now increasingly in the market for a smaller car, and may consequently consider European and Japanese designs as well as the US manufacturers' downsized offerings; the imported content of the US passenger car market at the start of 1980 suggests that this is happening on a wider scale than ever before.

Increasing penetration of the West European market from outside suppliers

The West European market in turn will become more attractive to outside suppliers. The Japanese are, of course, already well established and seem set to penetrate even further, particularly in West Germany which they have identified as a key area for sales growth. There is growing unease, however, over the imbalance of automotive trade between Japan and Europe, and it is possible that the pressures for protectionist measures may become too strong to resist. The Eastern Bloc too is gearing up to become a more significant supplier to West European markets, in some cases as a result of partnerships with Western companies.

Other countries, such as South Korea and Brazil, are expected to make stronger marketing efforts, but their impact is not expected to be significant. If they are to achieve a presence it will have to be on the basis of price, since the variety of designs produced in Western Europe is such that all consumer requirements are satisfactorily covered.

Energy is a key issue currently

Of all the issues facing the automotive sector at the present time probably the most urgent concerns energy. It is noticeable, for example, how the emphasis of the vehicle manufacturers has changed from safety and environmental considerations to energy saving measures. There is no foreseeable alternative in the short to medium term to the conventional internal combustion engine for motorised road transport, and thus throughout the 1980s oil will continue to be needed as a fuel for both passenger cars and commercial vehicles. However, it is fairly clear that during the next ten years the real cost of oil will probably increase, and that its availability will remain subject to political considerations.

In view of this, developments are required on two fronts. First, governments must ensure that oil is allocated to those uses - for example, transport - where substitute forms of energy are not readily available. This will involve decreasing the use of oil for such purposes as home heating and electricity generation. Secondly, it is expected that the automotive industry will utilise an increasing percentage of research and development resources towards bettering the fuel economy characteristics of its products.

Product change will emphasise the need for fuel economy

The majority of product changes are therefore expected to be related to improving fuel efficiency, and the industry has set self imposed targets aimed at raising average miles per gallon figures by, for example, 10 per cent by 1985. Two important ways of achieving this involve the redesign of vehicles to reduce aerodynamic drag, and the use of electronics in engine management systems to enable the power unit to keep in peak condition. The coming generation of passenger cars will reflect a growing understanding of the effect of aerodynamics on a vehicle's performance, and much knowledge has been gained from wind tunnel work. As an example, the new Opel Kadett is reported to have 15 per cent less aerodynamic drag than the model it superseded, while Ford's Erika will also be noticeably improved in this respect. Another method of improving fuel efficiency is through reducing weight; much work is currently taking place in the use of new, lighter materials. Passenger cars are forecast to become more reliable and need less servicing, but with a great deal more sophistication built in they are expected to cost more in real terms. The diesel car has made significant advances during the past five years and many manufacturers are obviously expecting this trend to continue. However, it is believed that much more can still be achieved to make the petrol engine more economical, and this may nullify to some extent the present advantage of diesel power units.

In the case of commercial vehicles the same pressures on energy conservation will be evident. The diesel engine will remain the norm, and there will be a growing demand for automatic transmissions. Fuel economy will be furthered by the design of better engines, reduction of vehicle weight, and better application of aerodynamic principles. Electronics will play an important role in taking over various functions from the driver to ensure optimum operating efficiency. Turbochargers will assume an ever greater importance.

Manufacturing techniques will become increasingly automated

On the manufacturing side, companies producing for volume markets will need to invest heavily in advanced production methods in order to remain viable. The use of robots will increase, and companies with the in house expertise for original thinking will be at an advantage against those which are dependent on outside support.

Diversification does not appear to be a pressing issue

Finally, diversification moves are not expected to feature strongly in the development of automotive companies in the 1980s. There will be exceptions, of course, and Volkswagen in particular is reported to be looking for suitable business opportunities. But many of the major vehicle producers are already highly diversified, and others have had bad experiences when moving out of their mainstream business.

Production and Sales Forecasts

FOR 1980, 1981 AND 1985

BACKGROUND TO THE FORECASTS

The previous section identified the principal features which are expected to determine the evolving structure of the West European automotive industry during the
1980s. Before examining the outlook for the individual major companies within
the sector. it is important to determine the volume of output and sales likely to
be prevailing in the short to medium term. For this purpose forecasts have been
provided of expected sales and production levels for passenger cars and commercial vehicles, by country. for 1980. 1981 and 1985.

The 1973 oil crisis was a watershed

As noted in the section headed "Structural Developments and Key Issues" the 1973
oil crisis and accompanying 1974/75 recession acted as a watershed to the motor
industry's postwar development. Up until that time the motor industry's fortunes
were governed by the business cycle and general economic conditions which
tended to vary from country to country. And, as a rule, the cost and availability
of energy were not particularly significant items in the demand equation. In 1973.
though. a completely new set of circumstances entered into the reckoning. Faced
with. initially, threats over oil supply and. subsequently, rapidly rising prices,
the Western economies went into a downturn in unison. For the motor industry
this development was double edged because, not only is the sector a substantial
energy user in its own right and dependent on a thriving economy for a high activity
level, but its products of course require oil for their use. The damage done during
this period is evident from Tables 1 and 2. Passenger car output fell from 11.5
mn units in 1973 to 9.9 mn in 1974 and 9.3 mn in 1975. Commercial vehicle output was less seriously affected. mainly because the sharp decline in West European
demand was partly offset by increased demand from oil producing nations as well
as higher sales to those developing countries which benefited from the general rise
in commodity prices. The 1973 oil crisis therefore was a watershed in that it
caused the Western economies to act in harmony. rather than altering the underlying demand trend for vehicles. Indeed, since that time the industry has made an
excellent recovery. Passenger car output moved up sharply in 1976 to 10.8 mn
units, and rose to 11.2 mn units in 1977. For the past two years it has stabilised
at the historically high level of 11.3 mn units - despite signs of another oil supply
problem in 1980 as a result of the Iranian revolution. In the commercial vehicle
sector. too. the depression of 1975 has been shaken off. After slumping to 1.26
mn units in 1975, commercial vehicle output in Western Europe increased to 1.41
mn in 1976, to 1.46 mn and 1.45 mn in 1977 and 1978, and recorded a new high of
1.5 mn in 1979.

Following a recovery in 1976-79 another downturn is in sight

There is now, however. a widespread expectation - confirmed by the research for this report - that a downturn is in prospect for 1980 and probably in 1981. This would fit into the four to five year cyclical pattern which has been a strong feature of vehicle demand - and hence production - in Western Europe. but the probability of a decline in activity is reinforced by developments in world oil supply during 1979/80. Oil shortages in 1979. coupled with higher prices of crude oil and cutbacks - or threats of cutbacks - in production from certain producing countries. are beginning to have an impact on the world economic scene. It is particularly disturbing that the USA - the economic powerhouse of the Western world - looks set for a recession of possibly quite severe proportions during 1980. The economies of Western Europe themselves face a trying time during 1980 with high (and generally rising) inflation. high interest rates. increasing unemployment. weak final demand. low business confidence and squeezed company profits. As the following table suggests. there is expected to be a widespread slowdown in economic growth rates with short term prospects for the most part distinctly subdued.

Table 64

Forecasts of Economic Growth in
Western Europe by Country, 1979 and 1980

	% change over previous year	
	1979	1980
Austria	4.4	2.2
Belgium	3.0	2.0
Denmark	3.0	-
Finland	7.5	5.0
France	2.8	1.8
Italy	4.3	1.3
Netherlands	3.3	0.5
Norway	3.0	3.5
Portugal	2.0	3.0
Republic of Ireland	3.0	3.0
Spain	2.5	1.5
Sweden	4.2	3.0
Switzerland	1.0	1.0
UK	1.3	-1.5
West Germany	4.1	2.6

Source: EIU World Outlook 1980.

Production forecasts conditioned by three broad factors

In forecasting West European vehicle production it is necessary to consider three broad factors: first. the likely development of demand in Western Europe's individual country markets; secondly. the extent to which this demand will be met by outside suppliers; and, thirdly. the prospects for exporting to markets outside Western Europe. These factors are discussed separately for passenger cars and commercial vehicles in the following pages. under the respective headings.

However, before doing so it is important to understand a basic premise which is built into the forecasts contained in Tables 65 to 74, namely that in Western Europe there is no foreseeable alternative to road transport as the principal mode for the movement of people and freight – <u>nor is there likely to be one in the longer term</u>. Observers who predict an end to current Western lifestyles at the first hint of oil supply problems have so far been proved in the event to be way off target. Energy economists confirm that there is no physical shortage of oil for medium term (early twenty first century) requirements, but that since the majority of easily recoverable resources are located in politically sensitive areas there are likely to be recurring short term hiccups until alternative energy supplies are sufficiently developed to neutralise this problem. In the meantime the vehicle manufacturers will go some way towards eking out oil supplies through the development of more fuel efficient vehicles. Although Opec appears to have the upper hand in negotiations with the West it is as well to bear in mind that certain principal oil producing nations need the West as much as the West needs their oil. It is for this reason that a fundamental change in the ground rules of forecasting for vehicle output and demand (which a substantially altered oil demand/supply equation could cause) is not expected. This is not to say, though, that the real cost of energy will not rise quite markedly during the next five to ten years. It will, but a variety of compensating factors – reduced utilisation per vehicle, more efficient designs, an acceptance of higher operating costs etc – are expected to work in a way which does not alter the underlying pattern of vehicle demand and production which has been evident in Western Europe since the postwar economic recovery. The maintenance, let alone an improvement, of living standards in Western Europe is dependent on an adequate, efficient and complex freight transport network in which road plays the major role. In addition, in the Western democracies it is not a policy alternative to ban personal motorised transport, and there is growing evidence of a willingness on the part of individuals to expend a high proportion of personal disposable income on the provision of private transport. With this in mind the following pages provide details of passenger car and commercial vehicle forecast demand and production for 1980, 1981 and 1985.

PASSENGER CARS

A record year for demand in 1979 –

1979, as already noted, was a peak year for passenger car demand in Western Europe; unit sales reached an estimated 10.5 mn units, 3.1 per cent above 1978's outturn which was also a record year. Of the major markets, conditions were especially bright in the UK – where a new high of 1.72 mn units were sold – and Italy. A record was also established in France but in West Germany demand, although strong by historical standards, fell slightly. Elsewhere, demand patterns fluctuated around 1978's level, except in Austria and Finland where strong recoveries from 1978's exceptionally low levels of demand were experienced.

Passenger car demand in Western Europe during the postwar period has exhibited strong underlying growth, but is characterised by pronounced cyclical downturns. The 1970s have been no exception to this general rule (see Table 23). The early part of the decade saw demand building up to the twin peak years of 1972 and 1973. The downturn in 1974 and 1975 was not unexpected, but was made considerably worse by the impact of the brief (yet traumatic) Arab oil embargo and subsequent massive rise of oil prices. Of the 15 West European markets only three - Sweden, Norway and Portugal - recorded an increase in 1974. During the depth of the 1974/75 recession it was easy to believe that things would never be quite the same again, but car demand has shown a rise every year since 1974 and, indeed, 1973's total was exceeded as soon as 1976.

– but a downturn is predicted for 1980 and 1981

It is not easy to become excited about the prospects for passenger car demand in 1980 and 1981. Even with a neutral economic outlook, the strong cyclical nature of motor vehicle demand would suggest a decline in sales. But the fundamentals point to a difficult couple of years in Western Europe as governments tackle the gathering recession; as indicated in Table 64 economic growth rates for eleven of the 15 countries are forecast to slacken in 1980, the exceptions being the relatively minor economies of the Republic of Ireland and Switzerland (where growth is expected to remain at the 1979 level), and Norway and Portugal (where only slightly higher growth rates are expected for 1980). The likelihood for the next 18 months therefore is one of generally poor economic performance which will be harmful to consumer and business confidence alike. Moreover, there is a possibility that this will be accompanied by renewed concern over the availability and price of oil. It would appear that consumers become quickly adjusted to higher oil prices and have come to expect them. The fact that individual motorists may choose to reduce their annual mileage does not change the need for a car - although, admittedly, cars which are used less may last longer and possibly remain with their first owners for a longer period too. On the other hand, shortages of fuel tend to have a more dramatic impact on the car market. In preparing the forecasts in Table 65 (and subsequent tables) account has been taken of the gloomier economic prospects facing Western Europe in the short term together with the probability of higher real energy costs, but it is assumed that the oil will remain in relatively free supply.

As will be seen in Table 65, passenger car demand in 1980 is forecast to decline by 9.3 per cent to 9.5 mn units. All principal markets are expected to witness a reversal, and most of the smaller markets are forecast to be dull in 1980 also. More contentiously perhaps, demand for passenger cars is forecast to weaken still further in 1981, by 1.6 per cent to 9.35 mn. This is because the effects of economic recession are expected to begin to be felt towards the middle of 1980 and the duration of the downturn is unlikely to be less than a year. Hence, conditions will continue to be difficult through the greater part of 1981, and it will be only towards the end of 1981 - or even in 1982 - before the next cyclical upturn can be realistically expected. Either that, or the coming recession is going to be a great deal less severe than many macroeconomic forecasts are suggesting.

By 1985 the market will probably be in the final phase of the next upswing. However, growth prospects in Western Europe are unquestionably slowing as a number of the principal markets - notably West Germany and France - reach saturation. Whereas the annual average growth in passenger car demand in Western Europe between the peaks of 1973 and 1979 amounted to 1.8 per cent, for the period 1979 to 1985 growth is forecast to decline to an annual average of 1.2 per cent. Obviously, some countries will perform better than others, especially those (such as Spain and Portugal) which are still a long way from saturation.

Table 65

Forecasts of Passenger Car Demand in Western Europe by Country, 1980, 1981 & 1985 ('000 units)

	Actual						Forecast		
	1970	1975	1976	1977	1978	1979	1980	1981	1985
West Germany	2,107	2,106	2,312	2,561	2,664	2,623	2,350	2,300	2,720
France	1,297	1,482	1,858	1,907	1,945	1,976	1,800	1,750	2,100
UK	1,077	1,194	1,286	1,324	1,592	1,716	1,550	1,530	1,850
Italy	1,364	1,055	1,188	1,219	1,216	1,350[a]	1,200	1,180	1,450
Spain	399	572	620	663	654	621	600	600	750
Netherlands	432	450	508	552	585	569	500	480	615
Belgium	301	365	421	429	424	424	380	370	450
Switzerland	211	190	204	234	272	296[a]	260	260	300
Sweden	203	285	313	241	201	215	205	225	230
Austria	127	185	225	296	158	220[a]	200	200	250
Denmark	108	116	152	141	133	130[a]	115	110	145
Republic of Ireland	54	52	70	82	106	96[a]	100	95	115
Finland	92	117	92	90	81	100	90	90	100
Norway	70	103	127	145	78	89	95	100	100
Portugal	60	84	98	76	53	50[a]	55	60	75
Total	7,902	8,356	9,474	9,960	10,162	10,475[a]	9,500	9,350	11,250

a   Estimated.

Source: EIU forecasts.

<u>Production will fall in 1980 and 1981 -</u>

The implications of these demand forecasts for production levels are given in
Table 67. After reaching a level of 11.32 mn units in 1979 (still below 1973's
11.47 mn units), passenger car output is forecast to decline by 8.7 per cent to
10.34 mn units in 1980, and by a further 1.8 per cent to 10.15 mn units in 1981.
These forecasts reflect the expectation of lower demand in Western Europe, but
also take account of the region's deteriorating net export position in the car sector.
Western Europe's passenger car output has traditionally been higher than demand,
but the gap has narrowed during the 1970s, and is expected to continue shrinking
in the early 1980s. The following table provides the details.

Table 66

Western Europe's Net
<u>Exports of Passenger Cars, 1970-85</u>

	'000 units
1970	2,475
1971	2,473
1972	1,858
1973	2,084
1974	1,817
1975	970
1976	1,286
1977	1,254
1978	1,141
1979[a]	852
1980[b]	835
1981[b]	800
1985[b]	550

a Estimated. b Forecast.

Source: EIU forecasts.

There are two main reasons for the pattern shown in Table 66. First, the West
European market has been increasingly penetrated by outside suppliers, notably
from Japan but also elsewhere including the Eastern Bloc. During the early 1980s
these outside suppliers are forecast to make further inroads, especially from the
Eastern Bloc where a number of West European companies have agreed to source
various models; for example, Fiat's Zero is to be sourced from Poland, while
Citroën has entered into a joint venture in Rumania to produce a new small car
which will be distributed in Western Europe through Citroën's dealers. Other
companies in countries such as Brazil and South Korea are eyeing West European
markets and presumably will achieve a certain - albeit minimal - volume of sales.
The Japanese too will remain strong contenders in the marketplace, but an as yet
unknown factor is the extent to which protectionist measures will be implemented
in Western Europe aimed at redressing the substantial deficit in vehicle trade
currently in Japan's favour. In theory, the US producers with their coming generation of downsized models ought to be in a good position to expand exports to
Western Europe, but it is believed that they will not in the event become significant suppliers to the region, mainly because they are likely to need the majority

of output to supply North American markets and, anyway, both Ford and General Motors have important European manufacturing operations which they would wish to see develop; any expansion in car imports from North America is therefore forecast to be modest.

The second reason for the pattern established in Table 66 is reduced opportunities for the direct export of built up vehicles. During the past couple of decades governments in developing countries have encouraged and, sometimes, legislated for the establishment of local assembly facilities. In addition, as Volkswagen found in the USA, it is in cases a necessity to set up local operations in order to maintain a reasonable market presence, and this trend is expected to intensify in the 1980s.

– but 1985 should see a new high

By 1985 Western Europe's passenger car output is forecast to amount to 11.8 mn units, implying a net export figure of 550,000 units. The overall production pattern of the 1970s is expected to remain largely unchanged with West Germany and France in the two top slots. However, Spain is forecast to overtake the UK. In arriving at the forecasts by country the following factors have been taken into consideration.

West Germany will remain the leading producer thanks to:

- the presence of five strong producers;

- the ability to achieve volume runs for certain models;

- the relatively settled state of labour relations;

- basic engineering and managerial competence;

- a high level of technical innovation;

- and a reputation for quality.

On the other hand, the West German companies suffer from high labour costs and a strong currency - factors which make sustaining exports in an increasingly competitive worldwide market a difficult business. In addition, there is evidence that their domestic market will come under heavy pressure from the importers - particularly the Japanese.

France's automotive industry will benefit from being concentrated into two major and powerful groups, both having strong encouragement from the government. With a good position in many key European markets, the French producers can look forward to a high level of activity when car demand is buoyant. In addition, the French government appears to be taking a strong line on the question of Japanese imports and, hence, the French producers should be able to continue supplying the lion's share of their domestic market.

In Italy too the manufacturers have benefited by protection from Japanese competition in the domestic market. But, with only one major supplier, imports have been a growing feature of domestic sales. Fiat's new models are expected to provide a firm base for the Italian industry,but the continuation of difficult labour relations will probably hold back the sector's true potential.

The UK's forecasts reflect the expectation that by 1985 there will be only two major producers - BL and Ford. Both Talbot and Vauxhall will be assemblers - and thus their output will not be counted as domestic production. It should also be noted that by 1985 BL is expected to be an important assembler due to its Honda connections; the Bounty is therefore not included in Table 67. The 1985 forecast also assumes that the DeLorean venture will be producing at the rate of around 30/40,000 units per year.

Spain's output in 1985 should reflect the growing build up of General Motors' new venture. Elsewhere within the country expansion is not expected to be dramatic. Entry into the EEC will be accompanied by an opening up of the Spanish market which, potentially, could have a far reaching impact on the domestic automotive industry.

Sweden, meanwhile, cannot expect to do more than maintain volume output. Much will depend on Volvo's new model to replace the 2 series.

Belgium's output in Table 67 consists of Ford's Taunus/Cortina production. So far as is known this arrangement will continue and, by 1985, with the introduction of a new model a couple of years previously, output is forecast to be at an historically high level.

The Netherlands is also dependent on a single facility - Volvo Car BV. It is assumed that Volvo and the Dutch government will work together to ensure the company's long term survival, although it remains to be seen whether an output level significantly higher than 100,000 units can be achieved.

COMMERCIAL VEHICLES

Long term demand prospects are bright,
but a short term downturn is expected

As with passenger cars, 1979 was a peak year for commercial vehicle demand in Western Europe. Sales amounted to an estimated 1.24 mn units, 9.2 per cent above 1978's level. However, in the context of deteriorating economic conditions the prospect for 1980 and 1981 is one of reduced demand. Business confidence will be affected by the economic slowdown, and the twin effects of reduced profits and high interest rates are expected to reduce capital spending plans. France and the UK will remain the biggest markets, followed by West Germany, Spain and Italy.

By 1985 business conditions should have improved in line with economic recovery, and commercial vehicle sales are forecast to reach 1.3 mn units. Full details are provided in Table 68.

Table 67

Forecasts of West European Passenger Car Production by Major Producing Country, 1980, 1981 & 1985
('000 units)

	Actual						Forecast		
	1970	1975	1976	1977	1978	1979	1980	1981	1985
West Germany	3,528	2,908	3,547	3,791	3,890	3,933	3,600	3,500	4,000
France	2,458[a]	2,546	2,980	3,092	3,111	3,222	2,900	2,800	3,350
Italy	1,720	1,349	1,471	1,440	1,509	1,481	1,350	1,300	1,550
UK	1,641	1,268	1,333	1,328	1,223	1,070	950	1,000	1,000
Spain	450	696	753	989	986	966	950	980	1,250
Sweden	279	316	317	235	254	297	260	260	280
Belgium	234	182	285	286	265	257	240	230	270
Netherlands	67	61	74	53	65	90	85	80	100
Total	10,377	9,326	10,760	11,214	11,303	11,316	10,335	10,150	11,800

a   See footnote to Table 1.

Source: EIU forecasts.

Table 68

Forecasts of Commercial Vehicle Demand in Western Europe by Country, 1980, 1981 & 1985

('000 units)

	Actual						Forecast		
	1970	1975	1976	1977	1978	1979	1980	1981	1985
France	208	206	293	298	300	315	290	284	325
UK	257	225	215	231	262	306	290	282	311
West Germany	165	109	137	138	156	170	160	155	180
Spain	78	94	93	101	104	106	100	104	118
Italy	85	76	95	110	98	108[a]	100	103	112
Netherlands	47	37	42	43	47	48	45	44	49
Belgium	25	21	24	26	29	36	32	31	35
Portugal	16	18	21	33	29	31[a]	30	30	38
Denmark	25	30	45	35	23	25[a]	22	23	28
Austria	16	12	18	19	19	20[a]	18	19	20
Sweden	19	17	19	20	17	17	16	16	19
Norway	16	12	14	17	14	16	16	17	18
Switzerland	13	8	8	11	14	17[a]	16	17	17
Republic of Ireland	10	7	8	10	13	13[a]	13	13	15
Finland	23	14	14	13	12	14	12	12	15
Total	1,003	886	1,046	1,105	1,137	1,242[a]	1,160	1,150	1,300

a Estimated.

Source: EIU forecasts.

The West European vehicle manufacturers have had greater success in preserving
their net export position in the commercial vehicle sector. Table 69 shows that
there was a substantial improvement in the period 1974-77, since when the gap
between production and domestic demand has slipped back to the levels of the early
1970s. This buoyant four year run is largely explained by high demand from the
oil exporting nations which benefited from vastly increased revenues after the 1973
oil crisis. Furthermore, other commodity prices followed in the wake of oil, and
hence there were increased shipments to developing nations in general. Towards
the end of the decade, though, the rise in commodity prices had worked through the
system and many markets - especially those in the Middle East - became saturated.

From Table 69 it will be noticed that the net export position in the commercial
vehicle sector is forecast to remain broadly unchanged for the period under review.
This is explained by two main factors.

First, European consumers are expected to remain basically loyal to domestic
products. The Japanese have made a certain amount of headway in the light goods
vehicle sector and are reported to be gearing up for an onslaught in the medium/
heavy sectors. But, apart from this, imports of commercial vehicles into Western
Europe from other regions have not been significant - and are not expected to
become so. In the choice process, consumers as a rule are governed by a combination of considerations including initial price, durability, reliability, running
costs and resale value. In many instances close relationships are built up between
users and distributors and the impact of goodwill should not be minimised. In
addition, all things being equal, businesses are more likely to buy from a national
supplier where possible in order to support local industry.

And, secondly, the commercial vehicle manufacturers appear to be quite well placed
to enjoy an active export trade in built up (or countable KD) units. In particular,
opportunities are opening up in the USA now that medium weight diesel powered
trucks are finding growing acceptance.

Table 69

Western Europe's Net
Exports of Commercial Vehicles, 1970-85

	'000 units
1970	328
1971	291
1972	... [a]
1973	248
1974	381
1975	376
1976	364
1977	359
1978	311

(continued)

Table 69 (continued)

Western Europe's Net
Exports of Commercial Vehicles, 1970-85

	'000 units
1979[b]	256
1980[c]	255
1981[c]	245
1985[c]	282

a 1972 figure not available due to lack of
UK data   (see Table 24). b Estimated.
c Forecast.

Source: EIU forecasts.

Declining output in 1980 and 1981, with recovery by 1985

Table 70 provides forecasts of West European commercial vehicle production by
country for 1980, 1981 and 1985. In the short term production will follow the
expected reduction in demand. Unit output in 1980 is scheduled to fall by 5.5 per
cent to just over 1.41 mn units, while a further slight fall in 1981 is expected to
see output drop to below 1.4 mn units. The heaviest losers will be the UK and
France. Assuming that 1985 represents the next peak, output is forecast to amount
to 1.58 mn units, implying an annual average growth of 0.9 per cent between 1979
and 1985.

Following Table 70, four further tables have been prepared to provide details of
commercial vehicle production forecasts by type for the UK, France, West Germany
and Italy. The analysis included in these tables corresponds to the classifications
in Tables 6, 10, 14 and 18. The following comments indicate the thinking behind
the individual country forecasts for 1985, compared with 1979's outturn.

The UK. By 1985 it is not expected that there will be a significant change in the
mix of UK commercial vehicle production. Car derived van output is forecast to
decline by 7.5 per cent to 86,000 units, but this reflects the buoyancy of 1979's
production performance rather than a weakening of the car derived van sector.
Little change is expected in output levels of other rigids up to 14 tons gvw where
markets are almost entirely dependent on replacement demand. Rather better
prospects, though, are predicted for the heavier end of the weight ranges where
rigids over 14 tons gvw and articulated units together are expected to account for
11.3 per cent of the UK's total commercial vehicle production in 1985 as against
8.6 per cent in 1979. There are three principal explanations behind this prediction:
first, the trend towards the use of heavier units for the movement of freight -
already well advanced - will continue, aided in part by (expected) legislation to
allow the use of combinations of 38 tons gtw (gross train weight); secondly, UK
vehicle manufacturers are expected to strengthen their competitive position vis-à-
vis the importers thanks to new models; and thirdly, export opportunities ought to
be improved in the context of new model offerings. The likelihood of higher bus
production stems from the continuing importance of public transport systems in
the UK's major cities, together with hopefully higher export sales.

105

France.   In France, too, there is expected to be a stronger emphasis in the higher weight categories, on the assumption that RVI's moves to rationalise and establish a more effective competitive position eventually begin to produce results. French commercial vehicle output is currently heavily concentrated in the up to 2.5 tons gvw category which accounted for 70.2 per cent of production in 1979, whereas rigids over 15 tons gvw and articulated units only amounted to 4.6 per cent of output; by 1985 this is forecast to increase to 6.3 per cent. Moreover, prospects in the middle weight range look bright in view of RVI's relationship with Mack.

West German goods vehicle production is forecast to remain relatively stable up to 1985. The Volkswagen/MAN partnership to produce mid range trucks explains the strength of the 6-16 tons gvw sector in Table 73. Following a downturn in the latter part of the 1970s, bus production is expected to pick up by the mid 1980s. In particular, MAN appears intent on expanding its activities in this sector, especially in export markets.

In Italy an across the board increase in all categories is predicted - except in the case of rigid goods vehicles from 6 to 12 tons gvw which are forecast to remain stable. In most sectors output rises are expected to be modest, and these forecasts reflect the growing opportunities for Iveco in increasingly competitive worldwide commercial vehicle markets.

Spain's commercial vehicle industry is expected to make slow but steady headway in the early 1980s as the present largely uncompetitive truck producing facilities become integrated with international groups. In theory export opportunities should be augmented, but Spain's membership of the EEC will be accompanied by an opening up of the Spanish market which will result in growing competition for domestic sales.

Sweden and the Netherlands are forecast to show gains up to 1985. In the case of Sweden both Volvo and Saab Scania have well entrenched positions and good reputations in the truck sector, while in the Netherlands DAF Truck should manage at least to hold its own during the next five years.

Table 70

Forecasts of West European Commercial Vehicle Production by Major Producing Country, 1980, 1981 & 1985
('000 units)

| | Actual | | | | | | Forecast | | |
	1970	1975	1976	1977	1978	1979	1980	1981	1985
UK	458	381	372	386	385	408	370	370	425
France	292a	315	423	415	397	392	375	365	410
West Germany	314	278	321	314	296	317	305	295	330
Spain	89	118	113	141	158	157	150	155	170
Italy	135	110	119	143	148	151	145	140	165
Sweden	31	50	51	52	51	58	55	55	65
Netherlands	12	10	11	13	13	15	15	15	17
Total	1,331	1,262	1,410	1,464	1,448	1,498	1,415	1,395	1,582

a See footnote to Table 2.

Source: EIU forecasts.

107

Table 71

Forecasts of UK Commercial Vehicle Production by Type, 1980, 1981 & 1985

('000 units)

	Actual						Forecast		
	1970	1975	1976	1977	1978	1979	1980	1981	1985
Rigid goods vehicles									
car derived vans	243[a]	81	82	86	82	93	83	85	86
others up to		121	139	153	165	173	155	149	175
3.5 tons gvw									
3.5-14 tons gvw	142[b]	111	88	87	78	82	75	75	86
over 14 tons gvw	31	23	21	21	24	25	23	25	32
Articulated units	18	9	9	12	12	10	9	10	16
Buses	23	36	33	28	23	26	25	26	30
Total	458	381	372	386	385	408	370	370	425

a Up to 3 tons. b 3-14 tons.

Source: EIU forecasts.

Table 72

Forecasts of French Commercial Vehicle Production by Type, 1980, 1981 & 1985
('000 units)

| | Actual | | | | | | Forecast | | |
	1970[a]	1975	1976	1977	1978	1979	1980	1981	1985
Rigid goods vehicles									
up to 2.5 tons gvw	187	204	287	291	275	275	261	259	270
2.5–6 tons gvw	60	62	83	75	73	63	62	55	75
6–15 tons gvw	17	22	24	23	27	32	28	31	35
over 15 tons gvw	18	17	15	13	10	10	10	10	14
Articulated units	7	7	10	10	9	8	7	7	12
Buses	3	3	4	3	4	3	3	3	4
Total	292	315	423	415	397	392	375	365	410

a See footnote to Table 10.

Source: EIU forecasts.

Table 73

Forecasts of West German Commercial Vehicle Production by Type, 1980, 1981 & 1985 ('000 units)

	Actual						Forecast		
	1970	1975	1976	1977	1978	1979	1980	1981	1985
Rigid goods vehicles									
up to 2 tons gvw	9	2	3	3	4	8	6	7	9
2–6 tons gvw	185	123	163	160	156	162	156	152	156
6–16 tons gvw	69	65	60	56	59	55	56	53	63
over 16 tons gvw	22	50	58	55	47	56	53	50	58
Articulated units	14	19	18	20	16	20	19	18	24
Buses	15	19	20	18	15	15	15	15	20
Total	314	278	321	314	296	317	305	295	330

Source: EIU forecasts.

Table 74

Forecasts of Italian Commercial Vehicle Production by Type, 1980, 1981 & 1985
('000 units)

| | Actual | | | | | | | Forecast | | |
	1970	1975	1976	1977	1978	1979	1980	1981	1985
Rigid goods vehicles									
up to 2 tons gvw	25	13	19	22	29	38	35	38	42
2-6 tons gvw	62	58	62	77	85	83	80	72	84
6-12 tons gvw	19	10	11	13	9	8	7	7	8
over 12 tons gvw	22	19	17	19	12	12	12	12	15
Articulated units	4	4	6	9	8	5	5	5	9
Buses	3	6	5	5	6	6	6	6	7
Total	135	110	119	143	148	151	145	140	165

Source: EIU forecasts.

111

Prospects for the Principal Vehicle Manufacturers

The increasingly global character of vehicle manufacturing operations

Following the preceding two sections of this special report which respectively
examine the main forces which are expected to shape the structure of the West
European automotive sector in the coming decade and present vehicle demand and
production forecasts for 1980, 1981 and 1985, it is now relevant to consider the
prospects for the individual manufacturers. It is worth recapping that the automotive industry is becoming increasingly international in its scope and character.
Whereas it was sufficient for a company to develop and prosper by operating
predominantly on the domestic level up until the early 1970s, the past few years
have been accompanied by the need to function on a wider European basis. But
today, at the beginning of the 1980s, even this is not enough. It is becoming more
evident that success in volume vehicle manufacturing requires a global involvement,
as exemplified by the world car concept. On the passenger car side, as worldwide
product specifications are harmonised, it is contended that only those companies
which are able to support an annual worldwide output base of 2 mn units plus - of
a rationalised product range - will be capable of securing the economies of scale
in component and subassembly manufacturing to retain an existence completely
independent from other groups. Below this volume it is doubtful whether cash flow
and profitability will be adequate for a comprehensive and all embracing research
and development facility to be maintained. This is not to suggest that there is no
future for independent middle rank - or, indeed, small - passenger car producing
companies, but that they will have to achieve by trading links or other means the
economies of scale afforded by the "world" companies. The likelihood, therefore,
is that by 1990 the global volume car industry will be heavily concentrated around
perhaps eight of these world companies, of which four are expected to be European
owned.

To a certain extent commercial vehicles, insofar as they are produced by the same
companies as passenger cars, will fall into the same pattern - although it is
probable that the scope for a company to sustain, and exist, on a strong local
presence will be greater than for passenger cars. This is because goods vehicle
and bus specifications are forecast to remain rather more varied between the North
American, Japanese and individual West European markets than is the case for
passenger cars. In addition, the proprietary component and subassembly suppliers
(for engines, transmissions, brakes etc) are expected to remain a significant force
in the marketplace, and hence there will be plenty of opportunity for a truck manufacturer to benefit from economies of scale and specify technologically advanced
equipment simply by outside sourcing from independent component suppliers.

But sheer volume is not everything

Another point to note arises over the question of size. Sheer volume alone will not provide a passport to success. As always return on capital and maintenance of employment will be of paramount importance.

The individual outlooks for the 19 companies which were identified in Table 25 are contained in the following pages. This section concludes with an assessment of the overall prospects for the smaller specialist manufacturers.

PEUGEOT CITROEN TALBOT (PSA GROUP)

The importance of rationalisation –

Having become Western Europe's largest vehicle producer through the acquisition of Chrysler Europe, the main issue facing the PSA group during the opening years of the 1980s is whether rationalisation can be achieved fast enough – especially in the context of falling demand in 1980 and 1981. With two distinct product ranges, each with their own distribution arrangements, Peugeot Citroën as an entity made a good deal of sense; in particular, the French company has been careful not to fall into the trap of rationalising dealer networks and thereby affording greater marketing opportunities for competitors. But the addition of Chrysler Europe (now renamed Talbot) adds a new and potentially unwieldy dimension.

The French government is undoubtedly delighted to see the emergence of a wholly French controlled vehicle manufacturing sector, and will provide whatever support (financial or otherwise) may become necessary to ensure PSA's continuing role as one of Europe's leaders. But as a private sector company, PSA needs to find a rationale for Talbot's inclusion within its ranks. From recent moves it is apparent that Talbot's image will become increasingly sporting. The association with Lotus to produce the Sunbeam Lotus is a minor manifestation of this trend but, more importantly (and surprisingly), Talbot has announced its intention to compete in the Formula 1 world motor racing championship during the 1981 season. The question remains, though, whether Talbot's range as presently constituted lends itself to this method of promotion. The Horizon and Sunbeam models are attractive in their own right, while the 1307/08/09 (Alpine) range has benefited from a recent facelift and addition of a three box version (the Solara). But no one would pretend that they are other than typical mid range family transport.

– brings into question the future of Talbot's UK operations –

Another thorny problem for PSA with Talbot arises over the future of the UK operations. As Europe's third largest car market the UK is of significance to any vehicle manufacturer with expansionist tendencies, and politically it is certainly useful to be seen to have a local presence in key markets. But will the continuation, let alone development, of Talbot's UK operations prove too costly for PSA? Indeed, will Talbot's UK business base be sufficient to justify a long term local presence? Even though business with Iran may pick up considerably in 1980 there are doubts over the long term prospects of this venture, and it is possible that the (Hunter based) Peykan model – currently assembled by Iran National from kits supplied by Talbot UK – will be replaced by a Peugeot design some time in the mid 1980s.

113

- but Peugeot and Citroën are unlikely to be troubled

Elsewhere on passenger cars there is no reason to suppose that Peugeot and Citroën will not continue along their individual - and hitherto successful - lines, while benefiting from a growing harmonisation of under the skin subassemblies, such as engines and gearboxes.

The basis for a viable commercial vehicle operation exists -

With regard to commercial vehicles, PSA has the basis of a full line product offering from its plants in the UK, France and Spain. As with passenger cars, there need to be moves towards rationalisation aimed at giving the various operations a common identity and, especially importantly, enhancing marketing opportunities. This need not necessarily mean removing the individual marque names in those markets - particularly Dodge in the UK and Barreiros in Spain - where goodwill exists. However, in other markets the establishment as quickly as possible of a group commercial vehicle identity - for example, selling the complete range under the Peugeot name - could be vitally important.

In addition, PSA would benefit from association with other groups in the sourcing of major components; the discussions with DAF Truck will probably be followed by talks with others as PSA attempts to bring together the nucleus of a European truck club in which it would be the leading partner.

- as well as the potential to become a world company

Whether or not PSA remains Europe's leading producer at the end of the 1980s will largely depend on the success achieved in becoming a world company. In practical terms this hinges on the group's development in North America which, compared with its European rivals (Renault, Volkswagen and, to a lesser extent, Fiat), has so far been minimal. Somehow PSA will need to begin car assembly in North America (in Chrysler plants?) if it is not to be overtaken.

RENAULT

Good prospects for cars -

Whatever else happens in the 1980s it is safe to assume that Renault's position as a state owned, independent and powerful group within the West European automotive sector will remain unchanged.

The company's passenger car lineup for the 1980s is well advanced with attractive new models already announced - R14, R18 and Fuego sporting coupé - and others scheduled to be introduced during the 1980s, starting with the R2 later in 1980. However, Renault still lacks a serious contender in the prestige luxury and executive car category. While this is a comparatively small market sector it is important from the standpoint of image, and Peugeot with its 604 model has shown that it is possible to enter this lucrative market by using the same engine (the V6 Douvrin unit) as is utilised by Renault in the R30.

During the 1980s Renault is expected to increase substantially its worldwide spread of interests, but with France remaining the nerve centre. The relationship with American Motors presents an excellent opportunity for Renault to gain greater influence and penetration in the all important US car market, but success will not come easily and is by no means guaranteed. It is, for example, not proven that Renault has in the R18 the right car to appeal to American buyers in sufficient volume to ensure that it is worthwhile for American Motors to assemble the model.

The agreement with Volvo, whereby Renault is to acquire a 20 per cent holding in the Swedish company's car manufacturing operations, is a pointer to future developments. Further alliances, and not only with European companies, are probable, but in all cases Renault is likely to be the dominant partner. These associations will provide a useful outlet for Renault's considerable in house production of components and subassemblies. Elsewhere associations will be formed with component suppliers, where the latter are able to offer technical expertise which Renault would not otherwise have access to. Moreover, a closer association with the PSA group cannot be ruled out, especially in the form of joint ventures to produce components.

– but commercial vehicles will remain a problem short term

When examining Renault's prospects in the commercial vehicle sector, however, the outlook becomes rather more cloudy. RVI is still not profitable, but the parent company obviously has sufficient financial and managerial muscle to continue the fight towards viability, and the potential is there given the consolidation of the past few years. But if success is to be achieved, marketing progress will be required on three broad fronts: first, RVI must increase market penetration in its domestic market; secondly, the company must get into other European markets properly, notably the UK, West Germany and Spain – Europe's major truck markets; and, thirdly, there needs to be a more effective push into international markets. Progress on this last point has been made by means of the connection with Mack of the USA; this linkup is of immense significance to both parties – but particularly RVI which is able to utilise its French production facilities more effectively through direct export of built up trucks to Mack's distribution network in North America.

In order to progress faster RVI needs to find European partners with whom it could secure an interchange of components. Also, a greater reliance on international proprietary component suppliers would help.

VOLKSWAGEN/AUDI NSU

Consolidation in Western Europe –

Following a heavy investment programme to update its model range in the second half of the 1970s, the next few years will see Volkswagen consolidate its position as a true world automotive company. With an attractive lineup of models which is expected to maintain the company's sales momentum up to the mid 1980s, Volkswagen will be able to refine its production and marketing arrangements while preparing for the next generation of cars. In addition, the company will maintain a high activity level on the technological innovation front, and the incorporation of advanced features is likely to be an increasing characteristic of Volkswagen's output. The diesel engined version of the Golf - which radically changed existing notions about the suitability of diesel powered passenger cars - is an example of what Volkswagen's research and development budget can achieve.

- and expansion in North America

In Western Europe Volkswagen is not expected to break out of its West German base, but elsewhere there could be major expansion. Nowhere are Volkswagen's ambitions greater than North America where the company is targeting to claw back to its market standing of ten years ago. The US assembly operation in Pennsylvania has been a great success and has encouraged the search for another site. Latest reports indicate that a second US factory will be operational during 1982, at which time Volkswagen will have a US assembly capability of around 0.5 mn units per year. Less dramatic progress is forecast for Latin America, but nevertheless this region will remain an important business area. In addition, Volkswagen's size and standing are such that it is one of the limited number of vehicle manu-facturing companies capable of handling major development projects on a global basis; for example, talks have taken place with China and it is possible that Volkswagen's sphere of influence will extend wide and far during the 1980s.

The biggest challenge over passenger car activities concerns Audi NSU which will require increasing attention if it is to acquire a BMW type image. The replace-ment 100 model, scheduled for introduction in 1980, will indicate the strength of Audi's response in the upmarket stakes.

Possibility of further links with MAN

Meanwhile, it would not be unexpected if links with MAN intensified during the next few years. The decision to cooperate in the design, development and pro-duction of a mid range truck represents an opportunity for both companies to come closer together and offer a full line commercial vehicle range. For Volkswagen and MAN distribution is a limiting factor - the former currently orientated towards light vehicles, the latter towards heavy ones.

FIAT

Outlook affected by prospects for Italy

Fiat's overall prospects for the 1980s are heavily conditioned by the difficult political, economic and social framework of Italy. However bright the fundamental aspects of Fiat's outlook may appear, there will always be the danger that - in Italy at least - the company may be blown off course by a period of labour unrest. Moreover, there would appear to be no clear solution to this problem. It is for this reason, presumably, that Iveco is headquartered in the Netherlands and Fiat is developing South America as a major centre of passenger car production in its own right.

Investment will pay off in passenger cars –

Following the doldrums of the mid 1970s when Fiat allowed its investment in passenger car operations to slip, the company is in the midst of an extensive and ambitious model renewal programme. The Ritmo (Strada) and Panda are – as noted in the earlier section on Fiat in Part 1 – only the beginnings of a revamp which promises at least one new model per year up to the mid 1980s. And, on the basis of these recent introductions, Fiat's prospects for maintaining market share in the medium term look good. But in the short term the company's showing in the European car market is unlikely to sparkle until a new mid range model (to replace the 131) makes its debut in 1981. Also, like Renault, Fiat has yet to come to grips with the luxury/executive market segment – and shows little signs of doing so.

It is difficult to see where Autobianchi will fit into the scheme of things when the new 127 supermini is launched in 1981. It is thought unlikely that the Autobianchi A112 model would be retained after that date – although an Autobianchi version of the revised 127 is a possibility.

On the international scene Fiat's position is good, although the company's presence in North America is clearly weak. There is no obvious candidate for Fiat to form an association with which would lead to greater marketing opportunities, and it is doubtful whether an assembly operation could be sustained in the USA by Fiat in its own right. Nevertheless, the build up of South American operations – already supplying engines to Fiat's European factories – could provide a useful additional sourcing point if the Italian company decided to increase its marketing thrust in North America. There is every likelihood that business ties with Eastern Bloc countries will intensify. and the decision to source the forthcoming Zero model exclusively from Poland for West European markets is a pointer that Fiat is thinking on a global basis.

– and commercial vehicles

The 1980s are expected to witness an intensive push by Fiat in commercial vehicles. Through Iveco – now wholly owned by Fiat – slow, but steady, headway has been achieved during the past five years. During the early 1980s Iveco will probably continue an aggressive export drive in European and international markets. Whether a serious role in Spain is achieved remains to be seen, but the fruits of recent efforts in the UK are beginning to come through. The same can be said of North America, where Iveco's products are marketed with a Magirus badge.

FORD

Parent company faces a difficult period –

The development of Ford's European operations during the 1980s will reflect their vital role in the US company's worldwide business interests. However, a burning issue concerns the extent to which Ford's problems in its domestic market will overspill – if at all – into Europe. It is worth recalling that Ford's loss in North America in 1979 amounted to about $1 bn, mainly as a consequence of the need to finance a gigantic capital investment programme – aimed at meeting the government's mandated fuel consumption targets which require that each supplier to the

US market must achieve a minimum 27.5 miles per (US) gallon fleet average by 1985 - coupled with a sudden swing in consumer choice towards smaller fuel efficient cars in the context of worries over the price and availability of oil, a development which has not helped Ford whose downsized models have yet to reach the dealers. Ford claims that this setback will not affect prospects in Europe but, with another sizeable loss predicted for US operations in 1980, it is natural for niggling worries to exist - albeit in the background.

- but momentum in Europe will be sustained in passenger cars -

Taking passenger cars, Ford begins the 1980s with one of Europe's best and most logical range of models. Furthermore, a phased model update programme, beginning with Erika (the new Escort) later in 1980 and including a revised Cortina and Granada around 1982/83, will ensure that Ford keeps up the pressure on competitors. But much more can be achieved in the penetration of key continental markets where Ford's performance to date has been disappointing, and it is to be expected that strenuous efforts will be made to promote its image. Quality, in general, is not a problem. In the UK car market Ford is unlikely to lose market leadership for the foreseeable future and, indeed, may well maintain it throughout the 1980s.

- and commercial vehicles

In the commercial vehicle sector, Ford is putting in the investment to ensure that it is not among the losers when the long predicted shake out of Western Europe's producers begins. A new range of light vehicles are scheduled for the early 1980s, together with a revamped 'D' series. The heavy duty 'H' range (Transcontinental) represents a worthwhile and praiseworthy entry into that fiercely competitive market sector, but a new model is needed before further progress can realistically be predicted. Meanwhile, the success story of the Transit van will continue - despite "copies" from other companies.

All in all, Ford faces an exciting future in Europe. The US reversal is serious and worrying - but temporary. By 1990 Ford will be one of the world companies mentioned on page 96. And as such the European operations could well be charged with playing a challenging role.

GENERAL MOTORS

A growing presence

As the world's largest vehicle manufacturer and with rock solid credentials, General Motors has the necessary financial, managerial and technical muscle to remain a growing force in Western Europe - especially since the corporation's policy is to be just that. Therefore, throughout the 1980s, and notably in the early years, General Motors' position will strengthen in both passenger cars and commercial vehicles. Additional factories for the assembly of passenger cars and manufacture of components will result in an increase in production capacity of an estimated 20-25 per cent by 1984. Thus, General Motors is set for a period of significant expansion; but even so, by 1990 the company is still expected to be trailing Ford in terms of West European vehicle output.

The most noteworthy development in General Motors' European passenger car activities will be the establishment of a greenfield production facility in Spain. Exact details are hazy but it is understood that a completely new model (the 'S' car) is to be produced there at the rate of 0.3 mn units per year, with full capacity working being achieved by the middle part of the decade. Opel, now with a well styled European model range, seems destined for a period of consolidation, at least during the next few years. But there must be doubts over whether Vauxhall remains even a car assembler long term to 1990. When the Chevette is deleted from Vauxhall's range - probably in 1981/82 - GM's UK subsidiary will cease to be a car producer and will become merely an assembler of Opel designs. However, at some stage during the 1980s the question must be posed as to whether the UK market's requirements could not be more economically supplied in built up form from Opel's West German and Belgian plants, which already furnish about 20 per cent of Vauxhall's sales. On the other hand, GM might give Vauxhall greater opportunities as an assembler, including perhaps a chance to export assembled Opels to the continent if demand outgrew the West German and Belgian plants' ability to supply; such a development would considerably enhance Vauxhall's ability to contribute to GM's fortunes.

Thanks to Vauxhall (Bedford), GM is forecast to achieve a growing position in Western Europe's commercial vehicle markets. In this it will face formidable competition from Daimler-Benz, Iveco and Ford - especially the latter in the UK market. Through GM connections Bedford will find greater marketing opportunities in international markets, although in certain areas it may come up against the claims of GM's Japanese associate - Isuzu.

BL

Three important short term objectives

Despite this company's well aired problems, BL is still - in unit terms - the seventh largest vehicle producer in Western Europe. The next few years are expected to be hectic as BL carries through its (hopefully successful) recovery programme. In the short term, progress is required in three key areas. First, the company must achieve success with its own new generation of vehicles - ranging from the Mini Metro car to the heavy duty T45 Roadtrain truck - in terms of both customer satisfaction and adequate market penetration. Secondly, there must be no slippage in the Honda Bounty project which is scheduled to come on stream in the middle of 1981. And thirdly, the search for new partners, or an intensification of existing links, requires to be pursued with full vigour.

Conditions could soon pick up in BL's car business -

After the introduction of the Mini Metro later in 1980, it is debatable whether BL will have sufficient financial and engineering resources to develop its own range of volume cars. Thus, the Honda association, far from being a means of plugging the mid range product gap, may be a foretaste of things to come. If so, this raises doubts over the proposed LC10 model - BL's own mid range successor to the Allegro/Marina/Maxi/Dolomite lineup - which, although given the go ahead by BL's board, is dependent on a sizeable injection of finance from the UK government. It is possible, therefore, that by the mid 1980s BL will be assembling other Honda models and carrying on extensive (and beneficial) reciprocal trading with the Japanese company.

In the specialist car sector BL should be able to capitalise on the goodwill which still exists for its products in many parts of the world. Indeed, with Jaguar Rover Triumph BL has the foundations of a specialist car range unequalled in scope by any other manufacturer. By concentrating on certain important markets - notably the USA - BL could do rather well. Another plus factor arises from the recent investment in the Land Rover division which will soon result in a significant boost of output.

- and in commercial vehicles -

In the commercial vehicle sector there are signs that a revival is under way, but for the short term BL will probably be vulnerable in several areas where either its lineup is weak (for example, light/medium goods vehicles) or the competition is making determined efforts (for example, double deck buses). The announcement of T45 Roadtrain and T43 Landtrain is an important step forward, and one which BL should exploit to the utmost over the next few years.

- but success will depend on the workforce

In the final analysis, there seems little likelihood of the UK government failing to support BL's recovery programme. The biggest challenge facing management, and the most obvious stumbling block to the successful implementation of Sir Michael Edwardes's proposals, is not lack of finance but the attitude and cooperation of the workforce. There have been encouraging pointers recently of an improvement in the industrial relations climate, but the situation is finely balanced and, on past trends, is capable of flaring up at any time. It is for this reason that BL's prospects for the 1980s - despite their underlying promise - need to be viewed with caution.

DAIMLER-BENZ

A solid foundation for future development

There is no reason to suppose that the managerial skill which has nurtured Daimler-Benz into a significant force in the West European automotive sector during the past 20 years will desert the company during the 1980s. Confidence in the future is expressed in the form of a huge investment programme for the group's domestic production facilities, aimed at reducing manufacturing costs and increasing capacity. Although not one of the motor industry's largest volume producers, Daimler-Benz's concentration in high value products - notably trucks - will ensure long term independence and development. In addition, the company's wide ranging and competent engineering base will be a pillar of strength.

Continuing strength with large
cars and a market entry with smaller ones

Although there is now no shortage of challengers, it is not believed that Daimler-Benz will lose its overall dominance in the European market for large prestige

120

saloons, at least in the first half of the 1980s. The second half of the 1970s saw various companies attempt - with varying degrees of success - to pick up sales in this market sector at Daimler-Benz's expense, including BMW with the 7 series, Peugeot with the 604, General Motors with Senator/Royale, and Ford with the revised Granada. In addition, the series 3 XJ range makes Jaguar an even more formidable opponent, especially now that the company's new painting facility is operational. The ability to offer diesel versions of many models is an aid to Daimler-Benz's sales in a number of markets, including the USA where, however, questions are being asked about the potential health hazards of diesel engine emissions.

Undoubtedly Daimler-Benz's biggest opportunity - and threat - in the next five years is the proposed introduction (in 1982/83) of a downsized car, probably to be equipped with a 1.8/2 litre engine and incorporating front wheel drive. A response to the fuel crisis, and regarded as a vital means of keeping up a worthwhile presence in the USA, this development is not without risk. It takes Daimler-Benz into an entirely new market segment which is already well supplied by existing designs. Also, the investment required represents a major commitment on the German company's part and there can be no turning back.

Daimler-Benz will remain Europe's number one in trucks

As the largest truck producer in Western Europe Daimler-Benz is an obvious target for those who wish to obtain incremental sales. Behind the company a number of powerful groups are building up, including Iveco, Ford and General Motors. International Harvester too has further ambitions in Europe. However, Daimler-Benz's response to date has been sufficient to keep it in the number one slot, and no change is forecast in the short to medium term. On the international front, the establishment of new local assembly operations for trucks seems a logical assumption.

VOLVO

Providing the basis for expansion

Equipped with the necessary ambition and engineering background to enter the 1980s in an expansionist manner, Volvo's principal problem is finding the finance to do so. After several false dawns, and in particular the breakdown of a proposed agreement whereby the Norwegian government would have used North Sea oil revenues to build up Volvo's capital base in exchange for 40 per cent of the company's equity, the recent association with Renault represents progress at last - albeit on a more limited scale than envisaged under earlier proposals. From Volvo's standpoint it is vitally necessary to ensure that Swedish employment is maintained, and that a distinctive product profile remains a characteristic of the company's output.

Success with passenger cars depends on a
replacement for the 2 series and developments with Renault

The biggest problems are faced in passenger cars. A revision to the 2 series is currently under development and is expected to make its debut in the early 1980s.

This will be a crucial model for Volvo and on it will rest the company's passenger car fortunes for the 1980s. Longer term, though, Volvo does not have the necessary wherewithal to establish a range in its own right and is likely to be essentially a one model company - as now - with regard to its Swedish operations. In retrospect, the move into smaller cars through the acquisition of DAF's passenger car operations in the Netherlands was the wrong move, although at the time there seemed to be a reasonable chance of success. A recent improvement in results at Volvo Car BV does not mask the fact that this operation is not essential for Volvo's long term passenger car strategy and hence continued assistance from the Dutch government will almost certainly be sought - and given - if required.

By the mid 1980s the benefits of Volvo's linkup with Renault should be working through. Cooperation will be in full swing on the manufacture of major subassemblies such as engines and gearboxes. Dependent on this arrangement, the likelihood is an even closer association with Renault on cars, although it is not at all certain that this need necessarily imply a full scale merger.

In the commercial vehicle sector
conditions will be tougher in the 1980s

In contrast, the pressures on commercial vehicle operations seem less pronounced and are not expected to lead Volvo to seek a similar solution as with cars. Growth is forecast to continue, and there are two areas which appear especially promising: medium weight goods vehicles, and buses.

However, Volvo's technical advances are now being matched and, in some cases, overtaken - both at the component supply and vehicle manufacturing levels. The company will find competition much tougher in the 1980s and will therefore need to adopt an increasingly international stance. The evidence points to the management's understanding of the risks and opportunities involved, and the necessary groundwork for greater export business - in the USA, for example, with Freightliner - has already been made.

BMW

Growth in the 1970s will be hard to sustain in the 1980s

BMW has had a phenomenally successful run in the 1970s. Not only did unit production double between 1970 and 1979, but the company established itself firmly as a strong contender in the upmarket stakes. The question now is whether this momentum can be kept up in the 1980s. One major worry is that BMW can look forward to only minimal growth - if any - in its domestic market. Moreover, competition is hotting up in the premium market niche where BMW specialises and, even if BMW secures a product advantage, margins could come under pressure. In particular, the forthcoming downsized Mercedes-Benz is seen as a big threat to BMW's smaller models.

It is probable that BMW will push much harder in the short term to develop export sales, especially in the USA which is becoming an ever more crucial market for a growing number of European vehicle manufacturers. BMW's desire to control more effectively its own destiny in export markets is demonstrated by moves to take over control of the importing organisation in various key markets (as in the UK).

An interesting question concerns whether BMW is large enough to develop the next generation of major subassemblies without forming links with other companies. Evidence elsewhere suggests not, but this need not imply that BMW would lose its independence, merely that joint ventures or swop arrangements will have to be established. And with BMW's traditionally strong engineering and technological base the company would be in a strong position to play a leading role in any proposed linkup.

ALFA ROMEO

The search for a partner is top priority

Without state backing Alfa Romeo's parlous position would have come to a head many years ago. It is also fair to say that without state pressure it is unlikely in the extreme that a greenfield site in southern Italy would have been chosen to locate major new investment for passenger car production. However, it is now obvious that serious steps have to be taken towards solving the dire financial situation in which the Italian company finds itself. In practical terms this means that the search for a partner is a top priority, and a proposed venture with Nissan seems a strong possibility. Despite understandable misgivings from Fiat, which regards the proposal as a way for the Japanese to enter the Italian market through the back door, the deal would make good sense for both partners. It should enable the Italian company to retain a fair measure of independence and individuality, while providing access to Nissan's economies of scale. Also, an association with Nissan ought to pave the way for greater worldwide marketing opportunities, as well as the benefits of access to extensive research and development facilities. Many observers feel that an alliance with Fiat would be the obvious solution, thereby creating an all embracing Italian motor sector. But in effect Fiat is that already, and the chances are that Alfa Romeo would be lost as just another part of the Fiat empire. What is needed instead is an arrangement whereby Alfa Romeo is as valuable an ally to its partner as the other way round, and Nissan - anxious to develop in Western Europe (see Motor Ibérica, page 109) - fits the requirement perfectly.

SAAB SCANIA

Car range will require a new body shape -

This Swedish company has shown remarkable skill and tenacity in both its passenger car and commercial vehicle activities. The management has demonstrated good judgement in keeping the business afloat, and in understanding the limitations - and opportunities - of being a small producer in an increasingly competitive and international manufacturing sector. Despite periodic rumblings of the inevitability of a merger with Volvo, this option is considered unlikely to be exercised. In a sense both companies are too similar in various fundamental ways for much advantage to be derived in the short to medium term.

On passenger cars Saab is forecast to strengthen its link with Lancia - possibly involving Fiat on a wider front. Technical excellence in terms of product specification will continue, but Saab urgently requires to progress on a new body style of its own if consumer interest is to be maintained in its specialist market niche in the early to mid 1980s when competitors will be unveiling futuristic wedge shaped body contours. It is not believed that a minor reskinning of the existing design will be adequate. And by using someone else's body shape a valuable - perhaps critical - element of product differentiation will be lost. Faced with this dilemma Saab's passenger car business appears too small for comfort, especially with other business divisions in Saab Scania competing strongly for the group's resources.

- and competition will intensify in the commercial vehicle sector

Commercial vehicles too face growing international competition. Again, the company needs to enter into a mutually beneficial partnership.

It would be wrong to write off Western Europe's smaller companies, and least of all Saab Scania - but the company's management faces an especially challenging start to the 1980s.

INNOCENTI

An uncertain outlook

Innocenti, dependent on a supply lifeline from another company for its existence, is in a vulnerable position. As such, it is difficult to predict with confidence either a strong or, indeed, long term future for the company. At the same time, though, it is unlikely that BL (Innocenti's supplier) would wish to terminate an agreement which represents a sizeable proportion of its passenger car export business - unless, of course, the terms and conditions for carrying on became unacceptable. But BL itself is in a precarious position, and clearly some of this must be reflected in Innocenti.

PORSCHE

Competence in a specialist market niche will ensure survival

Notwithstanding the twin prospects of a real increase in the cost of fuel throughout the 1980s and the likelihood of ever more restrictive speed limits, it is difficult to anticipate a time when there will be insufficient demand to support several small companies producing in Europe the type of specialist, high performance cars as exemplified in Porsche's current range. And since this West German company is as competent in its chosen market niche as anyone else, the odds must be on Porsche surviving the current decade relatively unscathed. On the other hand, a closer association with Volkswagen would not come as a surprise.

In the short term Porsche will be vulnerable (as always) to the development of recessionary economic conditions in its principal markets - North America and Western Europe - and for this reason the company's 1980 outlook looks decidedly lacklustre. It is not thought, though, that the Western world's economic prospects are so bad as to cause long term problems. In any case, Porsche is expected to experience strong and continuing demand for its consultancy services.

MOTOR IBERICA

The importance of Nissan's involvement

The pattern for Motor Ibérica to follow during the 1980s has been more or less established with the news that Nissan is to acquire a minority - yet substantial - equity stake in the Spanish company. Motor Ibérica, therefore, will act as a springboard for Nissan's considerable ambitions in the West European marketplace - ambitions which cannot realistically be achieved without a local assembly presence. This is a medium term strategy which takes into account Spain's intention to become a full member of the EEC.

It is almost certain that the Japanese company will make further moves in Western Europe, which means that longer term Motor Ibérica has the potential to become an important member of a pan European vehicle manufacturing network controlled by Nissan. The chances of developing strongly on exports look especially bright.

MAN

Closer links with Volkswagen are possible

MAN will remain a strong supplier in the heavy goods vehicle and bus sectors. A subsidiary of the giant West German based Gutehoffnungshütte company, it is possible that the commercial vehicle manufacturing activities of MAN will become more closely associated with another huge West German company - Volkswagen. The joint design, development and production of a medium weight goods vehicle range is an indication that both companies can work together - and each partner would probably concede the logic of a pooling of their entire commercial vehicle interests. Whether this would involve a full scale merger, an equity exchange, or some other arrangement is secondary to the point that in Volkswagen and MAN West Germany has the ingredients of a powerful, full range commercial vehicle group with worldwide connections.

Regardless of its relationship with Volkswagen, though, MAN is expected to become increasingly in evidence in two areas: first, the company will remain active in licensing foreign ventures; and, secondly, a greater role in bus markets is predicted, using domestic manufacturing facilities as a base. Furthermore, the desire to extend business activities in North America will be as strong as ever and, frustrated by the collapse of the White Motor deal, MAN is almost certain to seek discussions with other potential partners.

TALBOT MATRA

Future will depend on Talbot's policy

Although independent of the PSA group, Talbot Matra is heavily reliant on its
existing arrangement with Talbot to assemble the Bagheera and Rancho models.
It is unclear how this relationship will develop longer term since, presumably,
everything will depend on Talbot's policy decisions. It is impossible to see how
Talbot Matra could exist without its association with Talbot, and the chances of
being absorbed within the PSA group must be rated quite strongly.

ENASA

A brighter outlook now that International Harvester has a stake

Enasa's future lies as part of International Harvester's growing global commercial vehicle producing network, rather than as an independent Spanish based
company. Although International Harvester does not have a controlling interest -
yet - the US company's influence will be the guiding hand shaping Enasa's
development. As well as providing the Spanish company with strong product
support, export opportunities should be considerably enhanced. But it is vitally
important for International Harvester to seize the initiative quickly. Enasa
enters the 1980s in a poor state and urgently needs new products and a changed -
more aggressive - approach; hence the reason for International Harvester's
involvement in the first place.

Enasa, too, should be able to contribute to the partnership. International Harvester is forecast to benefit eventually from Enasa's business contacts in Latin
America, while its background in the bus sector could also assist IH's efforts
to develop in the supply of public service vehicles.

DAF TRUCK

Some unresolved questions, but survival prospects are good

As a major employer in the Netherlands DAF Truck's medium term survival is
not seriously in question, but it needs to make soon the moves which will enable
a reduction in production costs to be achieved. In effect, this means that the
company must either secure a higher volume of truck output to justify the current
quite extensive use of in house component and subassembly manufacture, or lean
more heavily towards buying in proprietary components and subassemblies. Most
probably the latter course of action will be adopted, which will not be disadvanta-
geous to the company's prospects.

Another interesting issue to be resolved concerns the ownership and control of
DAF Truck. International Harvester - currently owning 33.3 per cent - is
reported to be on the brink of exercising an option to acquire a further 4.5 per
cent of the Dutch company's equity. This would still not give IH control, but the
overall shareholding could be regarded as a good long term, low cost investment
which would give IH a potentially powerful voice over DAF Truck's future

development. The PSA group's intentions with DAF Truck are unclear, and these discussions have become somewhat protracted; in any case, an alliance with PSA would provide only a partial solution to DAF Truck's need to become more international in its approach and operations.

SMALL SPECIALIST MANUFACTURERS

A continuing role

In general, companies which fall into the broad category of small specialised vehicle manufacturers will survive the 1980s provided they are able to maintain, first, a product differentiation from their bigger rivals - either through excellence of design and quality, or because their chosen market niche is one which is unattractive to the larger producers - and, secondly, an even keel during times of market downturn; these two overall rules apply to the manufacture of both passenger cars and commercial vehicles.

It is a tribute to the inherent strength and character of their managements that so many of the small specialist producers were able to ride through the 1974/75 recession without too many long term bruises. There are three obvious danger areas which threaten survival. The first arises over the difficulty of financing new product development where volume output is low. In addition, the necessity of passing special legislative tests in order to sell in certain markets places an especially heavy burden on the smaller companies since the expense incurred has to be recovered from a limited number of units; unless the market for a company's product is relatively price inelastic, severe difficulties can occur. Secondly, except in special circumstances, governments are less inclined to help out a small vehicle manufacturer during times of financial hardship mainly because the unemployment ramifications of closure are usually quite minor; thus, when Jensen in the UK fell into difficulties during the mid 1970s government assistance was not forthcoming and the company eventually ceased operations - despite strong order books. And, thirdly, marketing support can, in places, become somewhat patchy due to lack of managerial and financial resources. Where a company becomes too stretched in the marketing function, field support can fail and reputation suffer. The result is that the smaller manufacturers are often forced to concentrate on a limited geographical spread or attempt to form an alliance with another company; a good example of the latter is Lotus's recent agreement with Rolls-Royce Motors whereby the Rolls-Royce distribution network in the USA will be utilised to market Lotus's cars.

Smaller companies have a number of advantages. They typically have a substantial bank of loyal customers. Furthermore, being small they have greater flexibility in responding to changed circumstances and altering product specification. It seems probable, therefore, that by 1990 there will continue to be a role for Western Europe's small specialist vehicle producers, and those who demonstrate the greatest flair, imagination and courage will be in the strongest position.

Effect on, and Prospects for, Component Suppliers

The components industry is a crucial
part of the West European automotive sector

The principal objective of this special report in the preceding pages has been to
examine the automotive industry's future with particular reference to the vehicle
manufacturers' scope of operations - the "front line" of the sector's activity. But
developments and change at this front line have a ripple effect on the myriad of
support companies which provide components, subassemblies and general services,
and, moreover, a number of these support companies are able to generate "reverse
ripples" either through technological leadership or by means of their dominant
position in the marketplace. Indeed, the components industry is a crucial part of
any automotive sector, but especially so in Western Europe where vehicle manufacturers have tended to rely on a bigger proportion of their component requirements from an _independent_ components industry than has been the case in North
America or Japan. From the standpoint of employment, too, the components
industry plays an important role and, as noted in the introduction, countries which
have been unable to attract vehicle assembly facilities are frequently capable of
sustaining a components manufacturing operation. And, with extensive state
ownership or financial support in West European vehicle manufacturing companies,
the independent automotive components industry provides the greatest opportunity
for private investors (individuals and institutions) to participate in the motor
industry's affairs.

It is not within the scope of this special report to examine in depth the automotive
components sector, but it is worth highlighting several of the more important
features which are expected to characterise the industry's development in the
1980s, as well as assessing how the main conclusions of the report will affect it.

Procurement habits vary from country to country

In Western Europe the automotive components industry has, not unexpectedly, been
traditionally located mainly in the four principal vehicle manufacturing countries.
New investment has tended to follow expanding country industries - as in Spain,
where a quite comprehensive supporting network has built up. Perhaps surprisingly,
the largest independent (in the sense of not being tied to, or owned by, a specific
vehicle manufacturing company) components industry is located not in France or
West Germany but in the UK, which provides the base for a powerful, technically
advanced and internationally minded automotive components sector. West Germany
has a technically strong components industry which is growing in its scope and
influence, while the French industry tends to be fragmented into clusters of strength
such as tyres and electrical items. In Italy and Spain the component companies
lean towards being essentially domestic in character.

The reason for this pattern relates to the operating philosophies of the principal vehicle manufacturers in each country. In the UK, for example, vehicle manufacturers - especially the US controlled ones - have depended heavily on bought in components from independent suppliers. This, in part, is a reflection of the historically fragmented nature of the UK motor industry, and the impossibility of individual vehicle producers financing the necessary research, development and production facilities for a wide range of items. Even those who have been strongest in their use of in house components and subassemblies have demonstrated an increasing propensity to source from outside in order to maintain a technologically advanced and/or cost effective product profile.

In contrast, many of the major continental vehicle producers have favoured manufacturing a high proportion of their component requirements, again for historical reasons. However, there is now strong evidence to suggest that this practice will soon be at least partially reversed. There are a growing number of linkups between vehicle producers for the joint production of components and subassemblies - a development which indicates that individual companies are finding it more and more difficult to justify in house facilities purely for their own requirements. In addition, independent component and proprietary assembly suppliers are noticing in general a greater willingness on the part of continental vehicle producers to discuss sourcing arrangements. Nevertheless, many continental vehicle producers manufacture a high percentage of their component needs, and companies such as Renault and Fiat have extensive networks of component producing subsidiaries within their respective groups.

The 1980s will present golden opportunities for expansion -

Looking to the future, the independent component and subassembly suppliers to the West European automotive industry are expected to be presented with several excellent opportunities in the 1980s which, if exploited to the full, could result in considerably widened activities for some of them in the short to medium term.

Most obviously, they should be able to derive increasing benefit from the economies of large scale manufacturing. This is of particular importance in an age when even the production of quite straightforward items can involve highly sophisticated, advanced and expensive machine tools. The benefits of long production runs will be further evident as customers agree to standardise on a limited and common range of part numbers per component.

Another principal advantage of the independents is that of specialisation. Technology is advancing so rapidly in many areas that only those companies capable of investing in comprehensive research and development facilities will stand a chance of remaining technically competent. Furthermore, because of their specialisation, it is contended that most of the technical innovation built into vehicles of the 1980s will originate from the component manufacturers; this is expected to be especially true in the field of electronics. It is doubtful, therefore, whether the vehicle manufacturers will have at their disposal the necessary finance - let alone technical skills - to match the research efforts of the component suppliers. Nor is this advantage likely to be restricted to advanced products. Even quite mundane items, such as leaf springs, have the potential to undergo radical change through the use of new materials.

Finally, certain already powerful component groups will become world companies in much the same way as a number of vehicle companies are developing on a global basis. Groups such as GKN and Lucas of the UK and Bosch of West Germany have established operations in the USA in anticipation of growing product convergence between North America and Western Europe. In all known examples, the key to success rests on being technologically proficient in a specific product area - in GKN's case with front wheel drive transmissions, and in the example of Lucas and Bosch with diesel fuel injection equipment. Of course, US companies have had a long standing role in Europe, and groups such as Cummins, Eaton, ITT, Dana, TRW and Rockwell have become important suppliers of components and sub-assemblies. The expected pattern for the 1980s has been recently set by the US Bendix group which intends to develop significant braking systems business in Europe following its takeover of Bendix Westinghouse in the UK. Bendix organises its automotive operations on a world basis, thereby providing considerable flexibility over sourcing arrangements.

- but also several serious threats

However, despite these opportunities the component suppliers will also come up against some formidable threats. It has already been noted that joint ventures for component manufacturing have been entered into in several instances by vehicle producers - a development which clearly poses questions in certain sectors; for example, it is probable that Renault's linkup with Volvo on passenger cars will eventually result in the French company supplying a substantial volume of components to Volvo, with potentially serious consequences for the UK's hitherto extensive components trade with the Swedish motor industry. In addition, as vehicle manufacturers become bigger and several others join the PSA group in the 2 mn units per year club, it is feasible for an extension of in house facilities to be at least considered.

Another danger concerns the growing fashion for reciprocal trading deals. In an effort to secure vehicle sales in what would otherwise be closed markets, vehicle manufacturers frequently enter into swop arrangements by exchanging finished vehicles for components. There is also the likelihood that world vehicle companies will increasingly establish a global sourcing policy for their worldwide output. This is happening already, and when reference is made to the world car concept what is really meant is world components. In other words, vehicle manufacturers are obtaining enormous manufacturing economies by concentrating component and subassembly output, which is then shipped to various worldwide locations for assembly into finished vehicles. As labour and other manufacturing costs in the Western nations escalate alternative sources will be used - for example, in Latin America and the Far East - for the supply of various items. Clearly, the evolving pattern of world sourcing will have a bigger impact on certain suppliers, while others may find their business opportunities improved. A good example of this is provided by BL's proposed deal with Honda to produce the new mid range Bounty model from the middle of 1981; since it is expected that complete engines will be sourced from Japan, suppliers of engine parts will effectively be cut out from the project, while others such as interior trim producers will probably find their level of business higher than if BL had continued with its own older model lineup.

Two basic conditions for success

To summarise, the independent automotive components industry of Western Europe can look forward to an exciting and challenging decade. As always, the sector's fortunes will be closely tied to those of the vehicle producers, but with the added complication of the ever deepening world dimension. For those who are powerful enough and bold enough to develop into world companies in their own right the future looks assured and bright - the more so if backed by a strong commitment to technical innovation.

Overall Conclusions:
Fortune or Failure?

An essential industrial activity –

It is impossible to carry out the type of research programme required for the preparation of an EIU special report such as this one without acquiring a strong regard and healthy respect for the individual companies – large and small – which in total make up the West European automotive sector. Motor vehicle manufacturing is a hideously complicated business in which one mistake of the wrong kind can now spell disaster. Fundamental market and economic changes have taken place during the past couple of decades which have altered the conditions for success, and the skill with which managements have responded to the new circumstances goes a long way towards explaining the current dynamic stance of the overall sector.

It is comparatively easy to be optimistic over the automotive industry's long term survival prospects. Whatever else Western societies require in the final two decades of the twentieth century, motorised road transport will come near the top of the list. In Western Europe there simply is no quick, viable or sensible alternative to road transport for the volume of freight which is currently transported by that mode, nor would it seem possible to reduce the strong desire of people to have their own means of transport.

Moreover, there is recognition by governments that the presence of a vehicle manufacturing sector, and/or supporting functions, provide a vital plank to a country's economic foundations. This is seen in terms of maintaining employment, retaining and developing technology, and as an integral part of a national manufacturing and taxable infrastructure.

– with an assured future

From the foregoing analysis two things are clear: first, that the future of the West European automotive sector is assured – and even promising; and, secondly, that the challenges facing the industry during the next five to ten years are as great as at any time in the sector's history. But it is unimaginable that the necessary responses will not be made in sufficient time.

Fortune or failure? Both will be experienced by individual companies in the 1980s but, for the sector as a whole, the bias is predicted to lean towards the former.

EUROPEAN VEHICLE PRODUCTION

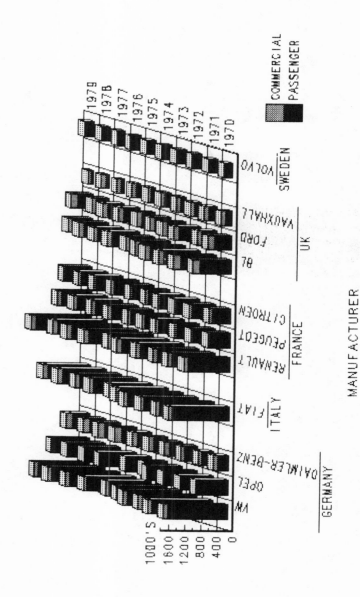

MANUFACTURER

COMMERCIAL
PASSENGER

Part Two:
Financial Assessment of the U.S. Automotive Industry

BACKGROUND TO THE US AUTOMOTIVE INDUSTRY

THE AUTOMOTIVE INDUSTRY AND THE ECONOMY

An important industrial sector –

There is a close relationship between the overall economy of the USA and its vast network of road transportation industries which – when the movement of goods, services and people, and the construction and maintenance of the road system are included – represents rather more than 18 per cent of the nation's GNP. Employment in the motor vehicle industry and allied sectors exceeded 14 mn in 1978 (the highest ever sales year). This represented about 20 per cent of the total job market in the USA, and indicates that the motor and related industries accounted for one in every five private, non-agricultural jobs in the country.

The most recent detailed statistics on employment, payrolls and receipts in the different sectors of the economy relating to the manufacture and use of motor vehicles cover 1977. They have been compiled by the Motor Vehicle Manufacturers' Association of the US Inc (MVMA) on the basis of material provided by the US Bureau of the Census and the American Trucking Association, and are provided in Table 1.   The data show that more than 1.6 mn employees and an $18.4 bn payroll are accounted for by vehicle and parts manufacturing alone. Vehicle sales and maintenance (including wholesale and retail), highway maintenance and construction, and related industries added 3.7 mn employees and a payroll of $38.8 bn. By industry sector, automotive wholesalers employed 423,000 persons with payrolls exceeding $5 bn; retail automotive establishments (both new and used vehicles) accounted for 1.8 mn jobs and paid $17 bn in wages and salaries; while automotive services added 483,000 jobs and $4 bn in payrolls.

The total US parc of motor vehicles topped 159 mn in 1980 (40 per cent of the world's total) – 123.4 mn passenger cars and 35.6 mn commercial vehicles.

Consumers spent nearly $225 bn on owning and operating motor vehicles in 1980. Petrol and oil accounted for nearly 40 per cent of expenditures – 10 percentage points higher than in 1970. Meanwhile, motor vehicle purchases accounted for 31 per cent, 10 percentage points down on 1970's level. Illustrative of the dependence of the USA on motor vehicles is the fact that 64.1 per cent of all communities with a population count lack passenger and freight rail services, and thus motor vehicles are vital economic links to the rest of the country.

Table 1

Employment, Payrolls and Receipts Related to the Manufacture and Use of Motor Vehicles in the USA in 1977

	Establishments	Employees	Payrolls ($ mn)	Receipts ($ mn)
Industry classification:				
Vehicle and parts manufacturing[a]				
Motor vehicles & car bodies	320	342,600	7,059.0	78,486.6
Truck & bus bodies	824	35,000	431.6	2,016.5
Motor vehicle parts & accessories	2,610	451,300	8,015.4	35,741.6
Truck trailers	351	27,900	319.2	1,898.3
Motorhomes on purchased chassis	103	16,200	170.9	1,312.6
Automotive stampings	579	132,000	2,440.7	9,470.3
Non-automotive industries producing automotive products	...	640,000[b]	...	33,121.9[b]
Total manufacturing	4,787[c]	1,645,000	18,436.8[c]	162,047.8
Wholesaling				
Automotive wholesaling	38,914	423,175	5,148.3	147,112.3
Total wholesaling	38,914	423,175	5,148.3	147,112.3
Retailing				
New & used motor vehicle dealers	30,793	790,381	10,279.3	121,883.3
Used motor vehicle dealers	37,016	42,281	374.2	6,945.2
Auto & home supply stores	46,957	205,497	1,928.3	12,861.0
Petrol dealers	176,465	672,673	3,829.9	56,468.1
Total retailing	291,231	1,710,832	16,411.7	198,157.6
Selected services				
Automotive retail, leasing without driver	12,385	75,480	834.3	6,407.0
Automobile parking	8,872	33,850	211.1	1,007.7
Automotive repair shops	154,194	316,302	3,090.1	12,770.4
Automotive service (except repair)	24,702	57,559	320.4	1,390.5
Total services	200,153	483,191	4,455.9	21,575.7

(continued)

137

Table 1 (continued)

Employment, Payrolls and Receipts Related to the Manufacture and Use of Motor Vehicles in the USA in 1977

	Establishments	Employees	Payrolls ($ mn)	Receipts ($ mn)
Highway and street construction and maintenance				
Highway & street construction	10,320	248,651	3,355.3	14,657.4
State,county & local highway departments	...	555,048	6,964.7	...
Total construction & maintenance	10,320^c	803,699	10,320.0	14,657.4^c
Related industries				
Petroleum & refining	349	103,000	206.1	91,832.9
Petroleum & petroleum products wholesalers	22,629	178,625	2,249.3	116,779.6
Total related industries	22,978	281,625	2,455.4	208,612.5
Transportation				
Local passenger transportation^d	13,716	260,277	2,050.0	...
Trucking, local & long distance	74,168	1,038,825	15,192.7	...
Trucking, terminal facilities	956	32,742	555.7	...
Trucking, private & not for hire	...	8,049,933	95,780.4	...
Total trucking	...	9,121,500	111,528.8	...
Total transportation	88,840^c	9,381,777	113,578.8	...

a Excludes basic material industries. b Automotive portion of employees and shipments only. c Partial total. d Includes some local transit rail and subway establishments, employees and payrolls.

Source: Compiled by the Motor Vehicle Manufacturers Association of the US from US Bureau of the Census and American Trucking Associations data.

<u>- which is heavily dependent on the domestic economy</u>

The major US vehicle manufacturers operate worldwide, but in all cases (other than Volkswagen of America which is West German owned) the US market is a prime determinant of overall sales volume and profitability. In 1980, sales in the USA accounted for the following percentages of the worldwide sales of the main manufacturers: General Motors, 70 per cent; Ford, 50 per cent; Chrysler, 75 per cent; American Motors Corporation, 85 per cent; International Harvester (truck division), 72 per cent; Mack Trucks, 80 per cent; Paccar, 85 per cent; and Freightliner, 90 per cent.

1980 was a year of recession for the US automotive industry with sales recording their lowest level since 1975; total sales of cars and trucks in the USA was 11,466,000 units, 25.7 per cent below the record 1978 figure of 15,422,000 units. The year was disastrous for the domestic industry which saw its sales drop to 8,582,000 units - the lowest in 19 years, and 34.4 per cent below the 1978 total of 13,085,000 units. In contrast, imports had their best ever year with total sales of 2,884,000 units, an increase of 23.4 per cent above the 1978 level.

The decline in the industry's domestic sales was fully reflected in the manufacturers' overall financial results for 1980 - a year when only one of the eight major US car and truck manufacturers (Paccar, with a surplus of $133.5 mn) registered a profit, and total net losses of the companies as a whole reached $4.3 bn; Chrysler's loss was $1.71 bn, Ford's $1.54 bn and General Motors' $762.5 mn. A ninth manufacturer, White Motor Corporation, declared bankruptcy in September, 1980. Moreover, the sales trends of 1980 have continued during the first three quarters of 1981, although the financial losses of the main manufacturers have been reduced.

PRINCIPAL DEVELOPMENTS IN
THE US MOTOR VEHICLE MARKET, 1971-80

<u>A decade of change -</u>

The decade from 1971 to 1980 was marked by unusually wide fluctuations in the fortunes of the US motor vehicle industry. This was a result not only of the traditionally cyclical character of demand for both passenger cars and trucks, but also of the effects of fuel shortages and higher prices following the Arab oil embargo of 1973 and the Iranian crisis of 1979. Moreover, the manufacturers have been faced with the substantial cost of installing in their product lines equipment mandated by the government for reasons of safety, fuel economy and environmental protection.

After the initial shock of the 1973 oil embargo had worn off, car buyers returned to the larger vehicles which had traditionally been the mainstay of the domestic industry. And, following the recessionary years of 1974 and 1975, the domestic industry recovered steadily to achieve record sales of both cars and trucks in 1978, at 9,312,000 and 3,773,000 units respectively. Thus, the industry entered 1979 at a near record sales pace. But at the end of March 1979 sales started to fall, and the decline was accentuated as fuel shortages led to queues at petrol stations and a sharp rise in petrol prices. By the end of the year sales had slumped once more to recession levels. The decline continued throughout 1980, and further slippage occurred during the first three quarters of 1981. Sales of the domestic industry in 1980 totalled only 6,581,000 passenger cars and 2,001,000 commercial vehicles, down 29.3 per cent and 47 per cent respectively from the 1978 levels. And, compared with the fairly average year of 1971, sales of passenger cars and commercial vehicles in 1980 were lower by 24.2 per cent and 0.5 per cent respectively.

– which has emphasised the need for fuel efficient vehicles –

Unlike the sequence of events which followed the oil crisis of 1973, the latest downturn has brought about a massive shift in consumer preference. There has been (and is) mounting concern over the price and availability of fuel and, as petrol prices continued to rise, domestic manufacturers found a reasonably ready market for their smaller models, but their larger models were tending to stick in the showrooms.   1980 brought the added problems of tight credit and high interest rates – both of which escalated further in 1981 and froze many potential buyers out of the market. Moreover, the general economic slowdown continued and, following a brief upturn towards the end of 1980, resumed in the second half of 1981 and seems set to continue at least into the early months of 1982.

– and helped the importers

The small car fever which gripped the country in 1979 acted as a sharp stimulus to foreign – particularly Japanese – manufacturers, who had always concentrated on the small car segment of the market. Import sales (other than those from Canada) reached new records in both 1979 and 1980; in the latter year they were 19.9 per cent higher than in 1978 and 52.9 per cent higher than in 1971.

As a result of the demand trend towards smaller cars, the distribution of sales among market classes changed rapidly during the decade. Between 1971 and 1980, the market share of domestic subcompacts rose from 7.42 per cent to 15.41 per cent, and that of compacts from 15.79 per cent to 20.96 per cent; the market penetration of intermediates rose fractionally from 20.84 per cent to 21.37 per cent. The share of standard size cars fell dramatically – from 37.07 per cent to 11.09 per cent. Luxury cars increased slightly – from 3.66 per cent to 4.48 per cent. The market share of imports (other than Canadian) rose from 15.22 per cent to 26.69 per cent.

Meanwhile, sales of domestic light trucks (including for recreational purposes) were hit particularly hard in 1979 – again for reasons of fuel availability and cost. Sales of imported small trucks (almost entirely of Japanese origin) bucked the trend, however, and continued to increase. The sharp drop in demand for domestic small trucks led to a steep decline in total truck sales in 1979 compared to 1978 – and to a further decrease in 1980 which continued into 1981. Sales in the two heaviest categories (classes 7 and 8, over 26,000 lb gvw) rose by 10.1 per cent to 223,166 units in 1979 from 202,640 units in 1978 and established a new record. Demand softened somewhat in the final quarter of 1979 with the onset of recession, and the decline continued through 1980 when total sales of these two weight categories fell by 21.3 per cent to 175,706; but sales of class 7 (26,001–33,000 lb gvw) rose by almost 18 per cent in 1980, to 58,436 units from 49,623 in 1979.

Table 2 contains details of US total retail sales of domestic type and imported passenger cars and trucks in the period 1971 to 1980, while Table 3 gives figures of total US production and factory sales of passenger cars and trucks over the decade. Passenger car market class comparisons, 1971-80, are contained in Table 4.

FORTUNES OF THE PRINCIPAL DOMESTIC MANUFACTURERS, 1971-80

Of the Big Three, General Motors has fared the best

The fortunes of the individual motor vehicle manufacturers varied during the decade 1971-80. General Motors consolidated its position as the leading manufacturer; the company's share of the total US market for passenger cars (including imports) increased a whisker from 45.8 per cent in 1971 to 45.9 per cent in 1980. In unit terms, though, General Motors' passenger car sales fell from 4,521,944 in 1971 to 4,116,482 in 1980, a decline of 9 per cent. Over the decade, sales of Chevrolet trucks (including the LUV captive import line from Japan) rose by 14 per cent, from 647,258 to 737,788, while GMC sales rose by 32.6 per cent from 144,112 to 181,252.

Ford's share of the total US passenger car market during the decade fell from 24 per cent to 17.2 per cent, while unit sales dropped by 37.6 per cent, from 2,363,277 to 1,475,232. Sales of Ford trucks (including the Courier captive import from Japan) rose from 700,635 to 784,132 units, an increase of 11.9 per cent.

The decline in Chrysler's fortunes was even more dramatic, with the corporation's share of the passenger car market declining from 14.2 per cent in 1971 to 8.8 per cent in 1980. Unit sales dropped from 1,401,184 in the earlier year to 660,017 in the latter, or by 52.9 per cent. Sales of trucks (including the Mitsubishi Ram 50 and Arrow import lines) rose by 60.7 per cent over the decade, from 159,778 to 256,829.

American Motors' market share fell from 2.4 per cent to 2 per cent, and unit sales by 39.2 per cent from 245,805 to 149,438.

Volkswagen has entered the manufacturing sector

Volkswagen Manufacturing Corporation of America started producing in the USA in 1978 and, by 1980, had acquired a 3.6 per cent share of the market for its domestically produced and imported (including Audi and Porsche) units.

Table 2

US Total Retail Sales of Domestic Type[a] and Imported Passenger Cars and Trucks, 1971–80 ('000)

	Passenger cars				Trucks			
	Domestic	Import	Total	Per cent imports	Domestic	Import	Total	Per cent imports
1971	8,681	1,568	10,250	15.3	2,011	85	2,096	4.1
1972	9,327	1,623	10,950	14.8	2,486	143	2,629	5.4
1973	9,676	1,763	11,439	15.4	2,915	233	3,148	7.4
1974	7,454	1,413	8,867	15.9	2,511	176	2,687	6.6
1975	7,053	1,587	8,640	18.4	2,248	229	2,477	9.3
1976	8,611	1,498	10,110	14.8	2,944	237	3,181	7.5
1977	9,109	2,076	11,185	18.6	3,352	323	3,675	8.8
1978	9,312	2,000	11,312	17.7	3,773	337	4,110	8.2
1979	8,341	2,329	10,671	21.8	3,010	470	3,480	13.5
1980	6,581	2,398	8,979	26.7	2,001	486	2,487	19.5
% change 1980/71	−24.2	52.9	−12.4		−0.5	471.8	18.7	

a Includes US domestic type vehicles imported from Canada under the terms of the US–Canadian Automotive Products Trade Act, 1965.

Source: Motor Vehicle Manufacturers Association of the US Inc.

Table 3

US Total Production and Factory Sales[a] of Passenger Cars and Trucks, 1971-80

	Production			Factory sales		
	Passenger cars	Trucks and buses	Total vehicles	Passenger cars	Trucks and buses	Total vehicles
1971	8,583,653	2,088,001	10,671,654	8,584,592	2,053,146	10,637,738
1972	8,828,205	2,482,503	11,310,708	8,823,938	2,446,807	11,270,745
1973	9,667,152	3,014,361	12,681,513	9,657,647	2,979,688	12,637,335
1974	7,324,504	2,746,538	10,071,042	7,331,256	2,727,313	10,058,569
1975	6,716,951	2,269,562	8,986,513	6,712,852	2,272,160	8,985,012
1976	8,497,893	2,999,703	11,497,596	8,500,305	2,979,476	11,479,781
1977	9,213,654	3,489,128	12,702,782	9,200,849	3,441,521	12,642,370
1978	9,176,635	3,722,567	12,899,202	9,165,190	3,706,239	12,871,429
1979	8,433,662	3,046,331	11,479,993	8,419,226	3,036,706	11,455,932
1980	6,375,506	1,634,335	8,009,841	6,400,026	1,667,283	8,067,309

a Factory sales are by source of manufacture in the USA and include all exports.

Source: Motor Vehicle Manufacturers Association of the US Inc.

Table 4

Market Class Comparisons of US Passenger Cars, 1971–80
(% of total market, including imports)

	Subcompact	Compact	Intermediate	Standard	Luxury	Import	Total sales
1971	7.42	15.79	20.84	37.07	3.66	15.22	10,234,027
1972	8.17	15.34	22.59	35.38	3.76	14.76	10,935,365
1973	10.74	16.77	23.37	29.80	3.94	15.83	11,427,478
1974	10.60	22.72	24.41	22.72	3.71	15.85	8,851,265
1975	12.26	22.92	23.85	17.94	4.74	18.29	8,627,883
1976	9.90	24.12	27.76	18.80	4.67	14.78	10,099,573
1977	8.52	21.16	26.40	20.37	5.00	18.55	11,178,554
1978	8.77	22.90	26.60	18.42	5.62	17.69	11,303,909
1979	12.86	20.89	23.79	15.14	5.47	21.85	10,641,679
1980	15.41	20.96	21.37	11.09	4.48	26.69	8,973,345

Source: Automotive News, 1981 market data book.

144

Table 5

US Retail Sales of Passenger Cars, by Manufacturer, 1971–80

	1971	1972	1973	1974	1975	1976	1977	1978	1979	1980	% change 1980/71
US sourced											
General Motors	4,521,944	4,635,656	5,053,540	3,645,056	3,747,009	4,800,716	5,148,131	5,385,282	4,917,911	4,116,482	-9.0
Ford	2,363,277	2,549,296	2,666,915	2,172,017	1,983,723	2,256,277	2,552,210	2,582,702	2,140,368	1,475,232	-37.6
Chrysler	1,401,184	1,466,141	1,512,520	1,180,202	997,116	1,301,940	1,219,752	1,146,258	949,598	660,017	-52.9
American Motors	245,805	301,973	392,105	329,431	322,272	247,640	184,361	170,739	162,057	149,438	-39.2
Checker Motors	4,673	5,326	6,002	5,240	2,896	4,681	4,568	4,103	4,629	3,020	-35.4
Volkswagen of America[a]	-	-	-	-	-	-	-	22,582	166,576	177,118	
Total domestic type	8,536,883	8,958,392	9,631,082	7,331,946	7,053,016	8,611,254	9,109,022	9,311,666	8,341,139	6,581,307	-22.9
Imports (other than from Canada)[b]											
General Motors	88,535	69,407	69,798	55,532	39,730	10,483	29,067	19,222	13,815	-	-100.0
Ford	56,118	91,995	115,153	76,894	55,112	29,904	63,007	80,224	78,109	68,595	22.2
Chrysler	28,381	34,057	35,523	42,925	60,356	78,972	121,262	103,292	138,053	129,350	355.8
American Motors	-	-	-	-	-	-	-	-	18,862	25,365	-
Other imports	1,360,602	1,401,989	1,539,936	1,227,684	1,429,471	1,379,386	1,861,054	1,799,675	2,083,457	2,174,973	59.9
Total imports	1,533,636	1,597,448	1,760,410	1,403,035	1,584,669	1,498,745	2,074,390	2,002,413	2,332,296	2,398,283	56.4
Total passenger cars	10,070,519	10,555,840	11,391,492	8,734,981	8,637,685	10,109,999	11,183,412	11,314,079	10,673,435	8,979,590	-10.8

a Volkswagen of America's sales do not include imports.   b Includes imports from Canada of domestic type cars.

Sources: Motor Vehicle Manufacturers Association of the US Inc; Automotive News. 1981 Market Data Book, for 1971–74.   As the bases of the two sources differ somewhat there are some discrepancies compared with the figures contained in Table 2. but such discrepancies are not material to the ten year trend.

Mixed fortunes among the truck producers

Among the companies producing commercial vehicles but not passenger cars, International Harvester was seriously affected by a strike in 1980 resulting in its sales falling by 52.9 per cent to 74,484 from the 158,194 units sold in 1971. During the decade Freightliner's sales rose from 6,495 units to 11,473 (by 76.9 per cent), Kenworth's from 6,739 to 11,163 (by 67.2 per cent), Peterbilt's from 4,296 to 7,008 (by 63 per cent) and Mack's from 15,582 to 21,743 (by 39.1 per cent). On the other hand, White's sales dropped by 27.4 per cent from 10,622 to 7,664.

Table 5 contains details of US retail sales of passenger cars, by manufacturer, for the period 1971 to 1980, while Table 6 gives total US passenger car market shares by domestic manufacturers and imports in 1971 and 1980. Table 7 contains figures relating to US retail sales by domestic manufacturers of new trucks, including their captive imports, by gvw and type, 1971-80.

Table 6

Total US Passenger Car Market Shares
by Domestic Manufacturers and Imports, 1971 and 1980

| | % share | |
Manufacturer	1971	1980
General Motors	45.8	45.9
Ford	24.0	17.2
Chrysler	14.2	8.8
American Motors	2.4	2.0
Volkswagen of America	-	3.6
Checker	0.1	0.1
"Other" imports	13.5	22.6

Note: Market shares refer to the total US market (i e domestic cars & imports) and include sales of imports by domestic manufacturers. "Other" imports therefore includes all imports other than the "captive" imports of General Motors, Ford and Chrysler, Renault cars imported by American Motors and Volkswagen, Audi and Porsche cars imported from West Germany by Volkswagen of America. Figures do not necessarily add up to 100 per cent due to rounding.

Table 7

US Retail Sales by Domestic Manufacturers of New Trucks, Including their "Captive Imports", by GVW and Type, 1971-80

Gvw category	1971[a]	1972[a]	1973[a]	1974	1975	1976	1977	1978	1979	1980	% change 1980/71
0-6,000 lb											
utility	...	...	...	157,014	65,156	60,968	68,674	79,588	74,878	50,842	...
Car type pickup	...	...	...	75,288	53,534	66,667	76,997	83,522	77,094	49,696	...
Compact imported pickup	...	...	...	74,819	102,153	100,251	133,291	140,736	225,410	254,403	...
Van & cutaway chassis	...	...	...	205,429	178,943	185,340	117,354	126,072	110,393	78,871	...
Conventional pickup (incl extended & crew cabs)	...	...	...	893,452	693,588	904,287	909,016	904,002	783,113	544,959	...
Stationwagon (truck chassis)	...	...	...	48,913	4,454	438	23	-	-	-	...
Passenger carrier	...	...	...	2,263	371	528	429	472	439	6,446[b]	...
Multi stop	...	...	...	2,229	93	5	-	-	-	-	...
Other	...	...	...	7,179	2,950	8	4	-	-	-	...
Total 0-6,000 lb	1,184,741	1,497,630	1,754,254	1,466,586	1,101,242	1,318,492	1,305,788	1,334,392	1,271,327	985,217	-16.8
6,001-10,000 lb											
utility	...	...	...	2,668	92,825	152,366	183,345	275,790	205,181	107,541	...
Vans	...	...	...	117,133	199,416	337,475	380,641	471,334	331,848	172,045	...
Van cutaway	...	...	...	}	}	}	77,978	76,277	43,797	19,918	...
Conventional pickup (incl extended & crew cabs)	...	...	...	469,195	540,580	799,564	1,032,190	1,171,257	884,551	545,720	...
Stationwagon (truck chassis)	...	...	...	15,487	50,128	72,832	87,764	100,395	73,294	38,807	...
Passenger carrier	...	...	...	1,243	3,228	4,746	5,632	6,398	4,792	65,917[b]	...
Multi stop	...	...	...	27,581	25,469	33,517	35,142	38,193	30,816	24,867	...
Other	...	...	...	62,941	40,064	447	-	-	-	-	...
Total 6,001-10,000 lb	487,663	598,813	758,236	696,248	951,710	1,400,947	1,802,692	2,139,644	1,574,279	974,815	99.9
10,001-14,000 lb	6,173	54,695	49,771	21,038	23,054	43,399	36,478	73,119	15,408	3,510	-43.1
14,001-16,000 lb	14,643	10,819	3,118	2,693	1,253	178	3,237	5,792	2,686	195	-98.7
16,001-19,500 lb	46,094	28,608	15,709	14,455	9,073	8,780	4,847	2,699	2,952	2,309	-95.0
19,501-26,000 lb	139,587	181,771	235,569	207,001	158,584	152,759	163,370	155,616	145,977	89,764	-35.7
26,001-33,000 lb	33,749	35,357	37,030	31,036	22,993	22,282	28,491	41,032	49,623	58,436	73.1
33,001 lb & over	98,664	126,225	154,571	147,533	83,148	97,286	140,643	161,608	173,543	117,270	18.9
Total	2,011,314	2,533,918	3,008,258	2,586,590	2,351,057	3,044,123	3,485,546	3,913,902	3,235,795	2,231,516	10.9

a Details by type are not available for the years 1971-73. b Starting in January 1980, Plymouth Voyager, Dodge Sportsman, Ford Club Wagon and Chevrolet Sportvan previously reported as passenger cars are now included with trucks.

Source: Motor Vehicle Manufacturers Association of the US Inc.

147

US PRODUCTION TRENDS, 1971-80

The decade ends on a low note

Passenger car production in the USA peaked in 1973 at 9,667,152 units but, follow-ing good years in both 1977 and 1978, dwindled in 1979 and fell sharply in 1980 when output amounted to only 6,375,506 units, 25.7 per cent below the 8,583,653 pro-duced in 1971 and 34 per cent below the 1973 record.

General Motors' production declined from 4,853,015 in 1971 to 4,064,556 in 1980, a fall of 16.2 per cent. The only individual marques to record increases over the decade were General Motors' Buick and Oldsmobile, up 4.2 per cent and 3.7 per cent respectively.

Production by Ford fell from 2,176,335 in 1971 to 1,306,948 in 1980, a rather serious decline of 39.9 per cent. Chrysler's production dropped from 1,313,306 to 638,974, an even more worrying 51.3 per cent reversal. American Motors' production slipped by 30.1 per cent from 235,669 in 1971 to 164,725 in 1980, and was surpassed in the latter year by Volkswagen which started US production only in 1978.

Chevrolet's production of commercial vehicles during the decade fell from 739,426 to 515,038 (by 30.3 per cent), but GMC's production rose by 1 per cent from 171,945 to 173,702. Ford's commercial vehicle production fell by 9.5 per cent, from 642,742 in 1971 to 581,507 in 1980, while Chrysler-Dodge's production was down over the decade from 204,766 to 119,232 - a fall of 41.8 per cent.

Mack was the only other listed manufacturer to increase production over the period 1971 to 1980, with a rise of 20 per cent from 19,453 to 23,387. International Harvester's output fell by a disastrous 64.5 per cent from 186,345 to 66,210, due to a six month strike in 1980; during 1979 its production was 115,453.

Table 8 contains statistics of US motor vehicle production, by manufacturer, for the period 1971-80.

THE US AUTOMOTIVE INDUSTRY'S
TRADE RELATIONS WITH OTHER COUNTRIES, 1971-80

A highly unfavourable balance of trade

The USA's balance of trade in motor vehicles was consistently unfavourable over the decade. In 1971 the balance for passenger cars and commercial vehicles combined reached a deficit of $4.1 bn, and, by 1980, the deficit had escalated to $14.4 bn. The details are set out in Table 9; 1971 figures are derived from the US International Trade Commission, the 1980 figures from the US Bureau of the Census.

Table 8

US Motor Vehicle Production, by Manufacturer, 1973-80

	1973	1974	1975	1976	1977	1978	1979	1980	% change 1980/71
Passenger cars									
American Motors	355.855	352.088	323.796	213.918	156.994	164.352	184.636	164.725	-30.1
Chrysler									
Plymouth	742.957	602.606	443.550	658.020	492.063	448.114	374.404	293.342	-53.9
Dodge	592.863	463.993	354.482	547.916	497.232	441.550	380.315	263.169	-44.4
Chrysler	220.557	110.063	104.870	127.466	247.064	236.504	181.427	82.463	-59.3
Total Chrysler	1.556.377	1.176.662	902.902	1.333.402	1.236.359	1.126.168	936.146	638.974	-51.3
Ford									
Ford	1.909.209	1.716.975	1.301.414	1.494.054	1.761.373	1.743.445	1.381.604	929.627	-47.2
Mercury	453.250	400.701	405.104	434.865	583.055	813.752	661.410	377.321	-9.1
Lincoln	133.394	87.569	101.520	124.880	211.439				
Total Ford	2.495.853	2.205.245	1.808.038	2.053.799	2.555.867	2.557.197	2.043.014	1.306.948	-39.9
General Motors									
Chevrolet	2.334.113	1.903.861	1.687.091	2.012.412	2.133.403	2.346.155	2.236.171	1.737.336	-25.1
Pontiac	866.598	502.083	523.469	784.631	875.957	867.010	714.511	556.429	-23.6
Oldsmobile	918.119	548.658	654.342	964.425	1.079.841	910.249	1.008.246	783.225	3.7
Buick	826.206	400.262	535.820	817.669	801.202	810.324	787.149	783.575	4.2
Cadillac	307.698	230.649	278.404	312.845	369.254	350.761	345.831	203.991	-26.2
Total GM	5.252.734	3.585.513	3.679.126	4.891.982	5.259.657	5.284.499	5.091.908	4.064.556	-16.2
Checker	6.333	4.996	3.181	4.792	4.777	4.225	4.766	3.197	-40.0
Volkswagen of America	-	-	-	-	-	40.194	173.192	197.106	-
Total passenger cars	9.667.152	7.324.504	6.717.043	8.497.893	9.213.654	9.176.635	8.433.662	6.375.506	-25.7
Trucks & buses									
AM General	38.364	40.780	30.081	27.917	27.497	20.922	23.934	8.201	-
Chevrolet	1.013.871	867.855	773.224	1.048.125	1.122.169	1.216.050	1.015.092	515.038	-30.3
Chrysler-Dodge	377.555	362.008	319.694	441.849	474.001	488.180	295.228	119.232	-41.8
Ford	946.470	892.736	692.200	888.162	1.186.013	1.233.243	1.032.117	581.507	-9.5
GMC	247.825	219.316	197.008	293.997	321.009	375.000	337.381	173.702	1.0
International	207.547	177.466	101.828	114.855	110.894	123.123	115.453	66.210	-64.5
Jeep	93.890	95.757	108.065	124.924	162.231	180.514	134.624	79.360	-7.0
Mack	30.916	30.999	24.597	23.230	30.178	33.114	35.937	23.387	20.0
Volkswagen of America	-	-	-	-	-	-	2.407	28.390	
White	28.533	28.558	11.993	17.730	25.195	13.217	11.251	b	
Others[a]	29.390	32.683	10.872	18.914	29.941	39.204	42.907	39.308	1.1
Total trucks & buses	3.014.361	2.748.158	2.269.562	2.999.703	3.489.128	3.722.567	3.046.331	1.634.335	-21.7
Total motor vehicles	12.681.513	10.072.662	8.986.605	11.497.596	12.702.782	12.899.202	11.479.993	8.009.841	-24.9

a Principally Freightliner, Peterbilt and Kenworth. b Included with "Others".

Source: Motor Vehicle Manufacturers Association of the US Inc.

Table 9

US Trade Balance in Motor Vehicles, 1971 and 1980
($ mn)

| | 1971 | | 1980 | |
	Passenger cars	Commercial vehicles	Passenger cars	Commercial vehicles
US imports	5,133.7	475.1	16,934.7	3,972.6
US exports	1,070.0	448.6	3,932.1	2,583.2
US trade balance	-4,063.7	-26.5	-13,002.6	-1,389.4

The USA's principal trading partners in motor vehicles are Canada and Japan.

US trade in motor vehicles with Canada –

Trade in automotive products between the USA and Canada is governed by the terms of the Automotive Products Trade Act, 1965, which provided for conditional duty free trade between the two countries in certain automotive products, including new passenger cars, buses and certain trucks, and in parts designed for them (but not replacement parts and tyres). Imports into the USA from Canada consist almost exclusively of US type vehicles and components produced by the major US (and Canadian) manufacturers in Canadian plants; they are indistinguishable from the US domestic product. Substantially, therefore, the USA and Canada constitute one market for the US type cars and commercial vehicles covered by the 1965 act.

Canadian production of passenger cars and commercial vehicles by manufacturer, for selected years between 1971 and 1980, is set out in Table 10. From this table it will be seen that, over the decade, Canada's production of passenger cars dropped from 1,083,201 in 1971 to 847,167 in 1980, while commercial vehicle production almost doubled – from 263,564 in 1971 to 531,010 in 1980. Production by General Motors in Canada increased from 406,186 cars and 101,020 commercial vehicles in 1971 to 514,396 cars and 255,092 commercial vehicles in 1980. In contrast, production of passenger cars by Ford, Chrysler and American Motors over the period all declined, while Volvo's output increased slightly. Canadian production of trucks by all the major manufacturers rose over the decade.

In 1971, the USA exported 348,404 cars and 65,087 commercial vehicles to Canada and, in return, imported 802,281 cars and 135,640 commercial vehicles. In 1980, US exports to Canada were 509,666 cars and 83,325 commercial vehicles, while imports amounted to 594,771 cars and 239,917 commercial vehicles. During the intervening years, the trade balance in vehicles has generally been favourable to Canada.

Table 10

Canadian Production of Passenger
Cars and Commercial Vehicles by
Manufacturer, for Selected Years Between 1971 and 1980

	1971	1974	1977	1979	1980
Passenger cars					
GM	406,186	478,255	522,291	558,548	514,396
Ford	392,527	413,579	376,785	286,400	248,199
Chrysler	232,749	225,478	214,808	134,083	71,530
AMC	42,209	57,467	41,717	-	3,077
Volvo	8,281	10,099	6,826	8,719	9,965
Total cars	1,083,201	1,165,635	1,162,519	987,753	847,167
Trucks & buses					
GM	101,020	167,026	256,351	287,210	255,092
Ford	144,397	159,775	212,582	219,373	186,177
Chrysler	17,010	25,228	117,260	55,602	52,917
AMC (Jeep)	-	-	-	51,924	12,450
International	12,103	16,666	19,862	20,446	16,413
White	1,440	2,703	2,392	3,982	2,808
Mack	860	4,999	4,009	3,845	2,305
Kenworth	...	...	...	4,071	2,150
Freightliner	...	...	...	542	698
Total trucks & buses	263,564	359,239	612,926	646,995	531,010

Sources: Motor Vehicle Manufacturers Association of Canada and Automotive News.

- Mexico -

The US automotive industry's relations with Mexico differ substantially from those with its northern neighbour, Canada, in that there is no free trade in built up motor vehicles between the two countries. Mexico, therefore, constitutes an entirely separate market from the USA, and is serviced by the major US manufacturers through local manufacturing and assembly facilities.

Chrysler Mexico has been the largest selling US affiliate company in Mexico during the eight years ending 1980 - a year when its sales exceeded $1 bn for the first time. Passenger car sales in 1980 reached 57,000 units and truck sales were 49,000. The company currently produces five car models, a light duty truck, and six and eight cylinder engines at its Toluca manufacturing and assembly complex. Two medium duty trucks are built at the company's other assembly plant in Mexico City. Chrysler Mexico was also constructing a plant to produce 2.2 litre, four cylinder, engines starting in late 1981. Some of these engines are to be used in the K cars which were scheduled to be launched in the Mexican market late in 1981.

Ford's plans include a new engine and a new assembly plant in Mexico. The company sees its problem as being to increase its exports from Mexico to balance its component imports from the USA, with the solution being to export built up or KD (knocked down) vehicles to other Latin American countries, and components to the USA.

General Motors is also erecting new engine production facilities in Mexico. Taken together, the new GM and Ford engine plants will reportedly be capable eventually of producing 800,000 units a year, 80 per cent of which may be destined for US assembly plants. American Motors also has assembly operations in the country. Among the heavy duty truck manufacturers, International Harvester and Mack have joint ventures - with Fansa and Fomento Industrial Somex respectively - for truck assembly in Mexico, and Paccar has a 49 per cent owned affiliate in the country.

US manufacturers will clearly continue to make a major contribution to Mexico's rapidly expanding automotive industry. The future of US-Mexican automotive relations is likely to involve an expanding trade between the two countries in vehicle components and not, as with Canada, in built up cars.

- and other countries, including Japan

With regard to trade in motor vehicles with all other countries, the USA has experienced a persistent and substantial unfavourable trade balance; imports of both passenger cars and commercial vehicles have far exceeded exports.

US imports from Japan in 1971 totalled 703,672 cars and 98,545 trucks. However, by 1980 imports of cars had more than doubled to 1,991,502 units, while truck imports (including bodies and chassis for assembly in the USA) totalled 480,547. US vehicle exports to Japan over the same period were negligible and, in 1980, totalled a mere 6,677 cars.

Apart from Canada and Japan, the principal sources of imports have been West Germany and - to a lesser extent - Sweden, France, Italy and the UK.

Passenger car exports (except to Canada) have been but a trickle. In recent years, Saudi Arabia and Kuwait have been the most promising markets in a mediocre export performance. Customers in these countries, as well as in Japan, have shown a strong preference for the US industry's heavy eight cylinder engined cars.

Statistics of US passenger car and commercial vehicle exports, 1971-80, are contained in Table 11, while Table 12 gives details of passenger car exports, by country of destination, for 1980. US imports of passenger cars and commercial vehicles (assembled) for the period 1971 to 1980 are set out in Table 13. US imports of commercial vehicles (assembled), bodies and chassis, by country of origin, for 1979 and 1980, are given in Table 14.

Table 11

US Exports of Passenger Cars and Commercial Vehicles, 1971–80

	1971	1972	1973	1974	1975	1976	1977	1978	1979	1980
Passenger cars										
US total exports	386,641	410,247	509,190	600,902	640,301	680,458	697,205	706,447	792,797	616,895
of which to										
Canada	348,404	376,231	452,370	516,588	550,808	573,470	591,509	542,341	600,840	509,666
Trucks & buses										
US total exports	96,341	117,977	149,461	211,543	218.696	197,237	197,971	248,162	255,147	190,247
of which to										
Canada	65,087	90,034	111,007	159,495	128,755	120,189	115,650	120.707	158,394	79,530

Source: Motor Vehicle Manufacturers Association of the US Inc.

Table 12

US New Passenger Car Exports by Country of Destination in 1980

	With piston engines		Other new passenger cars[a]	Passenger car chassis
	6 cylinders or less	Over 6 cylinders		
Argentina	1,172	325	382	1
Belgium	3,976	990	221	-
Canada	317,588	189,312	513	2,253
Colombia	2,044	726	511	816
W Germany	2,359	2,280	347	20
Japan	2,279	4,398	81	14
Kuwait	1,099	13,790	202	-
Mexico	320	2,806	185	937
Netherlands	1,344	1,374	212	-
Peru	1,143	782	435	-
Saudi Arabia	1,334	19,662	463	16
Switzerland	2,521	1,195	100	-
Taiwan	2,729	835	193	-
Venezuela	742	1,753	1,607	46
Others	11,501	11,246	3,646	69
Total	352,151	251,474	9,098	4,172

a Not specifically provided for elsewhere.

Table 14

US Imports of Commercial Vehicles
(Assembled), Bodies and Chassis, by Country of Origin, 1979-80

	1979			1980		
	Assembled	Unassembled		Assembled	Unassembled	
		Bodies	Chassis		Bodies	Chassis
Belgium	2	-	1,223	-	-	620
Brazil	-	814	3,041	-	12	5,262
Canada	267,732	15,168	22,122	239,917	8,499	26,820
France	3	35	43	10	7	1,792
Italy	2	-	9	-	33	1,397
Japan	7,635	271,224	389,816	102,829	363,904	379,987
Mexico	6	615	499	9	169	179
Sweden	2	1	559	393	11	137
UK	53	20	88	41	51	134
W Germany	121	62	973	143	865	788
Others	8	311	136	10	1,065	355
Total	275,564	288,250	418,509	343,352	374,616	417,471

Source: Motor Vehicle Manufacturers Association of the US Inc.

Table 13

US Imports of Passenger Cars and Commercial Vehicles (Assembled) by Principal Source, 1971-80

	1971	1972	1973	1974	1975	1976	1977	1978	1979	1980
Passenger cars										
US total imports	2,587,484	2,485,901	2,437,345	2,572,557	2,074,653	2,536,749	2,790,144	3,024,982	3,005,523	3,248,266
of which from:										
Canada	802.281	842,300	871,557	817,559	733.766	825,590	849.814	833,061	677,008	594,771
Japan	703.672	697,788	624,805	791.791	695,573	1,128.936	1,341.530	1,563.048	1,617,328	1,991,502
W Germany	770.807	676,967	677.465	619,757	370.012	349,804	423.492	416,231	495,565	470,528
Sweden	61,925	64,541	58,626	60,817	51,993	37,466	39,370	56,140	65,907	61,496
France	23,316	14,713	8,219	21,331	15,647	21,916	19,215	28,502	27,887	47,386
Italy	51,469	64,614	56,102	107,071	102,344	82,500	55,437	69,689	72,456	46,899
UK	106,710	72,038	64,140	72,512	67.106	77,190	56.889	54.478	46,911	32,517
Trucks & buses (assembled)										
US total imports	238,937	250,149	189,584	146,759	125,256	164,543	226,684	369.651	275,564	343,352
of which from:										
Canada	135,640	141,208	113,161	122,675	122,192	163,928	226,099	367.418	267,732	239,917
Japan[a]	98,545	104,775	62,346	23,158	2,650	394	...	1,259	7,635	102,829
W Germany	1,742	594	428	622	188	113	...	843	121	143

a See also Tables 14 and 16. The bulk of Japanese trucks sold in the USA are assembled in the USA from chassis and bodies imported from Japan.

Source: Motor Vehicle Manufacturers Association of the US Inc.

Principal import makes (other than Canadian)

As already noted, the Japanese manufacturers have achieved great success in the USA. Imports of Toyota passenger cars virtually doubled during the decade - from 264,850 in 1971 to 582,204 in 1980; the company has consistently been the best performer amongst the importers since 1975 when it overtook Volkswagen. Datsun overtook Volkswagen in 1976 and has retained second place ever since; its imports more than doubled - indeed, nearly trebled - over the decade, from 188,029 in 1971 to 516,890 in 1980. Honda's sales surpassed Volkswagen's in 1978 for the first time and have subsequently kept ahead. Honda's rate of expansion has been the greatest of all the importers; its sales have rocketed from 12,509 in 1971 to 375,388 in 1980. Mazda's and Subaru's sales have also risen sharply over the period - from 19,630 to 161,623, and from 14,162 to 142,968 respectively. The Mitsubishi imports Arrow/Champ and Colt - which are distributed in the USA by Chrysler - round out the list of Japanese makes which have come to play such an important role in the market.

Volkswagen was the leading import at the beginning of the decade, with sales of 532,906 in 1971. But the West German company's position slipped sharply in 1974 as the Japanese manufacturers stepped up their drive to capture the small car segment of the market. In 1978, Volkswagen commenced manufacturing in the USA in an attempt to recover its share of the US small car market. Among the other imports, Mercedes-Benz has been the steadiest performer with sales mounting from 35,085 in 1971 to 53,790 in 1980. Ford's captive Fiesta took the seventh place among the imports in 1980, with 68,595 units.

Statistics of the principal passenger car imports (other than Canadian), 1971-80, are contained in Table 15.

Imports of trucks more than doubled between 1971 and 1980, and sales rose from 230,731 to 487,567. The majority of these imports consisted of compact pickups from Japan, although medium and heavy trucks were sold by Mercedes-Benz, Volvo and Iveco.

Toyota captured first place among the "independents" in 1978, and its sales rose from 45,009 in 1975 to 131,648 in 1980. In second place, Datsun has seen its sales rise from 72,223 to 111,246 over the same period. Total sales of "captive" Japanese truck imports by the "Big 3" more than doubled between 1975 and 1980, from 102,444 to 228,878 units. Leadership has alternated between Chevrolet's LUV and Ford's Courier; sales of the former rose from 46,371 in 1971 to 88,447 in 1980, while sales of the latter increased from 56,073 to 77,375 over the same period.

Table 16 contains statistics of truck imports (other than Canadian), 1975-80.

Table 15

Principal Passenger Car Imports (Other than Canadian), 1971-80

	1971	1975	1979	1980
Toyota	294,850	283,909	507,616	582,204
Datsun	188,029	253,192	472,252	516,890
Honda	12,509	102,383	353,291	375,388
Mazda	19,630	65,351	156,533	161,623
Subaru	14,162	41,587	127,871	142,968
Volkswagen[a]	532,906	267,730	125,100	90,923
Fiesta	–	–	78,109	68,595
Volvo	51,826	60,338	56,027	56,999
Arrow/Champ	–	–	48,860	55,474
Mercedes-Benz	35,085	45,259	52,819	53,790
Colt	28,381	60,356	62,705	50,689

a Not including Audi and Porsche.

Table 16

Sales of Imported Trucks (Other than Canadian) in the USA, 1975-80

	1975	1976	1977	1978	1979	1980
Independents						
Toyota	45,009	49,838	83,680	94,882	130,075	131,648
Datsun	72,223	80,300	99,839	94,604	101,914	111,246
Mazda	9,837	5,819	4,519	4,696	8,304	8,775
Mercedes-Benz	1,218	1,169	1,820	2,251	3,713	4,051
Others	–	–	–	640	2,500	2,969
Total independents	128,287	137,126	189,858	197,073	246,506	258,689
Captives						
LUV (Chevrolet)	46,371	45,670	67,539	67,035	100,192	88,447
Courier (Ford)	56,073	54,589	65,755	70,557	78,088	77,375
Ram 50 (Dodge)	–	–	–	1,929	32,233	44,640
Arrow (Plymouth)	–	–	–	1,215	14,897	18,416
Total captives	102,444	100,259	133,294	140,736	225,410	228,878
Total imported trucks	230,731	237,385	323,152	337,809	471,916	487,567

THE PRINCIPAL US MOTOR
VEHICLE MANUFACTURING COMPANIES

Brief profiles are provided of the major vehicle manufacturers which make up the US automotive sector.

General Motors: the world's largest vehicle producer

General Motors is the world's largest producer of motor vehicles. Total world-wide sales amounted to $57.73 bn in 1980, against $66.31 bn in 1979. US sales account for 70 per cent, Canadian sales for 12 per cent and other sales for 18 per cent of the total.

Non-automotive products include diesel engines, diesel locomotives and other related products. Defence and space products include turbine aircraft engines and components, ordnance transmissions, inertial navigation, guidance and control systems and components, as well as commercial products delivered for use by the military. Non-automotive products accounted for 7.9 per cent of total sales in 1980.

Most of General Motors' products are marketed through retail dealers, distri-butors and jobbers in the USA and Canada, and through distributors and dealers elsewhere. At December 31, 1980, there were approximately 13,000 motor vehicle dealers in the USA and Canada, and approximately 5,000 outlets in other markets. To assist in the merchandising of General Motors' products, General Motors Acceptance Corporation (a wholly owned non-consolidated subsidiary) and its subsidiaries offer financial services and certain types of automobile insurance to dealers and customers.

General Motors purchases materials, parts, supplies, freight transportation, energy and other services from numerous unaffiliated firms. Purchases of such items in amounts of $5,000 or more per year are made from approximately 31,500 companies in the USA and Canada. Average worldwide employment totalled approximately 746,000 persons in 1980, with payrolls amounting to $17.8 bn. This included 14,800 employees of GM's financing and insurance subsidiaries, whose payroll amounted to $316.4 mn. GM's average US hourly rate employment in 1980 was 376,000 persons, with payrolls totalling $9.8 bn.

General Motors makes Cadillac, Oldsmobile, Buick, Pontiac and Chevrolet passenger cars, as well as Chevrolet and GMC trucks. Detroit Diesel Allison Division continues to be North America's largest producer of heavy and medium duty diesel engines. The company operates plants in 17 foreign countries and makes vehicles under the names Vauxhall, Bedford, Opel and Holden.

General Motors' worldwide retail sales of 7.3 mn vehicles in 1980 represented a decline of 17 per cent from 1979's level. Of the estimated 35 mn vehicles sold worldwide by all manufacturers[1] in 1980, General Motors accounted for 21 per cent compared with 23 per cent in the preceding year. Sales of GM trucks accounted

---

1 Estimated data exclude the USSR, parts of Eastern Europe, and China. Vehicle sales in these areas amounted to an estimated 4 mn units in 1980.

for 37 per cent of US sales in 1980, down from 40 per cent in 1979. Unit sales at 940,000 trucks, were 33 per cent below the 1979 level.

Outside the USA and Canada, General Motors' largest market areas in 1980 were: Europe, where total sales of passenger cars and trucks reached 946,000 units, a decline of 14 per cent from 1979; Latin America, with total sales of 373,000 units, a 5 per cent increase over 1979; the Pacific region, where 1980 sales of 209,000 units were 15 per cent lower than in 1979; and the Middle East and Africa, with sales retaining their 1979 level of 172,000 units. Foreign retail sales of North American produced vehicles in 1980 amounted to 211,000 units, a 6 per cent decrease from 1979.

Ford is number two in the USA –

Ford Motor Company is the second largest US automobile manufacturer with worldwide sales reaching $37,086 mn in 1980, compared with $43,514 mn in 1979. The manufacture, assembly and sale of cars and trucks, together with related parts and accessories, accounted for 90 per cent of Ford's worldwide sales in 1980 and 92 per cent in 1979. Other operations include the manufacture and sale of wheeled tractors, parts and components, for farm and industrial use. Ford Aerospace and its subsidiaries manufacture communications and electronic systems and equipment for industrial and governmental use. Ford Credit is a wholly owned unconsolidated subsidiary which provides wholesale financing to, and purchases retail instalment sales contracts from, franchised Ford vehicle dealers, as well as making loans to vehicle leasing companies and engaging in commercial, industrial, and real estate financing. Other wholly owned subsidiaries include the American Road Insurance Company, Ford Leasing Development Company and Ford Motor Land Development Corporation.

Raw and semi finished materials, supplies and parts are purchased from many suppliers. Ford plans to increase its dependence on outside suppliers for certain components in the future. Ford is negotiating the possible purchase of diesel engines from Toyo Kogyo, BMW-Steyr Motorem and International Harvester in the mid 1980s. In 1979, Ford acquired a 25 per cent equity interest in Toyo Kogyo, a Japanese automobile maker which markets products under the Mazda trademark.

The average number of employees at Ford and its consolidated subsidiaries was 426,735 in 1980, compared with 494,579 in 1979 and 506,531 in 1978. The total payroll amounted to $9.5 bn in 1980, compared with $10.2 bn in 1979 and $9.8 bn in 1978. In addition to the payroll, Ford makes substantial expenditures under employees' plans and programmes. Ford's total employee costs (including payroll, payroll taxes and fringe benefits) amounted to $12.4 bn in 1980, $13.2 bn in 1979 and $12.5 bn in 1978. The average number of employees at Ford and its consolidated subsidiaries working in US operations was 179,917 in 1980, compared with 239,475 in 1979 and 256,614 in 1978. Total payroll for these employees amounted to $5.2 bn in 1980, compared with $6.3 bn in 1979 and $6.6 bn in 1978.

The number of dealers in the USA declined from approximately 6,725 at the end of 1978 to 6,600 at the end of 1979, and to 6,050 as at December 31, 1980.

- and has foreign interests of growing importance

Since the early 1970s, Ford's operations outside the USA have accounted for a generally increasing percentage of total revenues and earnings. Sales outside the USA accounted for 30 per cent in 1971, but had risen by 1980 to 50 per cent, including 5 per cent in Canada. These sales contributed 14 per cent of net income in 1971 and 49 per cent in 1978. But the importance of non-US operations is demonstrated by the fact that they earned $475 mn in 1980 when Ford's worldwide results produced a loss of $1,543 mn.

Ford's sales in the USA and Canada totalled 1,560,007 cars and 862,201 trucks in 1980. Approximately 88 per cent of total truck unit sales were light trucks with a gross vehicle weight of 14,000 lb or less. Figures for US and Canadian sales in 1971 were 2,547,045 cars and 803,916 trucks.

Total car and truck sales outside the USA and Canada by Ford came to 1,906,242 units in 1980, and the company's share of total car and truck retail sales outside the USA and Canada was 9 per cent in that year. The 1971 figure for sales outside the USA and Canada was 1,581,971 vehicles.

Ford's main market areas outside the USA and Canada, including sales of units manufactured by other companies and sold by Ford were: Europe, with total car and truck sales of 1,392,252 in 1980; Latin America, 356,834; Australia, 93,490; and South Africa, 52,671. Ford's greatest market penetration in foreign markets was in the UK with a 30.7 per cent share, followed by Argentina (28.4 per cent), Australia (19.9 per cent) and Brazil (15.2 per cent).

Chrysler makes up the third member of the Big Three

The Chrysler Corporation is the third largest US automobile manufacturer, with total worldwide sales of $9,225 mn in 1980. Its market share has eroded in recent years in the face of strong competition from General Motors, Ford and the Japanese manufacturers.

The Chrysler Corporation operates principally in two segments, which can best be described as automotive and non-automotive operations. The corporation's domestic operations are engaged primarily in the manufacture, assembly, importation, sale and retail financing - in the USA and Canada - of passenger cars, trucks and related automotive parts and accessories. Foreign subsidiaries manufacture passenger cars, trucks and related parts and accessories which are sold outside the USA.

Chrysler holds an equity position of approximately 14 per cent in the PSA group (Peugeot/Citroën/Talbot) as a consequence of the purchase by the latter of Chrysler's principal European operations in 1978. In February 1980, Chrysler and Peugeot signed a memorandum of intent to explore cooperative industrial and commercial ventures. Discussions have subsequently taken place regarding the possibility of a joint venture under which Peugeot would build a subcompact in the USA, but no firm plans have been announced. Peugeot already sells engines to Chrysler for its compacts. Chrysler also holds a 15 per cent interest in the Mitsubishi Motors Corporation of Japan. Chrysler International SA assists in the distribution of Mitsubishi products in many world markets.

The number of Chrysler dealer locations has fallen to 3,500. Meanwhile, the Peugeot dealer network in the USA has expanded from 295 at the beginning of 1980 to 330 at the end of the year, and an additional 50 dealers were expected to be appointed during 1981.

In 1980, Chrysler's average number of employees worldwide was 92,596 against 157,958 in 1978.

Chrysler's defence operations are the major portion of non-automotive activities. Chrysler Defense is the main contractor for the turbo powered M-1, the US Army's new main battle tank. The remainder of non-automotive operations is composed of the manufacture and sale of outboard motors, inboard marine engines and industrial engines. Chrysler Financial Corporation sold virtually all of its European finance operations to the PSA group in 1978 and 1979; in 1979 it also sold its remaining interest in two associated companies in Venezuela and its operations in Argentina and Colombia. In December 1979, Chrysler Financial Corporation entered into an agreement to sell 75 per cent of its finance operations in Australia early in 1980.

Automotive operations worldwide accounted for 92.7 per cent of Chrysler's 1980 sales, leaving non-automotive operations with 7.3 per cent. Chrysler's worldwide sales of cars and trucks in 1980 totalled 1,224,923 - of which 783,510 were sold in the USA and 441,413 outside the USA. Of total sales, cars comprised 968,442 units and trucks 256,481. In 1973, total sales worldwide amounted to 2,423,099 units, of which 1,916,799 were in the USA and 506,300 outside. Of the 1973 total 1,994,394 represented car sales and 428,705 were truck sales.

American Motors: increasingly under French influence

American Motors Corporation's sales for fiscal 1980 (ending September 30, 1980) totalled $2,683 mn. The company's business consists principally of two segments: general automotive (accounting for 81.6 per cent of sales), and special government vehicles (15.4 per cent). The general automotive segment involves the manufacture, assembly and sale of passenger cars, four wheel drive Jeeps, utility and recreational vehicles, and their related parts and accessories in the USA, Canada and other foreign countries, together with the importation and sale of Renault passenger cars in the USA and Canada. The special government vehicle segment primarily involves the assembly and sale of specialised vehicles - including tactical trucks and postal service vehicles, principally to the agencies of the US and foreign governments. Other operations account for the remaining 3 per cent of sales, and comprise the manufacture and sale of plastic injection mouldings and the assembly and sale of lawn and garden tractors.

Worldwide automotive sales in fiscal 1980 reached 353,186 vehicles, of which 257,419 were in the USA and 95,767 in Canada and other foreign markets. During the last quarter of 1980 domestic retail unit sales accounted for 63.6 per cent of the small sports utility vehicle market and 23.1 per cent of the large sports utility vehicle market.

At December 31, 1980, the company had 2,154 franchised dealers in the USA, while the number of Renault franchised dealers was 1,302. The company's work-force at the same date was approximately 21,400 - of whom 14,700 were hourly rated and 6,700 salaried.

The company has facilities for the manufacture of major automotive components, including: forgings, stampings, engines, axles, bodies, differentials, plastic parts and interior trim. Even so, American Motors still purchases components from approximately 960 suppliers (including other automobile manufacturers), of which approximately 900 are single source suppliers. As a result of its relation-ship with Renault, the company will have increasing access to the French company's automotive technology and research capability.

International operations consist mainly of sales of domestically manufactured vehicles as KD units to independent licensees and distributors, or to local com-panies in which the company has a minority interest. In the twelve months ending September 30, 1980, sales outside the USA and Canada totalled 60,189 units, representing 10 per cent of the company's total sales in dollar terms. Principal international assembly facilities for the company's vehicles are located in Mexico, Egypt, Venezuela and Australia.

Beginning in 1979, the company signed an agreement with Renault to become the exclusive importer and distributor of Renault passenger cars in the USA and Canada (except Quebec). It was also expected that Renault would become the exclusive distributor of Jeeps in France and certain other markets. And, under a long term agreement signed in October 1979, American Motors will manufacture Renault designed cars beginning in 1982 - probably with a version of the R9. As a result of these agreements, Renault currently owns approximately 46 per cent of the capital stock of American Motors Corporation and, if the French company decides to exercise all its rights, it could end up owning more than 50 per cent. Nevertheless, Renault has informed American Motors that it has not made plans to increase its ownership to over 49.9 per cent.

The centrepiece of the company's future product plans is a new generation of front wheel drive, fuel efficient, Renault designed passenger cars which will be built by the company in the USA for introduction at the beginning of the 1983 model year. These cars will eventually be offered in multiple body styles and models, and are expected to have high volume sales potential. The company will continue to sell imported Renault cars and its own models.

Paccar: important in the heavy truck sector

Paccar's sales in 1980 amounted to $1,673.7 mn. The company manufactures for two main market sectors - trucks and related parts (75 per cent of sales) which are sold through a network of company appointed dealers, and railroad cars and related equipment (14.2 per cent of sales) which are sold directly to railroads and leasing companies. The geographical distribution of total sales in 1980 was as follows: 84.8 per cent in the USA, 10.4 per cent in Canada, and 4.8 per cent to other markets.

Paccar is the third largest heavy duty truck manufacturer in the USA. Its activities are dominated by the production of Kenworth and Peterbilt heavy duty trucks, most of which are built to customer specification. Both lines sell at a premium over equivalent standard trucks through having established a good image and following in the marketplace. Production facilities also exist in Canada and Australia and, in October 1980, the company acquired Foden in the UK (subsequently renamed Sandbach Engineering Company), and with it a modest share of the UK's heavy duty truck market together with a marketing network extending into the Middle East and Africa. Paccar also has a 49 per cent owned affiliate in Mexico. US and Canadian full service outlets exceed 300 in number, serving all 50 states and Canadian provinces. Paccar International, with regional offices, serves over 60 foreign dealerships. During 1980 important sales and deliveries were made to Egypt, China, Chile, Colombia, Malaysia, the Philippines and various Middle Eastern states.

Paccar's largest division, the Kenworth Truck Company, manufactures long hood and cab over engine models at plants in Seattle (Washington), Kansas City (Missouri) and Chillicothe (Ohio). Applications range from petroleum tankers to concrete mixers, and from general merchandise and refrigerated commodities trucks to off highway logging trucks. Special purpose designs include trucks engineered to operate in the rugged environments of Arctic and Middle Eastern oil fields, as well as on the typically more restricted roads of Western Europe. The Eurotruck incorporates a full complement of comfort and convenience features for the demanding long haul services from northern Europe to the Middle East. More than 35 per cent of Kenworth's worldwide production is destined for customers outside the USA.

Peterbilt Motors Company - with manufacturing facilities at Newark (California), Madison (Tennessee) and Denton (Texas) - produces long hood, cab over engine and special purpose models for a wide variety of customers including general highway haulers, logging and petroleum industries, and off highway users. Peterbilt of Canada is responsible for marketing north of the border, with emphasis on sales in Canada's western provinces.

Paccar's three wholly owned unconsolidated finance subsidiaries provide financing - principally to the trucking industry for customers of dealers in the USA, Canada and Mexico. Paccar Leasing Corporation assists dealers with truck leasing.

Signal Companies Incorporated: a diversified group -

Signal Companies Inc is a diversified group of businesses engaged in: the manufacture of transportation related equipment, primarily aerospace (Garrett); the design, engineering, manufacture and sale of heavy duty motor trucks and truck tractors (Mack Trucks); the manufacture of industrial products; and, through UOP, commercialised research and development resulting in processes, products and services having technologically based proprietary positions in the energy and environmental improvement markets. Ampex Corporation (acquired in January 1981) produces audio video systems, computer memories, data handling products and magnetic tape. Other activities of Signal include real estate and land development, and investments in radio and television broadcasting and shipping. Total sales in 1980 reached $4,285.3 mn; Mack accounted for 35.9 per cent, Garrett for 39.9 per cent and UOP for 22.4 per cent.

– represented in the truck sector by Mack

Mack Trucks is a leading manufacturer of heavy duty, diesel powered, trucks and truck tractors, custom built fire fighters, and components and replacement parts for these vehicles. In 1980, Mack ranked first among the seven major US manufacturers of class 8 diesel trucks in terms of North American factory sales, and maintains its position as the leading exporter of this product line. Since 1979, Mack has also marketed in North and Central America medium duty (classes 6 and 7) diesel trucks built by Renault. In May 1979, Renault acquired a 10 per cent common stock interest in Mack. Renault also holds subordinated debentures convertible into an additional 10 per cent common stock interest in Mack.

Mack Trucks are sold and serviced at 35 company owned branches, 211 independent distributors, and over 500 parts and service dealers in the USA. Canada has 78 outlets, and there are 104 international distributor locations in 80 countries. The company operates three manufacturing and assembly plants in the USA, and one each in Canada and Australia.

Over the five year period 1976–80, the composition of Mack's sales has remained relatively constant: domestic trucks account for about 60 per cent, while international deliveries and parts and services contribute about 20 per cent each. As at December 31, 1980, Mack had approximately 14,100 employees, reduced from 17,000 at the end of 1979.

Mack maintains a highly integrated manufacturing operation, building all of the major subassemblies for most of its trucks – engines, transmissions, axles, bodies, housings, carriers, axle shafts and cabs – and a substantial number of other component parts. A high degree of interchangeability of basic components among its truck models has been developed, thereby allowing flexibility in adapting trucks to a wide range of uses and, of course, helping the objective of reducing parts inventory. Although most trucks manufactured by Mack contain the company's own major components, when requested by a customer Mack will produce trucks utilising major components manufactured by others. However, Mack's engines and other major components are only available in its trucks, all of which are powered by diesel engines. Mack estimates that over 230,000 of its trucks were in operation in the USA at the end of 1980 – a parc which provides the major market for its replacement parts business.

An increasing number of Mack vehicles are shipped to foreign markets in KD form. KD assembly operations exist in nine countries with local companies – Mack having an equity interest in four of them. New KD assembly operations were opened during 1980 in Kenya and Ecuador, and Mack's joint venture with Fomento Industrial Somex of Mexico – which commenced production in August 1980 – is assembling six trucks per day for the Mexican market.

Mack's subsidiary, Mack Financial Corporation, and its Canadian subsidiary, finance Mack's instalment sales and also provide floor plan financing for the truck inventories of many Mack distributors in the USA and Canada. Approximately 21 per cent of Mack's domestic and Canadian new truck sales during 1980 were financed by Mack Financial Corporation and its Canadian subsidiary.

International Harvester (IH): important truck producing interests –

International Harvester manufactures self propelled heavy machinery and vehicles for use on and off the highway. It was organised into five worldwide groups, four of which – trucks, agricultural equipment, construction equipment and Solar Turbines [1] International (turbine machinery) – were responsible for the design, manufacture and marketing of their products. The fifth group – components – was responsible for the design and manufacture of axles, engines, castings and other parts for use primarily by the other four groups. In addition, the components group was responsible for directing the company's parts distribution system.

Total sales of the company in 1980 were $6,312 mn; 72 per cent represented sales in the USA, and 9.6 per cent sales in Canada. Sales of the truck group, at $2,722 mn, represented 43.1 per cent of the total. In 1980, the truck group lost its position as the largest manufacturer in the USA of medium and heavy trucks (classes 6, 7 and 8) due to a six month strike. Its principal products are diesel and petrol engined trucks ranging from 19,501 to 128,000 lb gvw. They are used for long distance and local hauls and for a variety of off highway applications such as energy exploration, mining and construction. International Harvester is the principal supplier of cabs and chassis for school buses in North America. School buses and straight trucks are normally forwarded to body building companies before final delivery to customers, while truck tractors are typically sold and delivered without bodies or trailers. I H purchases various components from outside suppliers worldwide, notably tyres, glass products, hydraulic and fuel injection systems, and electrical, plastic and drivetrain components.

– with widespread markets

The truck group of I H markets its products throughout North America, Europe, Africa, the Middle East, Asia, the Pacific Basin and Latin America. The principal sales, service and parts activities are carried out by approximately 2,000 dealers and distributors throughout the world, including approximately 1,650 in North America. In addition, sales, service and parts activities are conducted by about 125 company owned retail facilities worldwide.

About 40 per cent of I H's heavy duty truck sales are normally made to US fleets, where extreme price competition narrows profit margins. The company's share of the medium and heavy duty truck market in Canada is about 20 per cent, and there are plans to expand sales in Latin America where the medium and heavy truck market is expected to grow strongly up to 1985. The group has assembly operations in Mexico (through a joint venture with Fansa) and Venezuela. I H has medium and heavy truck producing interests in Western Europe through a 37.5 per cent interest in DAF Trucks (in the Netherlands) and its ownership of Seddon Atkinson in the UK. During 1980 I H acquired a 35 per cent interest in Enasa – a leading Spanish producer of trucks under the Pegaso and Sava marques; this involvement also envisaged the formation of a new company (with I H owning 65 per cent) which was to manufacture and market a line of diesel engines for automotive applications.

I H has finance subsidiaries in the USA and other countries which provide wholesale and retail financing for I H products. Other subsidiaries offer casualty and life insurance coverage and the leasing of I H products to dealers, distributors and customers.

---

1 Disposed of in 1981.

Nissan: truck assembly likely to begin in 1983

In 1980, Nissan exported 621,000 vehicles to the USA - almost three times the 1972 level; of the 1980 total, 111,000 were small trucks. Early in 1980, Nissan formed Nissan Motor Manufacturing Corporation USA, which is constructing a truck manufacturing facility in Smyrna, Tennessee, where production is scheduled to begin in August 1983. This facility will be equipped initially to build 120,000 vehicles per year, rising to 180,000 and, possibly, 480,000 in the longer term. The number of employees will be about 2,200 when production starts, and the plant will operate with only five levels of management. It is understood that the company will have only five Japanese staff members: vice president of quality assurance; director of in-process inspection; manager of US supplier quality; vice president of product design; and director of chassis design. The facility will initially import 62 per cent of its parts from Japan (including power trains), but 455 parts are reportedly to be sourced from US manufacturers. The plant's output will be distributed by Nissan Motor Corporation USA, which is also responsible for import sales.

One of Nissan's reservations about beginning US manufacturing in the past has been its inability to compete with the scale of operations of the American auto makers. But in deciding to manufacture trucks rather than cars, Nissan will be able to produce on the same scale as the US producers. The company will further mini- mise its risk by having fewer model changeovers than it would have had in the manufacture of cars. A further reason why Nissan decided to build trucks rather than cars in the USA is reported to be that there are fewer parts in a truck, and thus fewer chances for production failures.

Subaru of America Incorporated: an ambitious sales target

Subaru of America Inc, an independently owned US company and the country's fifth largest automobile import organisation,was founded in February 1968. American shareholders own a majority interest but, in 1975, Fuji Heavy Industries (the company's Japanese manufacturer) purchased a minority equity interest, at the company's urging, to forestall any takeover attempt.

Subaru of America has divided the US market into 15 distributor areas, each responsible for franchising dealers, of which there are now 750. The number of dealers will expand, though, as the company attempts to achieve its intermediate term sales target of doubling 1980 sales of 143,000 units. The company's main product lines are front wheel drive and four wheel drive vehicles; it has been particularly successful in selling the latter in rural, snowbelt and mountain areas.

Volvo White Truck Corporation: enhanced opportunities for the Swedish company

The Volvo White Truck Corporation was formed during the third quarter of 1981 following the purchase by AB Volvo (of Sweden) of most of the heavy truck manu- facturing and distribution assets of the White Motor Corporation, which had been in bankruptcy since September 1980. The purchase price was reportedly $70 mn. In the past Volvo's trucks had been marketed in the USA by the Freightliner Corporation (itself purchased in 1981 by Daimler-Benz of West Germany). In

1980 Volvo sold 1,020 medium and heavy trucks (valued at about $32 mn) in the USA, while sales of White Motor in the same year totalled approximately 6,000 heavy duty trucks. The new company will manufacture and distribute Volvo, White, Autocar and Western Star medium and heavy trucks in the USA, with production of Volvo's medium and heavy trucks scheduled to start in the USA during 1982.

Volvo's acquisition has given the Swedish company access to a range of trucks adapted to the special requirements of the US market for long haul operations, and this will complement Volvo's own truck exports. The principal customers for White trucks are common and private fleet carriers, owner operators specialising in over the road freight, construction companies, distributors of building materials, oil companies, and food and beverage distributors. White manufactures a variety of models with cab and chassis arrangements and special modifications designed to meet customer requirements.

White Motor Credit Corporation will continue to provide financing for Volvo White dealer organisations and their customers.

Freightliner/Daimler-Benz: potentially
a powerful new force in the medium to heavy truck sector

On July 31, 1981, Consolidated Freightways sold its truck manufacturing subsidiary, Freightliner, to Daimler-Benz for a total of $284 mn. The new company will manufacture and distribute the truck lines of both Freightliner and Daimler-Benz. Sales of Freightliner's heavy duty (class 8) trucks totalled approximately 9,000 in 1980, while sales of Daimler-Benz medium and heavy duty trucks (classes 6, 7 and 8) amounted to 4,051 units.

Freightliner was set up after the second world war to build trucks designed to meet the special needs of Consolidated Freightways' western freight routes, but in 1951 the company started selling to others under a marketing agreement with White Motor. And since December 1977, Freightliner has handled its own marketing, promotional and dealer support programmes to approximately 210 dealers. In August 1978, Freightliner signed an agreement with Volvo for exclusive marketing rights of Volvo's trucks and spare parts in the USA and Canada, but this agreement has now terminated. The facilities acquired by Daimler-Benz include three truck manufacturing plants in the USA, and one in Canada, three plants making truck parts, and other subsidiaries making light metal castings and plastic items. Daimler-Benz will also take over two credit subsidiaries of Freightliner, and will gain access to Freightliner's dealer network. Daimler-Benz has marketed its diesel powered medium and heavy trucks in the USA for some years, and sales have risen since its new assembly facility in Hampton, Virginia, started production in 1980; the investment involved was $8.1 mn and production capacity is 6,000 medium weight trucks per year. The Hampton, Virginia, plant performs a semi knocked down assembly operation, using components mainly manufactured by a Daimler-Benz subsidiary in Brazil; but the company is planning to increase purchases of locally sourced components in the longer term.

The two parts of the new group complement each other in a number of ways and together they should constitute a powerful manufacturing and marketing force in the US medium to heavy truck sector. Freightliner's plants and markets to a

167

large extent have been concentrated in the western USA, while Daimler-Benz's facilities and markets are located in the east. In the past, Freightliner has purchased its diesel engines, transmissions and axles from outside sources, but Daimler-Benz is strong in engineering with a substantial capability in diesel engine technology.

Volkswagen Manufacturing Corporation of America: a local presence

The Volkswagen Manufacturing Corporation of America was established as a wholly owned subsidiary of Volkswagenwerk AG (of Wolfsburg, West Germany) on July 6, 1976, and produces the Rabbit model (known in Europe as the Golf) for the US and Canadian markets at its Westmoreland assembly plant in East Huntington, Pennsylvania; the plant has a production capacity of 200,000 vehicles per year, and output in 1980 totalled 197,106 units. Volkswagen plans to have a second manufacturing facility in the Detroit area as a key element in its long term plan to regain 5 per cent of the US market. Engines and transmissions for the Rabbit are supplied from the parent company in West Germany, but an increasing proportion of other materials and parts are being purchased from US and Canadian suppliers.

Volkswagen Manufacturing Corporation sells its products to Volkswagen of America and Volkswagen Canada for distribution to authorised dealers who also handle sales of Volkswagen's imports, including small trucks. A separate dealer network handles sales of Porsche and Audi cars which are, of course, imported from West Germany.

Toyota Motor Sales, USA Inc: a truck assembly facility

Toyota Motor Sales, USA Inc, has its headquarters in Torrance, California, and is responsible for the sale throughout the nation of Toyota's passenger cars, pickups, trucks and components. Passenger cars are imported in built up form, but truck chassis and bodies are imported from Japan and assembled by Long Beach Fabricators of California - which is wholly owned by Toyota.

Company owned distributors are located in San Francisco, Los Angeles, New York, Chicago, Portland (Oregon) and Denver, while independent distributors operate from Houston, Pompano Beach (Florida), Woburn (Massachusetts) and Maryland. The company has over 1,000 franchised dealers, with sales somewhat heavily concentrated in the south east and the west; the heaviest concentration of truck sales is on the west coast.

Honda of America: the first Japanese producer of cars in the USA

Honda of America is a subsidiary of the Honda Motor Company. In addition to importing and marketing Honda Civic, Accord and Prelude cars, the company has a US manufacturing presence with its motorcycle plant at Marysville, Ohio, which is currently producing 60,000 motorcycles per year. Honda is now proceeding with plans to establish a passenger car assembly plant nearby, with an initial production capacity of 144,000 Honda Accords per year. This facility is scheduled to open in the latter part of 1982, and will be the first Japanese car assembly plant in the USA. But output will satisfy only part of the US demand for Honda Accords, and the balance will be imported from Japan. Honda's management will therefore be in a good position to monitor the extent to which the quality of US labour and its productivity measure up to Japanese standards. Bearing in mind that Japanese manufacturers have serious reservations about the quality of American labour, the result of Honda's experiment will almost certainly have an important influence on the thinking of other Japanese passenger car (as distinct from light truck) manufacturers contemplating manufacturing or assembly operations in the USA.

Iveco Trucks of North America Inc: a growing involvement

This is a wholly owned subsidiary of Iveco BV of the Netherlands, which itself is now wholly owned by Fiat. It markets class 6 and 7 trucks and, since the autumn of 1980, a class 2 truck. The vehicles are presently imported assembled, and only a few components are added locally. US sales in 1980 totalled 1,800 units, mainly medium weight trucks. More recently, a potentially far reaching agreement has been concluded with International Harvester involving the distribution of Iveco trucks in the USA.

Other manufacturers

For some time MAN has been seeking a manufacturing presence in the USA, but discussions with troubled White Motors came to nothing in 1979. However, MAN has gained contracts to supply articulated buses to Seattle and Chicago, and is building an assembly plant in Rowan County, North Carolina, to produce articulated buses.

The West German firm Auwarter has announced its entry into the US bus market and is building an assembly plant in Colorado.

Other manufacturers of cars and trucks in the USA are Checker (cars), Hendrickson Manufacturing Company (trucks and certain components), Oshkosh Truck Corporation (heavy duty trucks), the Flxible division of Grumman Corporation (buses for city transit), and Gillig (school buses).

Imported passenger cars - other than the lines specified above - are marketed in the USA through import and marketing companies which, in the main, are controlled by the overseas manufacturing parent.

CURRENT ISSUES

THE OIL CRISIS

Concern over the price and
availability of petrol leads to smaller cars -

The fuel shortages engendered by the oil embargo of 1973 led to the Energy Policy
and Conservation Act of 1975 which forced manufacturers selling more than 10,000
cars per year in the USA to meet a strict schedule of progressively higher average
fuel economy. For 1978, for example, the car manufacturers were required to
achieve a corporate average fuel economy (CAFE) of 18 miles per (US) gallon
(mpg). The CAFE standard for 1980 was 20 mpg, and the target for 1981 was set
at 22 mpg. The schedule stretches to 1985 when the CAFE standard is 27.5 mpg.

During the 1975-78 period, petrol prices actually declined in real terms, largely
as a consequence of government price controls which insulated the USA from prevailing world energy prices. However, the Iranian revolution caused an interruption
to petrol supplies in early 1979, and this was accompanied by rapidly rising prices
as the government finally began to remove price controls on petrol. As a consequence of these developments, the demand for small, fuel efficient cars increased
strongly. Imports from Japan - whose manufacturers had no difficulty in meeting
the CAFE standards - boomed, and the domestic manufacturers started to rewrite
their forward product plans and accelerate the development of new products.

General Motors has been able to raise its CAFE to 23 mpg for 1981, a 92 per cent
improvement over the base year of 1974. In July 1980, GM announced its intention
to achieve an estimated fleet fuel economy of 31 mpg for the 1985 model year -
nearly a 160 per cent improvement over 1974. Ford's CAFE for 1981 model year
cars was also projected to reach 23 mpg, representing a 65 per cent improvement
over 1975. On the assumption, though, that manufacturers will achieve no more
than the CAFE target by 1985, the fuel consumption rate of the average 1985 model
year car will be only 44 per cent of that of its 1974 predecessors. And as the
generations of "gas guzzlers" are scrapped year by year and replaced by the new
and increasingly fuel efficient cars, US petrol consumption for motoring will drop
significantly throughout the 1980s. In the meantime, both GM and Ford are
developing mini compact models which may achieve 70 mpg.

- and a search for alternative fuels

The quest for economy has also encouraged the use of diesel engines in passenger
cars, notably by GM and Volkswagen. GM estimates that by 1985 about 15 per
cent of its fleet will be diesel powered. Volkswagen manufactures diesel powered
cars in the USA and is reported to be testing a turbo charged three cylinder diesel
version of the Polo - reputed to have achieved 100 mpg.

170

The industry welcomed the easier oil supply conditions which developed at the end of 1981 and the recent decline in prices, but the vehicle manufacturers have clearly decided that they can no longer remain totally dependent on oil based fuels. Efforts are therefore being made to develop vehicles which run on alternative fuel supplies. Synthetic fuel production requires huge capital outlays and long lead times but, even so, industry sources believe that synthetic fuels could start taking the place of oil based fuels by the late 1980s. In the meantime, conventional engines can be modified to run efficiently on various other fuels - such as propane, compressed natural gas, ethanol (distilled from farm products and wastes) and methanol (derived from wood, coal or natural gas); emission control is also easier with such fuels. Progress in using them, however, is currently subject to their limited availability and the absence of distribution systems.

The electric car is also coming under renewed interest. GM, in particular, has a programme under way which aims to develop a commercially viable electric vehicle with sufficient range to capitalise on the availability of off peak power. One study has suggested that there is already sufficient off peak generating capacity in the USA to power between 10 and 13 mn electric vehicles. Considerable progress has already been made towards solving the substantial technical and design problems - involving, for example, battery life and safety - which lie in the way of producing a truly viable electric car.

GOVERNMENT REGULATION: SAFETY, THE
ENVIRONMENT, EQUAL OPPORTUNITY, AND ANTI-TRUST

An ever growing list of regulations since the mid 1960s -

The US automotive sector was virtually free of regulation at the federal level until the mid 1960s, since when it has been required to comply with a plethora of rules established by dozens of agencies. Currently, regulators in Washington set standards for exhaust emissions, safety and fuel consumption levels which affect the size, shape and performance of new cars, while noise regulations have been set for medium and heavy duty vehicles. Occupational safety inspectors inspect factories, while equal opportunity officials have a say in who gets hired and promoted. And until early 1981, the FTC was contemplating a suit aimed at dividing GM into a number of independent groups.

Apart from the aforementioned CAFE standards (established in order to conserve fuel), the principal federally mandated requirements which have directly affected the industry are related to safety and the environment. Regulations defining safety standards for motor vehicles include the National Traffic and Motor Vehicle Safety Act of 1966 and the 1972 Motor Vehicle Information and Cost Savings Act, as well as the related Federal Motor Vehicle Safety Standard 215 (the exterior protection standard); this was specifically designed to provide bumper systems which would protect safety related items such as lights, steering and cooling. Throughout the 1970s the National Highway Traffic Safety Administration examined the feasibility of making it a mandatory requirement for car manufacturers to offer passive restraints, which are intended to protect the vehicle's occupants from injury in an accident without them having to take any active step such as buckling a seat belt. In January 1977, GM, Ford and Daimler-Benz agreed to offer optional air bags on certain small to intermediate cars, beginning with the 1980 models. At the same time Volkswagen agreed to continue offering its passive belt - which stretches automatically across the occupants of front seats when the car doors are closed - for another three years.

The Clean Air Act of 1970, along with its 1977 amendments, constitutes the USA's most complex and far reaching environmental legislation. In line with the act's requirements, the US auto industry has achieved significant reductions in exhaust emission levels during the decade. Compared with an uncontrolled 1960 model car, levels of carbon monoxide and hydrocarbons have been reduced by 96 per cent, while those of oxides of nitrogen have decreased by 76 per cent. The automotive industry's manufacturing facilities are also subject to the stationary source provisions of the Clean Air Act. Efforts to reduce stationary source pollution have resulted in the replacement of older factories by new ones which incorporate modern pollution control technology. The act requires a case by case review of permit applications to build new facilities in order to determine if major, new sources of stationary emissions should be allowed to be added to the area in question. This requirement clearly adds an element of uncertainty for a company which plans to build a new plant or expand.

On the issue of noise reduction, standards set by the Environmental Protection Agency for medium and heavy vehicles stipulate that - compared to 1975 - noise levels should have been reduced by 50 per cent by 1978, and by a total of 75 per cent by 1982.

- has cost a lot of money -

The cost of meeting government regulations has had a severe impact on the industry. GM has estimated that it spent $10.3 bn in the period 1974-80 to comply with federal, state and local government requirements, analysed as follows:

	$ mn
Regulation of vehicles	
- safety	3,045
- emission control	2,840
- noise control	131
Sub total	6,016
Regulation of plant facilities	
- air pollution	931
- water pollution	578
- solid waste pollution	460
Sub total	1,969
Occupational safety & health	625
Government reports & administrative costs related to regulation	1,720
Grand total	10,330

In 1980, when GM lost $762.5 mn, total costs under the above headings reached $2.2 bn. And, at the consumer level, GM estimates that meeting the overall emission standards adds $725 to the price of a new car, while safety standards add a further $400.

– but relief has come with the Reagan administration

The Reagan administration, though, has brought a welcome respite for the automotive industry. On April 6, 1981, the federal government eased, eliminated or
delayed 34 automotive safety and environmental regulations. The cancellation of
new and more onerous regulations proposed by the previous administration has
proved to be at least as important to the industry as the deletion of existing regulations, but part of the problem of deregulation is the bureaucratic process needed
to rescind rules. Among the regulations rescinded was one which would have
required the installation of passive restraints starting in 1983.

PRODUCT CHANGE AND NEW TECHNOLOGY

Much effort has been directed towards downsizing cars

In order to meet the changes brought about by the demand for smaller cars and
the government mandated standards, the major US vehicle manufacturers have
launched programmes – based on the use of innovative technology – to redesign
most of their models and many of the plants which produce them.

In the quest to improve fuel economy, excess weight has clearly been identified as
the main area for attention and, since 1974, the US companies have been trying to
delete as much surplus metal out of their cars as possible. The first round of
downsizing lowered the average weight per car by 300 lb approximately, simply
by reducing vehicle size and installing smaller engines. But the second round of
downsizing has been more difficult; vehicles could not easily be further reduced
in size, and ingenious engineering was needed to lighten vehicle weight without
affecting strength. Between 1976 and 1979, General Motors spent $2.5 bn on
developing the 24 mpg X car, while Ford's Escort/Lynx model – which achieves
30 mpg – cost $3.3 bn. General Motors' J car series, which returns around 26
mpg, has cost about $5 bn to develop so far.

The US vehicle manufacturers are now well into their third round of downsizing,
with costs larger than ever. General Motors' current five year investment programme for new light weight models is expected to be completed by 1984 at a total
cost of $40 bn, while Ford is planning to spend $18 bn over the same period.
Chrysler's plans envisage the expenditure of $4.9 bn. Whether the companies are
able to maintain these spending levels remains to be seen; the disastrous financial
results of 1980 and 1981 are causing even General Motors to scale back its original
plans.

Part of the investment will go towards buying robots and refurbishing old factories
in an attempt to close the productivity gap between themselves and their highly
efficient Japanese competitors. But the bulk will be spent on prising yet more
weight out of vehicle structures, as well as designing new weight saving engines,
transmissions and suspension components. By 1985, the average weight of a US
car will have to be reduced by at least as much again as has already been shed if
the 27.5 mpg fleet average required by the CAFE standards is to be achieved.
General Motors' models averaged 4,460 lb in 1974 and achieved 12 mpg but the
corporation's average car is now down to 3,570 lb and delivers 23 mpg; by 1985,

173

it is expected to tip the scales at 2,800 lb and offer an average of 31 mpg. Ford anticipates that the average weight of its entire fleet – from subcompacts to large limousines and stationwagons – will have to come down to less than 3,000 lb by 1985 – implying about a further 1,000 lb or so out of its models.

A common feature of the new generation of US cars is that they are front wheel drive. Although the engineering is more complicated and the cost about $50 higher per car, front wheel drive enables the designer to provide more room inside the car and saves weight estimated at an average of 70 lb per car.

New materials will play an important role during the next few years

Between 1980 and 1985 there are likely to be significant changes in the use of materials by the US automotive industry. Currently, the industry accounts for 26 per cent of the country's consumption of iron and steel, 16 per cent of aluminium, 12 per cent of copper, 34 per cent of zinc, 54 per cent of lead and 40 per cent of platinum. It also uses 5 per cent of plastics production – or approximately 1 mn tons per year.

Conventional low carbon steel is gradually being replaced by lighter and stronger materials. The new contenders include special high strength steels, aluminium alloys and recently developed plastics; in 1978, Ford estimated that such materials accounted for about 15 per cent of the weight of one of its new models. A year later they accounted for 19 per cent and, by 1980, the proportion had risen to 23 per cent. Ford estimates that these new materials will constitute some 30 per cent of the weight of its average car and light truck by 1985.

Industry experts believe that high strength steels will account for between 12 and 15 per cent of a typical US car's weight by 1985. Using high strength steel to make suspension parts, body frames, indoor protection beams, bumpers and (even) wheels can lighten them by anything from 10 per cent to 25 per cent.

Aluminium will be used increasingly for components which are not overly stressed – especially castings such as cylinder heads, manifolds, gearbox casings, brake drums and pumps. Aluminium radiators could well replace conventional brass ones. Thus, a typical US car manufactured in 1985 will probably contain about 200 lb of aluminium – twice as much as in 1981. And every 1 lb of aluminium used will save about 1.4 lb in body weight.

In 1980, the average US produced car contained about 200 lb of plastic, while its counterpart in 1985 is likely to incorporate 300 lb of plastic parts – about 10 per cent of the vehicle's total weight. Plastic saves about 1 lb for every 1 lb used, and plastic parts are frequently cheaper and easier to make than comparable ones in steel or zinc. To date, plastics have been used in cars for components such as interior trim, radiator grills and flexible bumpers, but in the future they will also be used in more critical areas of the car where stresses occur. This will involve using aramid fibres and fibre reinforced plastics for load carrying parts such as driveshafts, springs and (possibly) wheels. The use of composite plastics such as carbon fibre – though currently much more expensive at $20 per lb – could save as much as 30 per cent of a car's total weight. In 1977, Ford engineers rebuilt an existing six seater saloon using about 600 lb of carbon fibre material for key parts; the car's weight came down from over 3,700 lb to less than 2,500 lb, and its fuel economy doubled. Meanwhile, quick setting adhesives are taking the place of metal fasteners.

The reduction of air drag also contributes substantially to fuel economy and the industry is accordingly laying great stress on aerodynamic design.

Developments are taking place in the truck sector too

In the commercial vehicle sector, the government and industry joint voluntary truck and bus fuel economy improvement programme has brought together motor carriers, manufacturers, labour, trade associations and the US Department of Transportation in order to achieve substantial fuel savings in the use of trucks and buses. This programme has provided a means for all members of the trucking industry to share information regarding practical ways of conserving fuel. Voluntary participation in the programme resulted in cumulative fuel savings – through the use of fuel efficient options such as variable fan drives, radial tyres, wind deflectors (and other aerodynamic devices) and diesel engines – estimated to be in excess of 1.7 bn gallons between 1973 and 1977; almost half of this was achieved in 1977 alone. And further progress in fuel saving has been made in subsequent years.

Moreover, the heavy truck manufacturers are developing further fuel saving re- finements for use on future vehicles. Onboard electronic systems are expected to become commonplace on trucks as well as cars, possibly combined with automatic transmissions to optimise gear selection for highest fuel economy. Attention to aerodynamic design and the use of light weight materials will continue, as will developments aimed at improving diesel engine efficiency. In the case of medium duty trucks, the trend towards the greater use of diesel engines is expected to grow. Manufacturers are also directing resources towards improving the fuel efficiency of their light trucks. In addition to programmes aimed at reducing weight from the traditional US light truck models (vans and pickups) through weight saving materials and more efficient engines, new US built mini pickups are now available, and others are planned.

COMPUTER APPLICATIONS IN
PRODUCTION METHODS AND NEW PRODUCTS

The vehicle manufacturers are
using advanced technology in their products –

The computer and microprocessor have become not only vital ingredients in new methods of production but also in the new products. The onboard computer became standard equipment on many models produced in 1980. The use of a computer in combination with electronic engine controls – as embodied in General Motors' computer command control system, which was introduced in all of the corporation's 1981 petrol powered cars in the USA to help control exhaust emis- sions and improve fuel economy – will gradually be extended to additional functions. One result will be the wider use of electronic fuel injection for petrol engines. The use of digital instrumentation will increase in the next few years and will provide such information as vehicle speed, fuel economy, and driving range available with fuel remaining in the tank. In some cases, the car's computer will control the shifting of the automatic transmission to improve its efficiency and reduce exhaust emissions. It will continue to be used to control converter clutches on more automatic transmissions, providing a mechanical lockup to eliminate slippage.

To help improve quality and serviceability, the onboard computer will also be used for more extensive end of line testing to verify engine and emission control system operation, and its self diagnostic capabilities will be expanded.

- and their businesses

Throughout the industry, data processing has become an integral part of doing business, from processing orders to maintaining inventories and performing a variety of other financial transactions. Computer assisted design makes it possible for the industry to redraw all the components of the new generation of smaller, more fuel efficient vehicles. A chassis, for example, can be drawn on the screen of a cathode ray computer terminal and linked to mathematical equations sufficiently sophisticated to simulate different operating conditions, and the terminal screen can then demonstrate how the chassis might flex or bend on different road surfaces. Once the design is perfected, computer assisted engineering techniques and computer assisted manufacturing processes aid in the production of the finished vehicle, either through numerical control (which permits an operator to instruct a machine to perform repetitive operations) or programmable controls (which enable an operator to instruct a machine to perform a sequence of operations). Such robots are the automotive industry's machines of the future for efficiency, productivity and quality. Not all robots are computer controlled, but the most sophisticated ones are - some by a large central computer, others by small individual microprocessors, and some by both. There were more than 3,000 robots in place in all US industrial plants in 1980, of which approximately 800 were located at the plants of the domestic motor vehicle manufacturers; worldwide, the motor industry had about 5,000 computer operated machines. In 1980, General Motors had 300 robots in use worldwide, but expects to be using 5,000 by 1985 - and 14,000 by 1990.

Through the use of robots and other innovations, the industry is seeking the ultimate goal of total flexibility in scheduling work, including the ability to shift production on a line quickly from one model to another to meet changing consumer demand.

At the moment robots perform seven major manufacturing functions: welding, painting, parts transfer, machine loading and unloading, die casting, parts assembly, and inspection. General Motors' robot paint spraying system uses photoelectronic detectors to identify different body styles; the robots have the capability to open the doors, trunk (boot) and hood (bonnet) so that paint can be applied to interior surfaces. The system is the most advanced in the world, even including Japanese methods. The wider use of robots will improve working conditions within plants by taking over repetitive, difficult and/or dirty jobs.

FURTHER RECESSION IN 1981

Passenger car sales fall for the third consecutive year

Total sales of passenger cars in the USA fell for the third consecutive year in
1981. At 8,535,175 units, sales in 1981 were 4.9 per cent below 1980's already
depressed total of 8,974,436 units.

As with the previous year, 1981 was disastrous for the domestic industry which
reported its lowest calendar year total in 20 years. Sales of domestic cars fell
to 6,208,760, a level 5.7 per cent below the 1980 total of 6,581,307 - and the
lowest recorded since the 1961 figure of 5,556,102. However, sales of imported
cars remained strong, and enjoyed their third best year; at 2,326,415 units, import sales were only 2.9 per cent below the record of 2,396,012 set in 1980.
Moreover, the market penetration of imported cars reached a new record at
27.3 per cent of total sales, compared with 26.7 per cent in 1980 and 21.9 per
cent in 1979.

The only domestic manufacturer to show rising sales was Chrysler which achieved
a 10.6 per cent sales increase with the assistance of price rebates. It should be
noted, though, that while these rebates contributed to the company's desperately
needed cashflow, they eroded working capital. In contrast, General Motors'
sales declined by 7.8 per cent and Ford's by 6.4 per cent, while Volkswagen and
American Motors were both down by 8.5 per cent.

Sales of North American produced cars were shared by the individual manufacturers
as follows in 1981: General Motors, 61.2 per cent (against 62.6 per cent in 1980);
Ford, 22.3 per cent (22.4 per cent); Chrysler, 11.8 per cent (10 per cent);
American Motors, 2.2 per cent (2.3 per cent); and Volkswagen, 2.6 per cent
(2.7 per cent).

Table 17

Sales of Passenger Cars in the USA by
Domestic Manufacturers (Excluding Captive Imports), 1980-81

Manufacturer	1980	1981	% change 1981/80
General Motors	4,116,482	3,796,696	-7.8
Ford	1,475,232	1,380,600	-6.4
Chrysler	660,017	729,873	10.6
Volkswagen	177,118	162,005	-8.5
American Motors	149,438	136,682	-8.5
Checker	3,020	2,904	-3.8
Total	6,581,307	6,208,760	-5.7

Car production continued to
fall but, even so, inventories increased

In 1981, US domestic passenger car production declined to 6,275,721 units, 2.2
per cent below the (revised) 1980 figure of 6,416,885 - which itself had already
been the lowest production total since the 5,522,004 cars built in 1961. Production

was cut back progressively throughout the year, accompanied by plant closures - some temporary, others likely to prove permanent - in a fruitless effort to prevent an excessive inventory build up.

By January 1, 1982, inventories of the industry as a whole had escalated to 107 new car days supply - compared with 80 a year earlier, and a "normal" level of 45 days supply. The situation deteriorated sharply in December when inventories rose by the equivalent of 24 new car days supply, from 83 to 107. On January 1, 1982, the domestic new car inventory totalled 1,471,053 units.

General Motors had a very poor December with inventories rising from 77 days supply to 107; this compares with 77 at the beginning of 1981. The corporation had particularly heavy stocks of its J car lines, while the newly introduced A body models were also in heavy supply - although the latter had not been on the market long enough to establish solid sales rates. The inventory position at Ford and American Motors also deteriorated sharply during December. Following the general industry pattern, Ford was heaviest in small cars and lightest in the larger sizes. Chrysler's inventory was already exceptionally high at the beginning of December, at 103 days supply, and had risen marginally (to 104) by January 1, 1982. Volkswagen alone reduced its exposure in December, as a result of increased sales; at 83 days supply its inventory nevertheless remained very high. With the exception of American Motors and Volkswagen, inventories of all the domestic manufacturers built up sharply during 1981.

Inventories rose to dangerous levels in all category sizes through 1981 except in the case of standard size, which rose only from 65 to 66 days supply over the year as a whole.

US passenger car production figures, by manufacturer, are contained in Table 18.

Table 18

US Passenger Car Production by Manufacturer, 1980-81

Manufacturer	1980	1981	% change 1981/80
General Motors	4,106,191	3,925,679	-4.4
Ford	1,306,948	1,320,197	1.0
Chrysler	638,555	749,687	17.4
Volkswagen	197,106	167,829	-14.9
American Motors	164,765	109,319	-33.7
Checker	3,340	3,101	-7.2
Total	6,416,885	6,275,812	-2.2

After 1980's severe downturn,
truck sales fell further in 1981 -

After their 28.5 per cent decline in 1980, truck sales in the USA fell by a further 9.3 per cent in 1981 to 2,259,039 units from 2,490,205 in 1980. The 1981 total comprised 1,812,750 North American produced vehicles and 446,289 imports from Japan and Europe. Sales of North American trucks dropped by 189,888 units from the 1980 level (by 9.5 per cent), while the import total declined by

41,278 units (8.5 per cent). The decline in sales of North American built trucks affected all weight classes. The decline in import sales was the result of a 30.3 per cent drop in captive imports; sales of the independent importers rose by 27,518 units to 286,738 in 1981, from 259,220 in 1980 – an increase of 10.6 per cent. Most of the decline in captive import sales occurred during the second half of the year.

Compact pickup sales, however, rallied during the second half of the year to reach a total of 523,619 units, an increase of 3.5 per cent over 1980's total of 506,079. The imports again secured the lion's share of this business and the independent imported compacts – Datsun, Toyota, Mazda and Isuzu – scored significant gains, notwithstanding the higher prices caused by an increase in import duty. Three new domestic models were launched on to the compact pickup market during the year – the Jeep Scrambler, the Chevrolet S-10 and the GMC S-15. The Scrambler was introduced in April 1981, and sold 7,815 units to the end of December. The S-10 and S-15 made their debut in November, and dealers sold 15,473 of the former and 2,314 of the latter before the end of the year. Chevrolet hopes to sell 225,000 S-10s in 1982, while GMC's target for the S-15 is 45,000. These new domestic entries are being followed in 1982 by Chrysler's (Omni/Horizon based) Dodge Rampage – which became available on January 4, 1982 – and Ford's new Ranger, with an introduction date scheduled for March.

Total sales of the heavier truck categories (classes 6, 7 and 8) fell by 41,741 units (15.7 per cent) to 223,729 from 265,470 in 1980; these sectors continued to be plagued by recession and high interest rates. The largest decline (of 19.8 per cent) occurred in class 6 trucks, partly because some class 6 trucks were reclassified into class 7; sales of the latter fell by 12 per cent, while sales of the heaviest (class 8) trucks dropped by 14.4 per cent during the year. For the first nine months of 1981, 97.4 per cent of class 8 trucks built in North America were diesel powered, compared with 63 per cent of class 7 trucks and 32.8 per cent of class 6 trucks; a year earlier only 19.3 per cent of class 6 trucks built in North America were equipped with a diesel engine.

For the fifth consecutive year, Ford retained its sales leadership over Chevrolet. Its dealers retailed 716,849 trucks (including the captive Courier), a decline of 9.8 per cent compared with the previous year's outturn of 794,520 units.

Chevrolet's dealers retailed 675,628 trucks (including the captive LUV), a drop of 10.7 per cent from the 756,491 sold in 1980. Chrysler's sales (including Dodge and the Ram 50 and Arrow captives) fell to 186,621 units, a decrease of 25.3 per cent from the 1980 total of 249,766. GMC's dealers sold 171,551 units in 1981, compared with 183,835 in 1980, a decline of 6.7 per cent. Meanwhile, Jeep's sales fell to 63,275 from 77,852 in 1980 – or by 18.7 per cent. But, bucking the general trend, sales of Volkswagen's Rabbit pickup increased to 33,879 in 1981 from 25,532 in 1980, a rise of 32.7 per cent.

– but production showed an increase on 1980's catastrophic level

US truck production rose to 1,670,488 in 1981 from the revised figure of 1,593,489 in 1980 – an increase of 4.8 per cent – thanks in the main to an almost 30 per cent reduction of inventories during 1980. Ford increased its lead over Chevrolet by registering a 6.2 per cent increase in production against Chevrolet's 4 per cent. The largest output increases in percentage terms were recorded by Jeep (46.8 per cent) and Volkswagen (31.7 per cent). But substantial production declines were suffered by AM General (estimated at 55.9 per cent) and Dodge (17.4 per cent). And International's production scarcely budged from its strike depressed 1980 level.

Table 19 provides details of truck (and van) production by make in 1981 compared with 1980.

Table 19

US Production of Trucks (Including Vans) by Make

Make	1980[a]	1981	% change 1981/80
Ford	581,507	617,375	6.2
Chevrolet	492,209	511,954	4.0
GMC	173,702	175,209	0.9
Dodge	118,959	98,240	-17.4
International	66,210	66,707	0.8
Jeep	62,841	92,248	46.8
Volkswagen	28,390	37,379	31.7
Mack	23,387	...	...
AM General	8,201	3,616[b]	-55.9[b]
Others[c]	38,083	67,760[b]	d
Total	1,593,489	1,670,488	4.8

a Revised.   b Estimated.   c Mainly Kenworth, Peterbilt and Freightliner; in 1981 also includes Mack.
d Not comparable.

Long term debt. From 1976 to 1979 long term debt was reduced from $1,044 mn to $880 mn, but in 1980 the total was increased to $1,886 mn - and further increases have been made in 1981. At the end of 1979, long term debt of the parent company accounted for 76.2 per cent of group debt and 90.8 per cent of all debt was denominated in dollars. However, in 1980 the greater part of the new debt (60.6 per cent) was raised through subsidiaries, with the result that the parent company's share of total debt was reduced to 56.6 per cent, and the dollar content of the debt fell to 73.4 per cent.

Unless retained earnings exceed capital expenditure over the next two to three years the corporation will face a refinancing problem in 1985 when $681.2 mn is repayable.

The weighted average rate of interest payable on long term debt as at December 31, 1980, was 13.5 per cent, compared with 9.1 per cent a year previously.

Current liabilities. Current liabilities rose by $2,589.7 mn in 1980 - from $9,683.3 mn to $12,273 mn. In particular, short term debt rose by $752.4 mn, while the increase in accrued liabilities of $1,065.9 mn included a rise in liabilities to dealers and customers of $750.2 mn. Current liabilities rose further in 1981, and loans payable are now at more than twice the level prevailing at the end of 1979.

CONSOLIDATED SALES

A steep fall in 1980 -

Reflecting both increasing unit sales of cars and trucks and higher prices, consolidated net sales rose during the period 1976-78. Despite a downturn in deliveries in 1979 net sales increased to record levels thanks to higher prices. However, in 1980 higher prices were inadequate to offset the 21 per cent fall in unit sales, and net sales revenue fell by 12.9 per cent. In the first nine months of 1981 unit sales were 1.6 per cent down on the equivalent period of 1980 - but revenue, due to higher prices per unit, was 13.5 per cent up.

- due to lower sales of automotive products

Consolidated sales may be divided into two major segments - automotive products and non-automotive products. Automotive products consist of passenger cars, trucks, buses and their major subassemblies, as well as parts and accessories, while non-automotive products consist broadly of two separate categories - diesel engines, locomotives and related products, and defence and space products. Automotive products dominate the corporation's revenue, and averaged 93.5 per cent of consolidated net sales in the period 1975-79. However, the fall of revenue in 1980 was entirely due to automotive products and, as a result, their share fell to 92.1 per cent in that year. Diesel engines, locomotives and related products probably account for around 85 per cent of revenue in the non-automotive products sector.

Table 26

General Motors Corporation: Long Term Debt, 1976-81
($ mn)

| | As at Dec 31 | | | | | |
	1976	1977	1978	1979	1980	1981ᵃ
General Motors						
10% 1984-86	-	-	-	-	200.0	...
8.05% 1985	300.0	300.0	300.0	300.0	300.0	...
12.2% 1986-88	-	-	-	-	200.0	...
8 5/8% 2005	300.0	300.0	300.0	300.0	300.0	...
Others	111.4	108.9	77.7	75.0	72.3	...
	711.4	708.9	677.7	675.0	1,072.3	...
Consolidated subsidiaries						
$ 16.4% 1982-89	254.0	256.0	231.9	128.5	318.0	...
£ 7.0% 1987-92	50.2	59.5	30.6	33.2	35.8	...
A$ 12.7% 1982-89	-	34.2	34.5	24.9	69.9	...
Ptas 16.1% 1982-88	-	-	-	-	38.5	...
C$ 18.3% 1985	-	-	-	-	284.4	...
Others	35.2	16.7	10.0	23.8	74.3	...
	339.4	366.4	307.0	210.4	820.9	...
Total of above	1,050.8	1,075.3	984.7	885.4	1,893.2	2,419.7
Less unamortised discount	6.8	7.1	5.8	5.4	7.2	
	1,044.0	1,068.2	978.9	880.0	1,886.0	2,419.7

a As at Sep 30.

Table 27

General Motors Corporation: Current Liabilities, 1976–81
($ mn)

	As at Dec 31					
	1976	1977	1978	1979	1980	1981[a]
Loans payable }	3,067.4	793.3	1,115.2	924.1	1,676.5	2,002.1
Accounts payable }		2,925.8	3,497.2	3,381.3	3,967.7	3,981.0
Accrued liabilities	4,848.6	4,607.8	5,438.2	5,562.9	6,628.8	6,885.9
	7,916.0	8,326.9	10,050.6	9,868.3	12,273.0	12,869.0

a As at Sep 30.

Table 28

General Motors Corporation: Consolidated Factory Sales, 1976–81
('000 units)

	Year ended Dec 31					
	1976	1977	1978	1979	1980	1981[a]
Cars	6,718	7,091	7,273	7,001	5,780 }	5,137
Trucks	1,850	1,977	2,209	1,992	1,321 }	
	8,568	9,068	9,482	8,993	7,101	5,137
Net sales ($ mn)	47,181.0	54,961.3	63,222.1	66,311.2	57,728.5	47,149.2

a Jan–Sep.

Table 29

General Motors Corporation: Consolidated Sales by Industry Segment, 1976–81
($ mn)

	Year ended Dec 31					
	1976	1977	1978	1979	1980	1981[a]
Automotive products	44,106.3	51,429.5	58,985.5	62,006.6	53,173.0	47,149.2
Non-automotive products	3,074.7	3,531.8	4,235.6	4,304.6	4,555.5	
	47,181.0	54,961.3	63,221.1	66,311.2	57,728.5	47,149.2

a Jan–Sep.

Table 30

General Motors Corporation: Consolidated Sales by Area, 1976–81
($ mn)

	Year ended Dec 31					
	1976	1977	1978	1979	1980	1981[a]
USA		43,514.3	49,048.8	49,559.9	41,637.4	
Canada		3,149.8	3,362.9	4,611.8	4,218.0	
Europe	47,181.0	5,573.3	7,421.0	8,338.2	7,437.6	47,149.2
Latin America		1,440.2	1,784.5	2,023.8	2,448.4	
Others		1,283.7	1,603.9	1,777.5	1,987.1	
	47,181.0	54,961.3	63,221.1	66,311.2	57,728.5	47,149.2

a Jan–Sep.

<u>Sales are heavily concentrated in the USA</u>

Although General Motors claimed 21 per cent of worldwide vehicle registrations in 1980 - and notwithstanding the corporation's significant subsidiaries in Canada, Europe, Latin America and Australia - sales are heavily concentrated in the USA; over the period 1977-80 General Motors' home base accounted for 77 per cent of consolidated sales. However, the group's declining US market share (46 per cent of vehicle registrations in 1978, and 44 per cent in 1980), coupled with falling demand, resulted in revenue in the USA falling to 72.8 per cent of the total in 1980.

Exports by General Motors from North America are limited (3.8 per cent of North American output in 1980) and foreign sales are achieved mainly through the overseas manufacturing companies and their international dealer networks.

CONSOLIDATED PROFIT AND LOSS ACCOUNT

<u>1980 saw the corporation's first loss since 1921</u>

Having shown a gently rising trend in earnings from 1976 to 1978 at a not altogether unacceptable level (profits before tax averaged 10.7 per cent of net sales), General Motors' earnings fell back in 1979 (when profits before tax were 7.3 per cent of net sales) and in 1980 the corporation recorded its first loss since 1921. While the first half of 1981 was profitable, there was a net loss of $468 mn in the third quarter, which reduced earnings for the first nine months of 1981 to $0.76 per share. Dividends for the first nine months of 1981 (totalling $1.80 per share) are thus - as in 1980 - uncovered by earnings.

Table 32 shows the consolidated profit and loss account on the basis of per unit sold.

<u>A rapid rise in the price per unit during 1981 -</u>

The compound annual growth rate in revenue per unit sold from 1976 to 1980 was 10.2 per cent compared with 9.7 per cent for the US consumer price index over the same period. Although such a comparison is undoubtedly superficial and does not take into account, for example, product improvements which justify a higher price, there is also no account taken of the sales trend towards smaller and lower priced cars - nor, indeed, of the fact that trucks and coaches accounted for only 18.6 per cent of unit sales in 1980 compared with an average of 22.2 per cent in the previous four years. Certainly the comparison would indicate that by 1980, irrespective of the ready availability of cheap imports, General Motors' prices had run ahead of the level which the market was likely to bear. Moreover, the trend towards higher prices continued in 1981; over the first nine months the average price per unit was no less than 15.4 per cent higher than in the comparable period of 1980.

Table 31

General Motors Corporation: Consolidated Profit and Loss Account, 1976–81

	Year ended Dec 31					
	1976	1977	1978	1979	1980	1981[a]
	('000 units)					
Cars	6,718	7,091	7,273	7,001	5,780	5,137
Trucks & coaches	1,850	1,977	2,209	1,992	1,321	5,137
	8,568	9,068	9,482	8,993	7,101	5,137
	($ mn)					
Net sales	47,181.0	54,961.3	63,221.1	66,311.2	57,728.5	47,149.2
Other income	555.9	349.8	214.5	560.3	348.7	269.9
	47,736.9	55,311.1	63,435.6	66,871.5	58,077.2	47,419.1
Less:						
cost of sales	38,031.4	44,441.1	51,275.7	55,848.7	52,099.8	41,404.4
selling, general & administration	1,759.7	1,997.3	2,255.8	2,475.5	2,636.7	2,039.7
depreciation & amortisation	2,236.2	2,380.4	3,036.3	3,187.3	4,177.7	3,368.0
bonus provision	139.7	161.0	168.4	133.8	–	–
interest paid	284.0	281.7	355.9	368.4	531.9	608.9
	5,285.9	6,049.6	6,343.5	4,857.8	(1,368.9)	(1.9)
Less taxation	2,567.8	2,934.2	3,088.5	2,183.4	(385.3)	(8.0)
	2,718.1	3,115.4	3,255.0	2,674.4	(983.6)	6.1
Equity income of non-consolidated subsidiaries & affiliates	184.7	222.1	253.0	218.3	221.1	230.6
	2,902.8	3,337.5	3,508.0	2,892.7	(762.5)	236.7
	($ per share)					
Earnings[b]	10.08	11.62	12.24	10.04	(2.65)	0.76
Dividend	5.55	6.80	6.00	5.30	2.95	1.80

a Jan–Sep.   b Based on the average number of shares outstanding – and calculated on the above earnings after deduction of dividends on preferred stocks: $12.9 mn in each full year, and $9.7 mn in the latest nine months.

Table 32

General Motors Corporation: Consolidated Profit and Loss Account Per Unit Sold, 1976-81

	Year ended Dec 31					
	1976	1977	1978	1979	1980	1981[a]
	('000 units)					
Cars	6,718	7,091	7,273	7,001	5,780 }	5,137
Trucks & coaches	1,850	1,977	2,209	1,992	1,321 }	
	8,568	9,068	9,482	8,993	7,101	5,137
	($ per unit sold)					
Net sales	5,506.7	6,061.0	6,667.5	7,373.7	8,129.6	9,178.4
Other income	64.9	38.6	22.6	62.3	49.1	52.5
	5,571.5	6,099.6	6,690.1	7,436.0	8,178.7	9,230.9
Less:						
cost of sales	4,438.8	4,900.9	5,407.7	6,210.2	7,337.0	8,060.0
selling, general & administration	205.4	220.2	237.9	275.3	371.3	397.1
depreciation & amortisation	261.0	262.5	320.2	354.4	588.3	655.7
bonus provision	16.3	17.7	17.8	14.9	-	-
interest paid	33.1	31.1	37.5	41.0	74.9	118.5
	616.9	667.2	669.0	540.2	(192.8)	(0.4)
Less taxation	299.7	323.6	325.7	242.8	(54.3)	(1.6)
	317.2	343.6	343.3	297.4	(138.5)	1.2
Equity income of non-consolidated subsidiaries & affiliates	21.6	24.5	26.7	24.3	31.1	44.9
	338.8	368.1	370.0	321.7	(107.4)	46.1

a Jan-Sep.

- in an attempt to improve margins

While net sales per unit sold rose by a compound annual growth rate of 10.2 per cent from 1976 to 1980, the cost of sales rose by 13.4 per cent per year. Thus, gross margins fell from 19.4 per cent to 9.8 per cent. In the first nine months of 1981 costs per unit sold increased by 9.9 per cent on the average for 1980 but, with revenue 12.9 per cent higher, margins have improved to 12.2 per cent.

Payroll costs of US hourly paid employees accounted for 18.8 per cent of the cost of sales in 1980, and the corporation has drawn attention to the fact that the total cost of an hour worked, including benefits, has risen from $11.20 per hour in 1976 to $18.45 per hour in 1980 - and to $19.55 per hour in the first nine months of 1981. On a compound basis the rate of growth from 1976 to 1980 was 13.3 per cent, almost exactly in line with the rate of increase in all costs per unit sold. However, it should be noted that in 1980 hourly costs rose by 21 per cent, from $15.25 per hour to $18.45 per hour, at a time when unit sales were showing a substantial decline. The increase in the first nine months of 1981, compared with the same period of 1980, was a more modest 8.6 per cent.

Selling, general and administration. Although selling, general and administrative costs are small in relation to the total activity of the corporation (4.6 per cent of net sales in 1980), they rose per vehicle sold by a rather worrying 16 per cent per year from 1976 to 1980. Had this been contained to the rate of increase in prices (10.2 per cent), $486 mn would have been saved from the 1980 loss of $762.5 mn.

Depreciation and amortisation. Continued increases in depreciation and amortisation costs reflect the capital expenditure programme of recent years.

Interest paid. Interest paid rose by 44.4 per cent in 1980, and the indications are that 1981 will be more than 50 per cent higher than 1980's outturn. Although of limited significance within the context of the whole group, interest paid in the first nine months of 1981 was nevertheless the equivalent of $118.5 per unit sold.

Equity income of non-consolidated subsidiaries and affiliates. This represents mainly the earnings of the wholly owned subsidiary, General Motors Acceptance Corporation, which increased gross revenue from $1,922.2 mn in 1976 to $4,566.8 mn in 1980; however, mainly because of higher interest rates, net income has shown little change over the past three years. In 1980, 88.4 per cent of GMAC's gross revenue was derived from financing activities (mainly retail and lease financing) and approximately 86 per cent was obtained in the USA.

Table 33

General Motors Corporation: Gross Profits, 1976–81
($ mn)

	Year ended Dec 31					
	1976	1977	1978	1979	1980	1981[a]
Net sales	47,181.0	54,961.3	63,221.1	66,311.2	57,728.5	47,149.2
Less cost of sales	38,031.4	44,441.4	51,275.7	55,848.7	52,099.8	41,404.4
	9,149.6	10,519.9	11,945.4	10,462.5	5,628.7	5,744.8
Gross margin (%)	19.4	19.1	18.9	15.8	9.8	12.2

a Jan–Sep.

Table 34

General Motors Corporation: Equity
Income of Non-Consolidated Subsidiaries and Affiliates, 1976–81
($ mn)

	Year ended Dec 31					
	1976	1977	1978	1979	1980	1981[a]
General Motors Acceptance Corporation	161.2	205.4	229.6	224.1	231.0	230.6
Other subsidiaries & affiliates	23.5	16.7	23.4	(5.8)	(9.9)	
	184.7	222.1	253.0	218.3	221.1	230.6

a Jan–Sep.

Net income by area: despite losses in 1980 –

From 1976 to 1979 inclusive, the USA contributed 84.8 per cent of net income compared with approximately 77 per cent of net sales. But in 1980 the domestic operations recorded a loss of $71.9 mn and, indeed, the only profitable area was Latin America. For General Motors the disaster in 1980 was Europe, where net income of $338.2 mn in 1979 changed to a loss of $559.3 mn; in West Germany Adam Opel recorded a net loss in 1980 of DM410.8 mn (approximately $226 mn) and, in the UK, the loss of Vauxhall Motors was £83.3 mn (about $194 mn).

– dividend payments continued

It has been General Motors' practice to pay quarterly dividends at an underlying rate, and to boost the underlying rate at the half year and year end according to the level of profits. The underlying rate was increased to $0.85 per share from $0.60 per share in the third quarter of 1976, to $1.00 per share in the first quarter of 1978, and to $1.15 per share in the third quarter of 1979. But this was reduced to $0.60 per share in the second quarter of 1980 – at which rate it has been maintained despite losses.

Table 36

General Motors Corporation: Quarterly Dividends, 1976–81
($ per share)

	Year ended Dec 31					
	1976	1977	1978	1979	1980	1981
1 Qtr	0.60	0.85	1.00	1.00	1.15	0.60
2 Qtr	1.10	1.85	1.50	1.65	0.60	0.60
3 Qtr	0.85	0.85	1.00	1.15	0.60	0.60
4 Qtr	3.00	3.25	2.50	1.50	0.60	0.60
	5.55	6.80	6.00	5.30	2.95	2.40

SOURCE AND APPLICATION OF FUNDS

Cashflow has become increasingly
inadequate to finance the capital expenditure programme

Until 1978, the corporation's cashflow (retained earnings plus depreciation and amortisation) more than covered the capital expenditure programme, and in 1979 84.4 per cent was covered. However, the trading loss in 1980 coincided with a 44.1 per cent increase in capital expenditure, with the result that cashflow of $2,541.1 mn covered only 32.7 per cent of capital expenditure of $7,761.5 mn. The balance of $5,220.4 mn was found mainly through current liabilities ($2,404.7 mn), long term debt ($1,006 mn) and a reduction in current assets ($1,135.2 mn).

In the first nine months of 1981, cashflow – at $3,058.3 mn – was higher than that for the whole of 1980, but the rate of capital expenditure has been increased, and the corporation has needed to find finance of $4,141 mn in addition to cashflow. Long term debt provided $533.7 mn and current liabilities $596 mn, but the greater part was supplied through a reduction in current assets. In particular, cash resources were reduced by $3,065.9 mn.

Table 35

General Motors Corporation: Net Income by Area, 1976-81
($ mn)

	Year ended Dec 31					
	1976	1977	1978	1979	1980	1981[a]
USA	2,380.3	2,976.2	3,073.2	2,320.5	(71.9)	...
Canada	174.2	116.7	157.5	224.1	(20.3)	...
Europe }		277.3	376.2	338.2	(559.3)	...
Latin America }	348.3	(4.9)	(96.2)	14.5	42.9	...
Others		(19.9)	15.6	13.9	(150.8)	...
	2,902.8	3,345.4	3,526.3	2,911.2	(759.4)	...
Less elimination of inter-area transactions	–	7.9	18.3	18.5	3.1	...
	2,902.8	3,337.5	3,508.0	2,892.7	(762.5)	236.7

a Jan–Sep.

197

Table 37

General Motors Corporation: Source and Application of Funds, 1976-81
($ mn)

	Year ended Dec 31					
	1976	1977	1978	1979	1980	1981[a]
Source						
Cashflow:						
retained earnings	1,299.4	1,379.8	1,782.5	1,359.5	(1,636.6)	(309.7)
depreciation	939.3	974.0	1,180.6	1,236.9	1,458.1 }	3,368.0
amortisation	1,296.9	1,406.4	1,855.7	1,950.4	2,719.6 }	
	3,535.6	3,760.2	4,818.8	4,546.8	2,541.1	3,058.3
Sale of property (net) etc[b]	92.8	24.5	125.5	166.9	235.2	–
Common stock	3.4	1.9	20.5	249.9	271.9	205.6
Long term debt	(153.2)	24.2	(89.3)	(98.9)	1,006.0	533.7
Current liabilities	1,470.5	410.9	1,723.7	(182.3)	2,404.7	596.0
Other liabilities	265.1	399.1	502.6	289.3	319.2	1,303.4
	5,214.2	4,620.8	7,101.8	4,971.7	6,778.1	5,697.0
Application						
Capital expenditure:						
property, plant & equipment	998.9	1,870.9	2,737.8	3,371.8	5,161.5 }	7,199.3
special tools	1,308.4	1,775.8	1,826.7	2,015.0	2,600.0 }	
	2,307.3	3,646.7	4,564.5	5,386.8	7,761.5	7,199.3
Current assets	2,633.1	484.6	2,042.3	(1,443.0)	(1,135.2)	(2,185.4)
Non-consolidated subsidiaries & affiliates	194.9	256.5	327.7	657.9	79.6	471.1
Other assets	78.9	233.0	167.3	370.0	72.2	212.0
	5,214.2	4,620.8	7,101.8	4,971.7	6,778.1	5,697.0

a Jan-Sep.   b Applied to capital expenditure.

198

Since 1978 there has been a marked swing of capital expenditure on property, plant and equipment away from the USA to foreign operations - particularly in Europe. In 1980, the USA accounted for 64 per cent of expenditure on property, plant and equipment, compared with an average from 1976 to 1978 of 85 per cent. However, it should nevertheless be appreciated that capital expenditure in the USA in 1980, at $3.3 bn, was more than four times the level of $0.8 bn in 1976.

Table 38

General Motors Corporation: Capital
Expenditure on Property, Plant and Equipment by Area, 1976-80

	Year ended Dec 31				
	1976	1977	1978	1979	1980
	($ mn)				
	998.9	1,870.9	2,737.8	3,371.8	5,161.5
	(%)				
USA	80	87	86	74	64
Canada	4	6	3	4	8
Elsewhere	16	7	11	22	28
	100	100	100	100	100

Note: A breakdown on the above basis for 1981 to date is not available.

ASSESSMENT OF CURRENT POSITION

An ambitious capital expenditure programme -

To date there has been no statement from the corporation to change the published intention to invest $40 bn worldwide during the five years 1980-84 on product redesign and plant construction and modernisation. Indeed, by the end of 1981's third quarter the amount spent was $15 bn, and the corporation is ahead of schedule. During the three years to the end of 1984 the annual rate needs to be around $8 bn. Assuming that depreciation and amortisation contribute an average annual $5 bn, the corporation must find from retained earnings, long or short term debt, or the reduction of other assets some $2.7 bn per year if the schedule is to be met - and around $3.4 bn per year if the dividend is maintained. On the basis of earnings from 1976 to 1979 this does not seem an unrealistic target, since during that period average annual earnings before dividends on common stock were $3.1 bn. However, there was no expectation that earnings at this rate could be achieved in the last quarter of 1981, nor probably at any time before mid 1983 at the earliest.

Even so, it would not necessarily be correct to assume that the capital expenditure programme and/or the dividend need be trimmed in the near future. If the management was to remain convinced (as it obviously was in early 1981) that the long term prospects of the corporation justified an investment of this scale - and if earnings could cover the dividend up to the end of 1982 - then additional finance would need to be around $3.5 bn. And even though the entire $3.5 bn might be raised in the form of long term debt, the long term debt to shareholders' funds ratio would still be only 0.33:1.

However, the indications are that the long term plans of the management are now subject to considerable revision. Although no statement had been made on cutting the capital expenditure programme, four major plant programmes were cancelled or delayed in 1981. Earlier in the year a major renovation at Baltimore was delayed indefinitely, and a decision on whether to build a replacement plant at Flint, Michigan, was put off for a year; in October, plans for a car assembly plant in Kansas City were cancelled and, in November, a one year delay in setting up an assembly plant in Detroit was announced.

Furthermore, it would appear that the thinking on the corporation's future model range is being questioned. Construction schedules for two plants planned for the 1984 model year have been delayed, and it seems at least possible that the corporation will place heavy reliance on its recent link with Suzuki (a 5 per cent equity stake has been acquired) to supply the US market with small cars.

It would thus appear that the management is giving considerable thought to reducing the planned level of expenditure in 1982. After all, if earnings were able to cover dividends, then depreciation and amortisation would be sufficient to finance a $6 bn programme over a 15 month period. Indeed, the $40 bn target could still be met if in 1983 expenditure rose to a rate of $9.5 bn per year - the rate in the first nine months of 1981.

In the meantime, considerable effort is being directed towards the preparations for the wage negotiations of September 1982, and it seems certain that labour will not be in a position to point at cash resources available to maintain wage rates over what will be a difficult period. On the other hand, management will be able to point to a capital expenditure programme some 50 per cent completed, and perhaps to an improving market. At the same time, if projected profitability cannot justify continued capital outlay, then the corporation will threaten the greater use of foreign suppliers.

On this basis, providing that capital expenditure is limited to the allowance for depreciation and amortisation in 1982, and that future development is financed either through higher profits from an improving US market or through foreign interests, there is no need for the corporation's balance sheet to deteriorate further - nor for a reduction in the current dividend rate.

Ford Motor Company

GROUP STRUCTURE

Important foreign interests

The manufacture, assembly and sale of cars and trucks, and related parts and accessories, constitute the principal business of Ford and its consolidated subsidiaries, and accounted for 89.8 per cent of sales in 1980. Other interests include

Tractor Operations, and the non-automotive products of the Steel Division, the Glass Division and Ford Aerospace.

Operations in the USA are wholly owned. The major foreign subsidiaries are Ford of Germany, Ford of Britain, Ford of Canada and Ford of Spain, in which Ford's capital stock interests on December 31, 1980, were substantially 100 per cent, 100 per cent, approximately 89 per cent and 100 per cent respectively.

Ford's expansion outside the USA has been markedly more successful than for any other US vehicle producer. In 1980, sales outside the USA represented 50.3 per cent of group sales and, for the first time, were more important in revenue terms than those in the USA. In terms of earnings, operations within North America have been loss making since 1979, whereas outside North America operations have been profitable.

CONSOLIDATED BALANCE SHEET

A sharp fall in shareholders' funds

From 1976 to 1980 total assets grew by 54.4 per cent, but - reflecting heavy capital expenditure in 1979 and 1980 - property, plant and equipment increased as a percentage of assets over the period from 35.4 per cent to 41.2 per cent; at the same time, current assets declined from 52.3 per cent to 47.5 per cent. In the first nine months of 1981, although the capital expenditure programme was lower, current assets as a proportion of total assets declined further, to 45.8 per cent.

Due to the trading losses of 1980 and the first nine months of 1981, shareholders' funds have fallen sharply, and on September 30, 1981, supported only 32.6 per cent of assets, compared with 45.1 per cent on December 31, 1976. Since the end of 1976, long term debt has increased by 59.4 per cent and other liabilities (to a large extent, deferred tax) by 139.8 per cent, while current liabilities have exceeded shareholders' funds since 1979.

Assets: the emphasis switches to foreign operations

Since 1978 the relative importance of assets in North America has declined, while those in Europe, Latin America and elsewhere have increased. Whereas North America (i e the USA and Canada) accounted for 61.8 per cent of all assets (before inter company receivables) in 1978, this proportion had fallen to 54 per cent by the end of 1980 - with less than 50 per cent of assets in the USA for the first time.

At the end of 1980 assets in Europe accounted for 29.3 per cent of all assets (before inter company receivables) compared with 25.2 per cent two years previously, and over the same period assets in Latin America have increased from 6.6 per cent to 9.1 per cent of the total.

Table 39

Ford Motor Company: Consolidated Balance Sheet, 1976–81
($ mn)

	As at Dec 31					
	1976	1977	1978	1979	1980	1981[a]
Assets						
Property, plant & equipment	5,579.8	6,207.5	7,418.5	9,227.0	10,025.9	9,979.7
Current assets	8,242.5	10,872.4	12,370.6	11,571.3	11,559.0	10,879.0
Non-consolidated subsidiaries & affiliates	1,385.9	1,598.6	1,721.1	2,041.8	2,142.2	2,300.1
Other assets	559.9	562.8	591.2	684.5	620.5	594.1
	15,768.1	19,241.3	22,101.4	23,524.6	24,347.6	23,752.9
Liabilities						
Stockholders' equity	7,107.0	8,456.9	9,686.3	10,420.7	8,567.5	7,746.6
Long term debt	1,411.4	1,359.7	1,144.5	1,274.6	2,058.8	2,250.1
Current liabilities	5,996.8	7,883.8	9,278.0	9,263.0	11,072.0	10,751.4
Other liabilities	1,252.9	1,540.9	1,992.6	2,566.3	2,649.3	3,004.8
	15,768.1	19,241.3	22,101.4	23,524.6	24,347.6	23,752.9

a As at Sep 30.

Table 40

Ford Motor Company: Consolidated Assets by Area, 1976-81
($ mn)

	As at Dec 31					
	1976	1977	1978	1979	1980	1981[a]
USA	8,636	10,933	12,907	13,354	12,547)	
Canada	1,653	1,668	1,699	1,730	1,617)	
Europe	4,297	5,409	5,949	7,607	7,691)	
Latin America	1,195	1,376	1,566	1,755	2,374)	23,753
Others	1,227	1,286	1,516	1,722	2,000)	
	17,008	20,672	23,637	26,168	26,229)	
Less inter company receivables	1,240	1,431	1,536	2,643	1,881)	
	15,768	19,241	22,101	23,525	24,348	23,753

a As at Sep 30.

Current assets. From 1976 to 1979 inventories rose consistently, but from the end of 1979 the group has achieved a reduction of 15.4 per cent. Cash and marketable securities reached a peak of $3,799 mn at the end of 1978 but, as a result of the capital expenditure in 1979 and trading losses in 1980 and 1981, the level had fallen by the end of September 1981, to $2,358.2 mn.

Property, plant and equipment. Particular emphasis has been laid on expenditure for special tools; these accounted for 24.2 per cent of property, plant and equipment on September 30, 1981, compared with 18.3 per cent on December 31, 1976.

The extent of the capital expenditure programme as at the end of 1979 can be seen from the fact that construction in progress accounted for 10 per cent of land, buildings and machinery compared with 5.6 per cent three years previously, and 6.9 per cent a year later.

Non-consolidated subsidiaries and affiliates. The major non-consolidated subsidiary is the Ford Motor Credit Company, which derives most of its revenue by providing wholesale and lease financing to, and purchasing retail instalments from, franchised Ford dealers.

On November 1, 1979, shares in Ford Industries Co Ltd (Japan) - a wholly owned consolidated subsidiary of the Ford Motor Company - were exchanged for shares in Toyo Kogyo Co Ltd. The exchange in shares provided the Ford Motor Company with a 25 per cent equity interest in Toyo Kogyo, which is included with "others" in Table 43.

Table 41

Ford Motor Company: Current Assets, 1976-81
($ mn)

	As at Dec 31					
	1976	1977	1978	1979	1980	1981[a]
Inventories	4,356.0	4,914.0	5,647.2	5,891.9	5,129.6	4,984.0
Cash & marketable securities	1,664.3	3,371.5	3,799.0	2,192.6	2,587.2	2,358.2
Receivables	1,702.5	2,013.0	2,105.6	2,723.7	2,998.1	2,580.1
Others	519.7	573.9	818.8	763.1	844.1	956.7
	8,242.5	10,872.4	12,370.6	11,571.3	11,559.0	10,879.0

a As at Sep 30.

Table 42

Ford Motor Company: Property, Plant and Equipment (Net of Depreciation), 1976-81
($ mn)

	As at Dec 31					
	1976	1977	1978	1979	1980	1981[a]
Land, building & machinery	4,305.1	4,549.6	5,326.7	6,344.8	7,049.9 }	7,559.8
Construction in progress	253.0	451.2	493.1	704.0	525.2	
	4,558.1	5,000.8	5,819.8	7,048.8	7,575.1	7,559.8
Special tools	1,021.7	1,206.7	1,598.7	2,178.2	2,450.8	2,419.9
	5,579.8	6,207.5	7,418.5	9,227.0	10,025.9	9,979.7

a As at Sep 30.

Table 43

Ford Motor Company: Non-Consolidated Subsidiaries and Affiliates, 1976–81
($ mn)

| | As at Dec 31 | | | | | |
	1976	1977	1978	1979	1980	1981[a]
Ford Motor Credit Company	1,087.9	1,239.9	1,343.8	1,567.3	1,599.8	2,300.1
Others	298.0	358.7	377.3	474.5	542.4	
	1,385.9	1,598.6	1,721.1	2,041.8	2,142.2	2,300.1

a As at Sep 30.

Table 44

Ford Motor Company: Stockholders' Equity, 1976–81
($ mn)

| | As at Dec 31 | | | | | |
	1976	1977	1978	1979	1980	1981[a]
Capital stock (incl capital surplus)	635.6	675.5	732.6	765.3	768.1	767.3
Retained earnings	6,471.4	7,781.4	8,953.7	9,655.4	7,799.4	6,977.3
	7,107.0	8,456.9	9,686.3	10,420.7	8,567.5	7,744.6

a As at Sep 30.

Liabilities: stockholders' equity suffers

Stockholders' equity. On September 30, 1981, the outstanding capital of the company was 120.6 mn shares, composed of 107.4 mn shares of common stock and 13.2 mn shares of class B stock.

The holders of the common stock are entitled to one vote per share and in aggregate have 60 per cent of the general voting power. Meanwhile, the holders of class B stock are entitled to the number of votes per share which will give them 40 per cent of the general voting power. All shares of common stock and class B stock are entitled equally to the assets upon liquidation and to dividends, except that any dividends in the form of stock are payable in shares of common stock to holders of that class and in class B stock to holders of that class.

Although there is no quoted market for the class B stock, shares of class B stock may be converted at any time into an equal number of shares of common stock for the purpose of effecting a sale. The common stock is registered in the USA on the Boston, Midwest, New York, Pacific and Philadelphia stock exchanges. It is also listed on the Montreal and Toronto stock exchanges in Canada, and on certain stock exchanges in the UK and continental Europe.

At the recent price of $17, the common stock was capitalised at $1,826 mn.

Long term debt. Having remained little changed from 1976 to 1979, long term debt was increased by 61.5 per cent in 1980, and by a further 9.3 per cent in the first nine months of 1981. During 1980, the greater part of long term debt raised was in dollars. The group may face a refinancing problem in 1985 when $623 mn of long term debt is repayable.

Table 45

Ford Motor Company: Long Term Debt, 1976-81
($ mn)

	As at Dec 31					
	1976	1977	1978	1979	1980	1981[a]
Denomination						
$	1,118.5	1,110.4	936.0	1,078.4	1,808.9)	
Ptas	165.6	117.8	100.2	83.1)	)	
£	79.3	70.7	56.5	58.1)	) 249.9)	2,250.1
Ffr	23.5	41.6	28.9)	55.0)	)	
Others	24.5	19.2	22.9)		)	
	1,411.4	1,359.7	1,144.5	1,274.6	2,058.8	2,250.1

a As at Sep 30.

Current liabilities. Loans payable rose by 74.8 per cent from 1977 to 1979, and by a further 102.1 per cent in 1980 to $2,405.6 mn (compared with long term debt at that time of $2,058.8 mn). In the nine months to the end of September 1981, loans payable were reduced to $2,133 mn.

Table 46

Ford Motor Company: Current Liabilities, 1976-81
($ mn)

	As at Dec 31					
	1976	1977	1978	1979	1980	1981[a]
Loans payable	619.8	681.1	865.6	1,190.4	2,405.6	2,133.0
Accounts payable } Accrued liabilities }	5,377.0	7,202.7	8,412.4	4,886.5 3,186.1	4,955.1 3,711.3	8,618.4
	5,996.8	7,883.8	9,278.0	9,263.0	11,072.0	10,751.4

a As at Sep 30.

Table 47

Ford Motor Company: Consolidated Factory Sales, 1976-81
('000 units)

	Year ended Dec 31					
	1976	1977	1978	1979	1980	1981[a]
Cars	5,304	6,422	6,462	5,810	4,328	3,309
Trucks } Tractors }	118	131	95	134	98	68
	5,422	6,553	6,557	5,944	4,426	3,377
Net sales ($ mn)	28,839.6	37,841.5	42,784.1	43,513.7	37,085.5	29,233.5

a Jan-Sep.

CONSOLIDATED SALES

Rising net sales until 1980 –

Net sales revenue rose in every year up to 1979, despite static unit sales in 1978 and a 9.3 per cent fall in 1979. However, higher prices could not fully offset the 25.5 per cent decline in unit sales in 1980, but over the first three quarters of 1981 unit sales were 3.3 per cent up and net revenue 8.7 per cent up.

– when the automotive interests went sharply into reverse –

The fall in sales from 1978 to 1980 was entirely due to a poorer performance from automotive products. Over the two year period "others" increased their share of the company's revenue from 6.4 per cent to 10.2 per cent.

– notably in the USA

Sales in the USA since 1978 have been a disaster – with revenue falling by 12.2 per cent in 1979 and by a further 25.5 per cent in 1980. Revenue in Canada (particularly) and Europe suffered a setback in 1980, but Latin America and "others" have consistently improved, and increased their share of the company's sales from 10.9 per cent in 1976 to 17.8 per cent in 1980.

CONSOLIDATED PROFIT AND LOSS ACCOUNT

Costs have been racing ahead of revenue –

In 1977 profits before tax had represented 7.5 per cent of net sales, but margins fell to 6.1 per cent in 1978, and pretax losses were recorded in the last two quarters of 1979, throughout 1980, and in two of the first three quarters of 1981 (the second quarter of 1981 was profitable). Throughout the period from 1976 to 1980 the cost of sales rose at higher rate than net sales, and in 1980 was 41.7 per cent higher than in 1976 despite the fact that unit sales were 18.4 per cent lower. However, all costs other than the cost of sales (excluding taxation) rose from 1976 to 1980 by no less than 71.3 per cent. In particular, depreciation and amortisation increased by 92.9 per cent because of the capital expenditure programme, and interest paid rose by 99.7 per cent. In the first nine months of 1981 the cost of sales showed little change, but – with other expenses continuing to rise – the increased revenue was not high enough to avert losses.

In the period 1976-80, the average price per unit sold rose at a compound annual growth rate of 12 per cent, but the cost of sales increased by 14.8 per cent over the same period, with the result that the margin fell from $801.3 to $538.8 per unit sold. If all other costs (excluding taxation) had remained stable from 1976 to 1980 the company would have been profitable just (taking into account "other" income), but in fact they rose from $548.6 to $1,151.2 per unit sold – an increase of 109.8 per cent.

In the first nine months of 1981 net sales per unit sold were 3.3 per cent above the average for 1980, but the cost of sales per unit was virtually unchanged. With the exception of interest, all other costs per unit sold have also been contained.

Table 48

Ford Motor Company: Consolidated Sales by Industry Segment, 1976–81
($ mn)

	Year ended Dec 31					1981[a]
	1976	1977	1978	1979	1980	
Automotive	26,499	35,073	40,040	39,899	33,303 }	29,234
All others	2,341	2,768	2,744	3,615	3,783 }	
	28,840	37,841	42,784	43,514	37,086	29,234

a Jan–Sep.

Table 49

Ford Motor Company: Consolidated Sales by Area, 1976–81
($ mn)

	Year ended Dec 31					1981[a]
	1976	1977	1978	1979	1980	
USA	18,199	24,769	27,799	24,408	18,429 }	
Canada	1,659	1,950	2,030	2,382	1,855 }	
Europe	5,847	7,621	8,433	11,050	10,209 }	29,234
Latin America	1,783	2,104	2,754	3,723	4,521 }	
Others	1,352	1,397	1,768	1,951	2,072 }	
	28,840	37,841	42,784	43,514	37,086	29,234

a Jan–Sep.

Table 50

Ford Motor Company: Consolidated Profit and Loss Account, 1976-81

	Year ended Dec 31					
	1976	1977	1978	1979	1980	1981[a]
	('000 units)					
Cars & commercial vehicles	5,304	6,422	6,462	5,810	4,328	3,309
Tractors	118	131	95	134	98	68
	5,422	6,553	6,557	5,944	4,426	3,377
	($ mn)					
Net sales	28,839.6	37,841.5	42,784.1	43,513.7	37,085.5	29,233.5
Other income	232.6	299.1	456.0	693.0	543.1	483.1
	29,072.2	38,140.6	43,240.1	44,206.7	37,628.6	29,716.6
Less:						
cost of sales	24,494.7	31,930.6	36,806.5	38,448.3	34,700.6	26,480.5
selling, general & administration	1,166.5	1,285.7	1,490.6	1,701.8	1,930.7	1,495.2
depreciation & amortisation	1,020.7	1,116.4	1,313.7	1,604.4	1,969.3	1,576.0
pensions & compensation provisions	570.8	763.2	814.8	842.2	763.2	570.2
interest paid	216.6	192.7	194.8	246.8	432.5	502.1
	1,602.9	2,852.0	2,619.7	1,363.2	(2,167.7)	(907.4)
Less taxation	730.6	1,325.6	1,175.0	330.1	(435.4)	(69.0)
	872.3	1,526.4	1,444.7	1,033.1	(1,732.3)	(838.4)
Equity income in non-consolidated subsidiaries & affiliates	136.3	150.0	159.0	146.2	187.0	119.6
Minorities	(25.5)	(3.6)	(14.8)	(10.0)	2.0	5.0
	983.1	1,672.8	1,588.9	1,169.3	(1,543.3)	(713.8)
	($ per share)					
Earnings [b]	8.36[c]	14.16[c]	13.35	9.75	(12.83)	(5.93)
Dividend	2.24[c]	3.04[c]	3.50	3.90	2.60	0.90

a Jan-Sep.　b Based on the average number of shares outstanding.　c Adjusted to take account of the five for four stock split of May 1977.

Table 51

Ford Motor Company: Consolidated Profit and Loss Account Per Unit Sold, 1976–81

	1976	1977	1978	1979	1980	1981[a]
	Year ended Dec 31					
	('000 units)					
Cars & commercial vehicles	5,304	6,422	6,462	5,810	4,328	3,309
Tractors	118	131	95	134	98	68
	5,422	6,553	6,557	5,944	4,426	3,377
	($ per unit sold)					
Net sales	5,319.0	5,774.7	6,525.0	7,320.6	8,379.0	8,656.6
Other income	42.9	45.6	69.5	116.6	122.7	143.1
	5,361.9	5,820.3	6,594.5	7,437.2	8,501.7	8,799.7
Less:						
cost of sales	4,517.7	4,872.6	5,613.3	6,468.4	7,840.2	7,841.4
selling, general & administration	215.1	196.2	227.3	286.3	436.2	442.8
depreciation & amortisation	188.3	170.4	200.4	269.9	444.9	466.7
pensions & compensation provisions	105.3	116.5	124.3	141.7	172.4	168.8
interest paid	39.9	29.4	29.7	41.6	97.7	148.7
	295.6	435.2	399.5	229.3	(489.7)	(268.7)
Less taxation	134.7	202.3	179.2	55.5	(98.3)	(20.4)
	160.9	232.9	220.3	173.8	(391.3)	(248.3)
Equity income in non-consolidated subsidiaries & affiliates	25.1	22.9	24.3	24.6	42.2	35.4
Minorities	(4.7)	(0.5)	(2.3)	(1.7)	0.5	1.5
	181.3	255.3	242.3	196.7	(348.7)	(211.4)

a Jan–Sep.

211

<u>- and have led to a serious erosion of margins</u>

Reflecting the continuing higher increase in costs than in revenue, gross margins fell from a peak of 15.6 per cent in 1977 to 6.4 per cent in 1980. However, in the first nine months of 1981 there was a recovery to 9.4 per cent.

The average US hourly employees' labour cost per hour worked (including benefits) increased from $12.01 in 1976 to $19.99 in 1980. Nevertheless, total worldwide labour costs - which rose from $10,839 mn in 1976 to $12,417 mn in 1980 - accounted for only 31 per cent of all costs in 1980 compared with 39 per cent in 1976.

The greater part of equity income of non-consolidated subsidiaries and affiliates is provided by the Ford Motor Credit Company.

Net income: foreign operations
<u>help out in 1979, but not in 1980 -</u>

The USA and Canada were loss making in 1979,but net income from foreign operations was more than sufficient to give the company a positive total. Severe losses in the USA in 1980 were the major cause of the downturn in the company's fortunes in that year, but net income from Europe also suffered a serious fall - mainly because Ford of Germany recorded a loss of DM462.8 mn ($255 mn) compared with a profit in 1979 of DM483 mn ($264 mn). Losses in North America continued in 1981.

Table 54

Ford Motor Company: Net Income by Area, 1976-81
($ mn)

| | Year ended Dec 31 | | | | | |
	1976	1977	1978	1979	1980	1981[a]
USA	429	942	809	(199)	(2,018))	
Canada	117	26	10	(9)	(101))	
Europe	305	609	581	1,219	323)	(714)
Latin					)	
America	71	79	93	132	196)	
Others	61	17	96	26	57)	
	983	1,673	1,589	1,169	(1,543)	(714)

a Jan-Sep.

<u>- yet the company has continued to pay a quarterly dividend</u>

The company continued to pay increasing annual dividends up to 1979, and even maintained the peak rate during the first half of 1980 despite continued losses. In the third quarter of 1980 a 70 per cent reduction in the quarterly rate was made, but this lower rate has continued to be paid in 1981.

Current assets. The sale of the European operations reduced the significance of inventories from 63.2 per cent of current assets in 1977 to 55.6 per cent in 1978. From 1978 to 1980, while other current assets declined, inventories remained at a similar level, with the result that at the end of 1980 they accounted for 67 per cent of current assets. In the first nine months of 1981 inventories were reduced by 11.5 per cent, so that at the end of September, 1981, they accounted for 63.7 per cent of current assets. The recent problems have meant that current assets (excluding inventories) have declined from $1,581 mn to $966.8 mn in the past two and three quarter years.

Non-consolidated subsidiaries and affiliates. In 1978 Chrysler disposed of a number of its wholly owned retail sales outlets, and in 1979 Chrysler Realty Corporation was sold. As a result, holdings in non-consolidated subsidiaries have fallen from $932.8 mn at the end of 1976 to $702.3 mn at the end of 1980.

Affiliates increased in 1978 when Volkswagen purchased 67 per cent of the previously wholly owned Chrysler Motors do Brasil, and when 51.3 per cent of Chrysler Fevre Argentina was sold. The balances retained in both these two companies have subsequently been disposed of.

Investments. For its European operations and certain other assets, Chrysler received $230 mn in cash, plus about 15 per cent of the issued share capital of Peugeot SA valued at $323.9 mn.

Table 63

Chrysler Corporation: Investments at Cost, 1976-80
($ mn)

	As at Dec 31				
	1976	1977	1978	1979	1980
Mitsubishi Motors Corporation	28.5	28.5	28.5	28.5	28.5
Peugeot SA	-	-	323.9	323.9	323.9
	28.5	28.5	352.4	352.4	352.4

Liabilities: shareholders' equity
plummets and long term debt rises sharply

Stockholders' equity. As at September 30, 1981, stockholders' equity was represented by the following:

	$ mn
Preferred stock:	
10,000,000 $2.75 cumulative	221.5
342,951 8 1/8% 1981	902.5
73,092,346 shares of $6.25 par value	1,152.5
	2,276.5
Retained earnings	(1,652.3)
	624.2

5 mn warrants were issued with the $2.75 cumulative preferred stock in 1978, and in February, 1981, a further 27,686,000 warrants were issued to the US government and certain other tenders in connection with the debt restructuring programme. All of the warrants are exercisable at $13 per share. The $2.75 cumulative preferred stock is redeemable at a price of $25 per share at any time on or after July 1, 1983.

The 8 1/8 preferred stock, issued at an equivalent price of $2,000 per share, is redeemable at the equivalent of $3,200 per share in ten equal instalments commencing one year after certain government guaranteed loans are paid in full (the last date for payment being December 31,1990) and after all dividend arrears on all outstanding series of preferred stock have been paid; as at February, 1981, the US government was guaranteeing $1.2 bn of long term debt, while dividend payments on the $2.75 preferred stock were suspended in the fourth quarter of 1979.

All of the corporation's stock (including the warrants) is registered on the New York stock exchange, while the common stock is also registered on the Midwest, Pacific Coast and Philadelphia stock exchanges in the USA, and listed elsewhere in Montreal, Toronto, London, Paris, Geneva, Basle, Zürich and Frankfurt. At the recent price of 4\frac{1}{4}$ the common stock, despite its negative value according to the balance sheet, was capitalised at $310.6 mn.

Long term debt. Until 1979, financing problems caused by trading losses and the capital expenditure programme were overcome from sources other than long term debt. But in 1980 the corporation was forced into a drastic restructuring, which was followed by a second restructuring in February, 1981. In essence, the position at the end of 1980 was that the corporation's long term debt -- together with the debt of foreign subsidiaries - stood at $1,657.4 mn, compared with $976.5 mn a year previously. In addition, at the end of 1980 there was further debt totalling $1,309 mn to be restructured in February, 1981.

Under the terms of the February, 1981, restructuring, $685.9 mn was convertible into 8 1/8 per cent preferred shares (the conversions were made in February, 1981, and June, 1981) and - of the balance of $623.1 mn - Chrysler is committed to repaying in direct form only $190 mn, leaving an outstanding $433.1 mn. Of this balance, $21.6 mn is to be credited to operations, and the final $411.5 mn is to be repaid with the 8 1/8 preferred shares - making the redemption value of the 8 1/8 per cent preferred shares $1,097.4 mn ($685.9 mn plus $411.5 mn).

Current liabilities. Short term debt rose sharply in 1979, but was reduced when long term debt was increased in 1980.

Other liabilities. A significant boost to funding was provided by an increase in deferred employee benefits in 1979.

Table 64

Chrysler Corporation: Stockholders' Equity, 1976-81
($ mn)

| | As at Dec 31 | | | | | |
	1976	1977	1978	1979	1980	1981[a]
Preferred stock $2.75	-	-	217.0	218.7	220.3	221.5
8 1/8 % 1981	-	-	-	-	-	902.5
Common stock (incl capital surplus)	1,025.1	1,025.5	1,080.8	1,109.1	1,111.0	1,152.5
Retained earnings	1,790.2	1,899.1	1,628.7	496.3	(1,215.0)	(1,652.3)
	2,815.3	2,924.6	2,926.5	1,824.1	116.3	624.2

a As at Sep 30.

Table 65

Chrysler Corporation: Long Term Debt, 1976–81
($ mn)

	As at Dec 31					
	1976	1977	1978	1979	1980	1981[a]
Convertible	120.0	120.0	105.9	96.0	161.9	
Non-convertible	511.4	493.4	638.3	660.2	334.1	
Revolving credit	175.0	250.7	262.9	40.0	–	
Loans from:						
US government	–	–	–	–	800.0	
State of Michigan	–	–	–	–	150.0	2,251.1
State of Indiana	–	–	–	–	32.0	
State of Delaware	–	–	–	–	5.0	
	806.4	864.1	1,007.1	796.2	1,483.0	
Subsidiaries outside USA	241.3	376.2	181.4	180.5	174.4	
	1,047.7	1,240.3	1,188.5	976.7	1,657.4	2,251.1
Long term debt to be restructured	–	–	–	–	1,309.0	–
	1,047.7	1,240.3	1,188.5	976.7	2,966.4	2,251.1

a As at Sep 30.

Table 66

Chrysler Corporation: Current Liabilities, 1976–81
($ mn)

	As at Dec 31					
	1976	1977	1978	1979	1980	1981ᵃ
Loans payable	241.1	340.7	61.6	876.5	316.7	292.5
Accounts payable	1,856.0	1,975.8	1,726.2	1,547.2	1,921.8	1,689.6
Accrued liabilities	728.8	773.4	698.0	807.9	790.8	741.5
	2,825.9	3,089.9	2,485.8	3,231.6	3,029.3	2,723.6

a As at Sep 30.

Table 67

Chrysler Corporation: Other Liabilities, 1976–80
($ mn)

	As at Dec 31				
	1976	1977	1978	1979	1980
Deferred employee benefits	83.3	91.1	91.0	301.4	353.0
Others	302.2	322.3	289.4	319.3	293.0
	385.5	413.4	380.4	620.7	646.0

CONSOLIDATED SALES

Deconsolidation of European operations has a marked effect

Sales fell sharply in 1978 due to the deconsolidation of the European operations; on a comparable basis the number of units sold declined by 5.1 per cent in that year, while net sales revenue rose by 4.3 per cent. The higher prices per unit sold in 1979 and 1980 could not in any way offset a decline in unit sales of 44.6 per cent over the two year period, and net sales revenue fell by 32.3 per cent - from $13,618.3 mn to $9,225.3 mn. A significant recovery was made in the first nine months of 1981, despite the market conditions; unit sales were 11.4 per cent up on the same period of 1980, and net revenue was 25 per cent higher.

The decline in sales since 1978 is almost entirely due to automotive operations. Non-automotive operations have increased their share of the corporation's net revenue from 5 per cent in 1978 to 7.4 per cent in 1980.

Reflecting the sale of European operations in 1978, sales in the USA accounted for 81.3 per cent of revenue in that year, compared with 63.8 per cent in the previous year. However, since 1978 the disappointing US market resulted in the proportion of revenue generated there declining to 77.5 per cent in 1980.

CONSOLIDATED PROFIT AND LOSS ACCOUNT

Profitability, when achieved, has been inadequate

The corporation recorded losses in 1974 and 1975, but returned to an inadequate level of profitability in 1976. Quarterly losses commenced in the fourth quarter of 1977 (although there were small profits in the second and fourth quarters of 1978, and in the second quarter of 1981). The scale of losses since 1977 is well illustrated by the fact that (as noted previously) the entire retained earnings of the group have been eliminated. Losses in the first three quarters of 1981 were reduced through a mixture of increasing prices and containing the cost of sales.

While the average price per unit sold rose consistently from 1976 to 1980 (at a compound rate of 11 per cent) the cost of sales rose at an annual rate of 14.4 per cent, with the result that by 1980 - bearing in mind the slim profits of 1976 - costs of sales alone were effectively equivalent to the selling price. And to compound the problem, all costs other than costs of sales rose at the remarkable compound rate of 32.9 per cent. In particular, depreciation and amortisation rose by 3.6 times (reflecting the heavy capital expenditure), and interest paid (despite the restructurings of 1980) by 4.7 times. In the first nine months of 1981 the cost of sales per unit sold has been reduced - but, even with increased prices, this has not been sufficient. Interest paid accounted for $271.7 per unit sold in 1980, but has fallen (as a result of the debt restructuring programme) to probably around $250 per unit in the first nine months of 1981.

Table 68

Chrysler Corporation: Consolidated Sales, 1976–81

	Year ended Dec 31					
	1976	1977	1978	1979	1980	1981[a]
	('000 units)					
Passenger cars	2,489	2,375	1,577	1,345	917 ⎫	⎫
Trucks	637	690	635	451	308 ⎬	982 ⎬
Tractors	4	4	–	–	– ⎭	⎭
	3,130	3,069	2,212[b]	1,796	1,225	982
($ mn)						
Net sales	15,537.8	16,708.3	13,618.3[b]	12,001.9	9,225.3	8,077.5

a Jan–Sep. b Excludes 392,010 units sold through European operations and 87,397 through South American operations, since these were deconsolidated in 1978; the value of these sales was $2,722.4 mn.

Table 69

Chrysler Corporation: Consolidated Sales by Industry Segment, 1976–81
($ mn)

	Year ended Dec 31					
	1976	1977	1978	1979	1980	1981[a]
Automotive ⎫	15,537.8	16,101.6	12,938.8	11,289.6	8,540.0 ⎫	8,077.5
Non-automotive ⎭		606.7	679.5	712.3	685.3 ⎭	
	15,537.8	16,708.3	13,618.3	12,001.9	9,225.3	8,077.5

a Jan–Sep.

Table 70

Chrysler Corporation: Consolidated Sales by Area, 1976-81 ($ mn)

| | Year ended Dec 31 | | | | | |
	1976	1977	1978	1979	1980	1981[a]
USA }	11,146.5	10,664.6	11,066.0	9,367.2	7,149.4 }	8,077.5
Canada }		1,282.9	1,156.3	1,150.3	923.5 }	
Europe }	4,391.3 }	3,413.5 }	1,396.0	1,484.4	1,152.4 }	
Others }		1,347.3 }				
	15,537.8	16,708.3	13,618.3	12,001.9	9,225.3	8,077.5

a Jan–Sep.

Table 71

Chrysler Corporation: Consolidated Profit and Loss Account, 1976-81

| | Year ended Dec 31 | | | | | |
| | 1976 | 1977 | 1978 | 1979 | 1980 | 1981[a] |
	('000 units)					
Passenger cars	2,489	2,375	1,577	1,345	917 }	982
Trucks	637	690	635	451	308 }	
Tractors	4	4	-	-	-	
	3,130	3,069	2,212	1,796	1,225	982

(continued)

Table 71 (continued)

Chrysler Corporation: Consolidated Profit and Loss Account, 1976–81

	Year ended Dec 31					
	1976	1977	1978	1979	1980	1981[a]
	($ mn)					
Net sales	15,537.8	16,708.3	13,618.3	12,001.9	9,225.3	8,077.5
Other income	51.2	62.0	37.3	60.0	57.3	–[b]
	15,589.0	16,770.3	13,655.6	12,061.9	9,282.6	8,077.5
Less:						
cost of sales	13,624.8	15,083.1	12,640.1	11,631.5	9,132.5	7,233.9
selling, general & administration	566.2	612.8	572.1	598.5	561.3	446.7
depreciation & amortisation	402.1	388.0	352.2	400.6	567.3	344.2
incentives & pension plans	295.2	302.4	262.3	260.6	302.4	225.9
interest paid	181.0	202.0	166.2	275.4	332.8	209.5[b]
	519.7	182.0	(337.3)	(1,104.7)	(1,613.7)	(382.7)
Less taxation	212.3	93.5	(81.2)	(5.0)	39.5	23.4
	307.4	88.5	(256.1)	(1,099.7)	(1,653.2)	(406.1)
Equity income in non-consolidated subsidiaries & affiliates	20.8	36.3	22.1	2.4	(56.5)	(30.0)
Equity income in deconsolidated operations	–	–	29.4	–	–	–
	328.2	124.8	(204.6)	(1,097.3)	(1,709.7)	(436.1)
	($ per share)					
Earnings[c]	5.45	2.07	(3.54)	(17.18)	(26.00)	(6.60)
Dividends	0.30	0.90	0.85	0.20	–	–

a Jan–Sep. b Interest paid in the nine months to September 30, 1981, includes any credit from "other income". c Based on the average number of common stock shares outstanding, and after dividend and amortisation requirements on cumulative preferred shares as follows: 1978, $12.6 mn; 1979, $29.1 mn; 1980, $29.1 mn; 1981 (first three quarters), $21.7 mn.

Table 72

Chrysler Corporation: Consolidated Profit and Loss Account Per Unit Sold, 1976–81

	Year ended Dec 31					
	1976	1977	1978	1979	1980	1981[a]
	('000 units)					
Passenger cars	2,489	2,375	1,577	1,345	917	982
Trucks	637	690	635	451	308	
Tractors	4	4	-	-	-	-
	3,130	3,069	2,212	1,796	1,225	982
	($ per unit sold)					
Net sales	4,964.1	5,444.2	6,156.5	6,682.6	7,530.8	8,225.5
Other income	16.4	20.2	16.9	33.4	46.8	-
	4,980.5	5,464.4	6,173.4	6,716.0	7,577.6	8,225.5
Less:						
cost of sales	4,353.0	4,914.7	5,714.3	6,476.3	7,455.1	7,366.5
selling, general & administration	180.9	199.7	258.6	333.2	458.2	454.9
depreciation & amortisation	128.5	126.4	159.2	223.1	463.1	350.5
incentives & pension plans	94.3	98.5	118.6	145.1	246.8	230.0
interest paid	57.8	65.8	75.2	153.3	271.7	213.3
	166.0	59.3	(152.5)	(615.0)	(1,317.3)	(389.7)
Less taxation	67.8	30.5	(36.7)	(2.8)	32.3	23.8
	98.2	28.8	(115.8)	(612.3)	(1,349.6)	(413.5)
Equity income in non-consolidated subsidiaries & affiliates	6.7	11.8	10.0	1.3	(46.1)	(30.6)
Equity income in deconsolidated operations	-	-	13.3	-	-	-
	104.9	40.6	(92.5)	(611.0)	(1,395.7)	(444.1)

a Jan–Sep.

Cost of sales. The continued faster rise in costs than in sales meant that gross profits fell in every year from 1976 to 1980 - from 12.3 per cent to 1 per cent. However, there was a significant recovery in the first nine months of 1981, with margins rising to 10.4 per cent.

Despite concessions granted by the unions, the average total hourly labour cost per hour worked by US employees (including their benefits) have risen consistently and substantially, from $11.28 per hour in 1976 to $19.14 per hour in 1980. Nevertheless, total payroll costs of worldwide operations declined from a peak of 24.8 per cent of all costs in 1977 to 21.6 per cent in 1980.

Equity income of non-consolidated subsidiaries and affiliates. Losses in the retail sales outlets were the main reason for the static performance from 1976 to 1979. With no contribution from Chrysler Realty (which had been sold) and even heavier losses by the retail outlets, earnings were reduced to $3.7 mn in 1980, and, after the elimination of the fee paid by Chrysler Corporation under the income maintenance agreement to Chrysler Financial, a deficit of $56.5 mn was recorded.

Net income by area. Losses have been due primarily to activities in the USA - although Canada also has a disappointing record. Outside North America the corporation has remained profitable since 1977.

Dividend payments. Although recording losses, the corporation maintained dividend payments on its common stock until the second quarter of 1979. Dividend payments on the $2.75 cumulative preferred stock became payable from the second quarter of 1978, but the fourth quarter payment of 1979 was omitted and no payments have been made since. Furthermore, under the Loan Guarantee Act of 1979, the corporation may not pay any dividend on its common or preferred stock until loan guarantees issued under the act are no longer outstanding.

SOURCE AND APPLICATION OF FUNDS

An ambitious capital expenditure
programme which could not be maintained

Until the end of 1980, and throughout the trading difficulties from 1978 onwards, Chrysler's capital expenditure programme was maintained. Even in 1977 it had been necessary to increase long term debt, and in 1978 the expenditure was met through the sale of assets and the issue of the $2.75 cumulative preferred stock. In 1979, the trading losses were offset by short term debt, while the capital expenditure needs were met through the reduction of current assets and the sale of non-consolidated subsidiaries (mainly Chrysler Realty). However, in 1980 (when capital expenditure reached a record level) the methods previously used - the sale of assets, the raising of preferred stock, increases in short term debt and a reduction of current assets - were no longer able to meet the corporation's needs. Because of this, the corporation needed to raise some $2 bn in long term debt, and - in the context of a weak profits outlook - was forced into the hands of the government and the debt restructuring programme of 1981.

In the first nine months of 1981 capital expenditure was sharply reduced, and has effectively been met through a reduction in current assets (particularly inventories).

Table 73

Chrysler Corporation: Gross Profits, 1976–81
($ mn)

| | Year ended Dec 31 | | | | | |
	1976	1977	1978	1979	1980	1981[a]
Net sales	15,537.8	16,708.3	13,618.3	12,001.9	9,225.3	8,077.5
Less cost of sales	13,624.8	15,083.1	12,640.1	11,631.5	9,132.5	7,233.9
	1,913.0	1,625.2	978.2	370.4	92.8	843.6
Gross margin (%)	12.3	9.7	7.2	3.1	1.0	10.4

a Jan–Sep.

Table 74

Chrysler Corporation: Equity Income of Non-Consolidated Subsidiaries and Affiliates, 1976–81
($ mn)

| | Year ended Dec 31 | | | | | |
	1976	1977	1978	1979	1980	1981[a]
Chrysler Financial Corporation	32.5	43.0	48.5	57.6	57.0	
Chrysler Realty Corporation	(2.0)	12.6	12.7	7.3	–	
Others	(9.7)	(19.3)	(39.1)	(32.7)	(53.3)	
	20.8	36.3	22.1	32.2	3.7	(30.0)
Less reclassification of certain amounts received by Chrysler Financial	–	–	–	29.8[b]	60.2[b]	
	20.8	36.3	22.1	2.4	(56.5)	(30.0)

a Jan–Sep. b Effectively the fee paid by Chrysler Corporation under the income maintenance agreement.

234

Table 75

Chrysler Corporation: Net Income by Area, 1976-81
($ mn)

	Year ended Dec 31					
	1976	1977	1978	1979	1980	1981[a]
USA)	283.1	174.0	(219.9)	(1,072.3)	(1,573.3))	
Canada)			(38.2)	(81.3)	(161.8))	(436.1)
Elsewhere	45.1	(49.2)	53.5	56.3	25.4)	
	328.2	124.8	(204.6)	(1,097.3)	(1,709.7)	(436.1)

a Jan-Sep.

Table 76

Chrysler Corporation: Quarterly Dividends on Common Stock, 1976-81
($ per share)

	Year ended Dec 31					
	1976	1977	1978	1979	1980	1981
1 Qtr	–	0.15	0.25	0.10	–	–
2 Qtr	–	0.25	0.25	0.10	–	–
3 Qtr	0.15	0.25	0.25	–	–	–
4 Qtr	0.15	0.25	0.10	–	–	–
	0.30	0.90	0.85	0.20	–	–

ASSESSMENT OF CURRENT POSITION

Pressures on profitability and the balance sheet –

Unless Chrysler can report net income of $161.1 mn in the fourth quarter of 1981, thus bringing the net loss for the year to $275 mn, its future lies in the hands of the US government loan board – since a provision under the loan agreement states that the net loss for 1981 must be limited to $275 mn. If this provision is not met the board has the right technically to call in loans totalling $1.2 bn. Since it is more likely that Chrysler will report a net loss (up to perhaps $100 mn) for the fourth quarter of 1981 (before taking account of any tax credits that may have been negotiated under new laws), management will need to persuade the board that a new operating plan will justify a waiver of previous agreements. It is understood that a plan for submission in December, 1981, had been approved by the corporation's directors, in which a profit for 1982 was forecast.

In the first nine months of 1981 Chrysler lost $444 on every unit sold, and it is extremely difficult to see how – in the relatively depressed market expected in 1982 – prices can be increased and/or costs reduced in such a way that the loss can be turned into any meaningful profit. Assuming, however, that the corporation manages to show a small profit for the year, pressures on its balance sheet will continue. The long term plan calls for capital expenditure of $6.5 bn over the period 1981-85, of which $1.1 bn had been undertaken by September 30, 1981. With $5.4 bn to be spent over three and three quarter years, Chrysler would need a

Table 77

Chrysler Corporation: Source and Application of Funds, 1976-81
($ mn)

	Year ended Dec 31					
	1976	1977	1978	1979	1980	1981[a]
Source						
Cashflow:						
retained earnings	310.1	70.5	(270.4)	(1,132.4)	(1,711.3)	(437.3)
tax benefits	94.4	38.4	-	-	-	-
depreciation & amortisation	402.1	388.0	352.2	400.6	567.3	244.2
	806.6	496.9	81.8	(731.8)	(1,144.0)	(193.1)
Common stock	1.6	0.4	55.3	28.3	1.9	41.5
Preferred stock	-	-	217.0	1.7	1.6	903.7
Sale of property etc (net)[b]	49.7	(2.9)	720.8	21.9	96.2	51.4
Long term debt	(5.8)	192.6	(51.8)	(211.8)	1,989.7	(715.3)
Current liabilities	363.6	264.0	(604.1)	745.8	(342.5)	(165.5)
Other liabilities	43.8	27.9	(33.0)	240.3	25.3	94.4
	1,259.5	978.9	386.0	94.4	628.2	17.1
Application						
Capital expenditure	424.1	723.1	670.7	748.5	834.6	210.4
Current assets	761.6	274.5	(591.0)	(441.1)	(259.5)	(199.1)
Non-consolidated subsidiaries & affiliates	86.7	(11.6)	47.4	(231.7)	(28.2)	5.8
Investments	-	-	323.9	-	-	
Other assets	(12.9)	(7.1)	(65.0)	18.7	81.3	17.1
	1,259.5	978.9	386.0	94.4	628.2	17.1

a Jan-Sep. b Applied to capital expenditure.

positive cashflow of around \$1.4 bn per year to meet the programme. Of this, depreciation and amortisation could account for perhaps \$0.6 bn. leaving \$0.8 bn per year to be found.

- point to a sale of assets -

It would seem quite unrealistic to expect earnings at this level for the foreseeable future (even if boosted by tax credits) and, if the capital expenditure programme is to be met, other forms of financing will be necessary. Under the terms of the Loan Guarantee Act of 1979, the corporation still has available \$300 mn which could be borrowed from the government - assuming that the current plan is approved. But it would seem that the sale of assets will become essential. The directors have already stated that the sale of a majority interest in Chrysler Financial Corporation (where assets attributable to shareholders were \$667.9 mn as at the end of 1980) is under consideration; other major assets - besides unutilised facilities in the USA and Chrysler Defense Inc[1] - include the manufacturing subsidiary Chrysler de México, and the investments in Peugeot SA, Mitsubishi Motor Corporation and Sigma Motor Corporation of South Africa.

- and perhaps a close association with another group

Nevertheless, unless substantial profits are forthcoming by mid 1983, even the sale of assets will not be sufficient for the capital expenditure programme to be met. In these circumstances it would seem likely that large sections of the corporation would have to be closed. which could mean that the smaller part remaining would not be sufficient to carry the overhead of a national organisation. If this were to occur it is probable that those parts of the organisation still in business would be effectively absorbed - perhaps by Peugeot, Mitsubishi, General Motors or Ford - or perhaps even by American Motors backed by Renault.

In conclusion. if Chrysler is to remain an independent corporation holding almost 10 per cent of the US car market. it appears essential that the group should achieve at least close to breakeven in 1982. and earn substantial profits from around the middle of 1983. While success should not be ruled out. it does seem that the balance of the odds is against.

American Motors Corporation

GROUP STRUCTURE

A growing French influence

American Motors Corporation is 46.4 per cent owned by Régie Nationale des Usines Renault of France. Under various agreements made, Renault has the right to acquire capital stock in the corporation which could increase its percentage ownership to up to 59 per cent, but Renault has informed American Motors that it has not made plans to increase its ownership to over 49.9 per cent.

---

1 On February 19. 1982. it was announced that Chrysler had reached an agreement to sell Chrysler Defense to General Dynamics for \$348 mn.

The business of American Motors may be divided into three segments: general automotive, special government vehicles and others. The general automotive segment involves the manufacture, assembly and sale of passenger cars, four wheel drive units, utility and recreational vehicles, and their related accessories, and the importation and sale of Renault passenger cars in the USA and Canada. The special government vehicles segment is primarily involved in the assembly and sale of specialised vehicles - including tactical trucks and postal service vehicles - principally to agencies of the USA and foreign governments. The third segment (others) manufactures and sells plastic injection mouldings, and assembles and sells lawn and garden tractors. In 1979/80, general automotive accounted for 81.6 per cent of net sales, special government vehicles for 15.4 per cent, and others for 3 per cent.

The corporation's general automotive business may itself be subdivided into three parts: domestically produced passenger cars, Jeeps and Renault passenger cars. The manufacture of cars is conducted through the corporation's wholly owned operations in the USA and Canada. The Jeep Corporation, whose products are manufactured in the USA only, became a wholly owned subsidiary in 1970. After a number of years of not entirely satisfactory trading in the early 1970s, the corporation decided actively to seek an affiliation with a leading foreign manufacturer, and an agreement was made with Renault in January, 1979. The corporation commenced selling Renault cars in April, 1979, and in October, 1979, acquired the exclusive right to manufacture Renault designed cars in the USA and Canada: production is scheduled to commence in 1982 with a version of the R9.

Special government vehicles activities are conducted through the wholly owned subsidiary AM General Corporation, while "other" activities are also conducted through wholly owned subsidiaries.

American Motors' international business consists primarily of sales of domestically manufactured vehicles as knocked down kits to independent licensees, distributors and local companies in which the corporation has a minority interest.

CONSOLIDATED BALANCE SHEET

Conditioned by Renault's funds and heavy trading losses

The structure of the corporation's balance sheet has shown signs of change since 1978/79. On the one hand it has benefited from the funds provided by Renault and their application to capital expenditure, but on the other hand there have been heavy trading losses as the capital expenditure programme has been implemented. On September 30, 1981, total assets - at $1,100.3 mn - were effectively the same as two years previously ($1,123.5 mn). But, whereas on September 30, 1979, property, plant and equipment accounted for 19.4 per cent of total assets, the proportion had risen by September 30, 1981, to 27.9 per cent.

Overall, stockholders' equity has declined over the past two years (despite contributions from Renault totalling $226.6 mn) due to trading losses; in the nine months to September 1981, it was necessary to increase long term debt significantly.

Table 78

American Motors Corporation: Consolidated Balance Sheet, 1976-81
($ mn)

| | As at Sep 30 | | | | | | |
	1976	1977	1978	1979	1980	1980[a]	1981[b]
Assets							
Property, plant & equipment	271.6	241.3	221.6	217.8	249.4	263.1	306.6
Current assets	597.3	618.0	668.6	793.6	659.9	640.9	666.9
Non-consolidated subsidiaries	94.0	78.2	78.3	85.8	85.6	86.4 }	126.8
Other assets	28.7	19.8	25.6	26.3	38.9	38.6 }	
	991.6	957.3	994.1	1,123.5	1,033.8	1,029.0	1,100.3
Liabilities							
Stockholders' equity	311.4	320.8	357.9	440.8	296.6	434.3	373.4
Long term debt	111.7	86.3	78.9	56.5	121.9	108.8	275.6
Current liabilities	537.6	515.1	516.7	557.8	565.2	434.3	402.2
Other liabilities	30.9	35.1	40.6	68.4	50.1	51.6	49.1
	991.6	957.3	994.1	1,123.5	1,033.8	1,029.0	1,100.3

a As at Dec 31; in 1980 the corporation changed its financial year end to December 31.
b As at Sep 30.

239

Assets: little change in their level during the past two years

Current assets. Since 1976/77 inventories have steadily increased. On September 30, 1981, they accounted for 61.6 per cent of current assets.

Non-consolidated subsidiaries. The major non-consolidated subsidiary is American Motors Realty Corporation. In addition, American Motors owns a number of retail sales outlets, and provides wholesale financing to certain of its dealers through American Motors Financial Corporation (AMFC). In March 1981, Renault purchased new shares in AMFC representing 50 per cent of the company, and granted it a credit line of $17.5 mn. The business of AMFC is to be expanded to include the financing of fleet sales and the making of capital loans to dealers, with the objective of establishing a full service finance company to support American Motors', Jeep's and Renault's sales in the USA and Canada.

Liabilities: help from Renault

Stockholders' equity. As at September 30, 1981, the outstanding capital of the corporation was 56.98 mn shares of capital stock (of which Renault owned 26.43 mn) and 1,607,143 $2.80 cumulative preferred shares (all of which were issued to Renault). With each of the $2.80 cumulative preferred shares there was attached a warrant to subscribe to four shares of capital stock at $7 per share. If Renault decided to exercise these warrants, it would receive a further 6.43 mn shares and – assuming no other additions to the outstanding shares – would own 51.8 per cent of the corporation.

Under the 1979 purchase agreement, Renault has the option to purchase from the corporation (and the corporation the option to sell to Renault) $40 mn 10 per cent convertible subordinated debentures due March 15, 2000, up to December 31, 1982 for $40 mn. The convertible debentures will be convertible into 3,333,333 shares of capital stock at $12 per share. If Renault purchases the convertible debentures, it then has the option to buy within three years $50 mn subordinated debentures for $50 mn.

Under the 1980 purchase agreement, Renault also had an option to require the corporation to sell – and the corporation an option to require Renault to purchase – 2,767,857 shares of the corporation's $2.80 cumulative preferred stock, and a warrant to subscribe to four shares of capital stock for each share of preferred stock so purchased. The purchase price for the preferred stock and warrants is $28 per share of preferred stock, and the warrants may be exercised at $7 per share. In addition, Renault had the option to buy 714,286 additional shares of preferred stock – and warrants to subscribe to four shares of capital stock for each share of preferred stock at $7 per share – for $28 per share.

The 1,607,143 $2.80 cumulative preferred shares now owned by Renault were part of the above options, and were purchased at a cost of $45 mn in the September 1981 quarter. Options over 1,875,000 preferred shares therefore remain. Assuming that there are no issues of capital stock other than to Renault under the terms of the agreements, and that Renault provides finance through the convertible debentures and preferred shares, Renault's share of the increased capital stock would be 59 per cent.

Table 79

American Motors Corporation: Current Assets, 1976–81
($ mn)

	As at Sep 30					1980[a]	1981[b]
	1976	1977	1978	1979	1980		
Inventories	340.2	328.5	340.1	388.6	371.7	403.3	410.9
Cash & marketable securities	91.3	60.2	75.1	100.1	64.7	71.8	36.2
Accounts receivable	159.0	216.9	239.9	258.0	188.4	144.3	214.1
Others	6.8	12.4	13.5	46.9	35.1	21.5	5.7
	597.3	618.0	668.6	793.6	659.9	640.9	666.9

a As at Dec 31; in 1980 the corporation changed its financial year end to December 31.   b As at Sep 30.

Table 80

American Motors Corporation: Non-Consolidated Subsidiaries, 1976–81
($ mn)

	As at Sep 30					1980[a]	1981[b]
	1976	1977	1978	1979	1980		
American Motors Realty Corporation							
Equity	16.6	16.3	15.2	13.8	12.5	12.2	...
Loan	50.4	30.8	29.5	32.1	32.8	34.6	...
	67.0	47.1	44.7	45.9	45.3	46.8	...
Others (equity & loan)	27.0	31.1	33.6	39.9	40.3	39.6	...
	94.0	78.2	78.3	85.8	85.6	86.4	...

a As at Dec 31; in 1980 the corporation changed its financial year end to December 31.   b As at Sep 30.

241

Table 81

American Motors Corporation: Stockholders' Equity, 1976–81
($ mn)

| | As at Sep 30 | | | | | | |
	1976	1977	1978	1979	1980	1980[a]	1981[b]
Preference (incl surplus) subscribed by Renault	–	–	–	–	–	–	44.9
Capital stock (incl surplus)	179.7	180.8	181.2	182.5	183.7	183.7	183.7
Capital stock subscribed by Renault (incl surplus)	–	–	–	–	15.0	181.7[c]	181.7
	179.7	180.8	181.2	182.5	198.7	365.4	410.3
Retained earnings	131.7	140.0	176.7	258.3	97.9	68.9	(36.9)
	311.4	320.8	357.9	440.8	296.6	434.3	373.4

a As at Dec 31; in 1980 the corporation changed its financial year end to December 31.
b As at Sep 30.   c Including $44.7 mn (net) on conversion of 9 per cent convertible note.

Table 82

American Motors Corporation: Current Liabilities, 1976–81
($ mn)

| | As at Sep 30 | | | | | | |
	1976	1977	1978	1979	1980	1980[a]	1981[b]
Short term debt	84.6	83.5	73.8	9.0	130.4	54.4	45.8
Accounts payable	349.9	350.6	301.7	378.8	284.5	241.9	194.1
Others	103.1	81.0	141.2	170.0	150.3	138.0	162.3
	537.6	515.1	516.7	557.8	565.2	434.3	402.2

a As at Dec 31; in 1980 the corporation changed its financial year end to December 31.   b As at Sep 30.

The corporation's shares are registered on the New York and Midwest stock exchanges, and at the recent price of 2\frac{3}{4}$ were capitalised at $156.7 mn.

Current liabilities. From 1975/76 to 1978/79 the corporation's current liabilities showed little change. But within the mix, the position became considerably more favourable in that short term debt had fallen to a mere $9 mn.

In March 1980, the corporation entered into a credit agreement with 13 banks whereby it obtained an unsecured seven year revolving and term credit facility of $150 mn. But a combination of poor trading conditions during the latter part of 1979/80, the need to meet a significant level of accounts payable, plus the demands of the capital expenditure programme, placed the corporation in an extremely difficult position, and it seemed possible at the time that there could be a default on the credit agreement. In these circumstances Renault agreed (in June 1980) to provide a $90 mn line of credit to the corporation, payable on demand on or after October 31, 1980, and the March credit agreement was reduced to $90 mn. Over the three months to December 1980, short term debt was reduced despite continued losses, and further small reductions were made during the first nine months of 1981.

CONSOLIDATED SALES

A source of much disappointment

Unit sales over the past few years have been extremely disappointing, with the low point of 323,000 units reached over the twelve months to September 30, 1981. Within this total, sales of passenger cars have been relatively static (albeit boosted by sales of 33,284 Renault cars), but sales of Jeep vehicles have declined alarmingly. Higher prices ensured that,in revenue terms, 1979 was a record year, but since then revenue has fallen despite still further price increases (although there have been reductions from the higher levels in recent months).

With regard to sales by industry segment, no part of the corporation can claim a record of success.

From 1975/76 until 1978/79 international sales represented 7 per cent of the corporation's revenue, but this proportion increased to 10 per cent in 1979/80, thereby significantly helping to mitigate the problems of a bad year. To a large extent the increase in 1979/80 was due to a contribution of $135.6 mn from AM General (compared with $112 mn in the previous year). In 1979/80 AM General received 32.7 per cent of its revenue from exports, and accounted for approximately 51 per cent of the corporation's exports.

Table 83

American Motors Corporation: Consolidated Sales, 1975/76-81

	Year ended Sep 30					1980ᵃ	1981ᵇ
	1975/76	1976/77	1977/78	1978/79	1979/80		
('000 units)							
Passenger cars }	440	227	214	208	242	58	163
Jeep vehicles }		154	181	207	111	20	82
	440	381	395	415	353	78	245
($ mn)							
	2,315.5	2,236.9	2,585.4	3,117.0	2,684.0	657.9	1,967.8

a Oct-Dec; in 1980 the corporation changed its financial year end to December 31. b Jan-Sep.

Table 84

American Motors Corporation: Consolidated Sales by Industry Segment, 1975/76-81 ($ mn)

	Year ended Sep 30					1980ᵃ	1981ᵇ
	1975/76	1976/77	1977/78	1978/79	1979/80		
General automotive	1,845.5	1,791.6	2,165.2	2,528.9	2,189.6	571.4 }	
Special government vehicles	401.7	377.1	348.3	503.9	414.5	72.6 }	1,967.8
Other operations	68.3	68.2	71.9	84.2	79.9	13.9 }	
	2,315.5	2,236.9	2,585.4	3,117.0	2,684.0	657.9	1,967.8

a Oct-Dec; in 1980 the corporation changed its year end to December 31. b Jan-Sep.

Table 85

American Motors Corporation: Consolidated Sales by Area, 1975/76-81

	Year ended Sep 30					1980[a]	1981[b]
	1975/76	1976/77	1977/78	1978/79	1979/80		
	($ mn)						
	2,315.5	2,236.9	2,585.4	3,117.0	2,684.0	657.9	1,967.8
	(%)						
USA	86	87	87	87	83	83	...
Canada	7	6	6	6	7	9	...
Elsewhere	7	7	7	7	10	8	...
	100	100	100	100	100	100	100

a Oct–Dec; in 1980 the corporation changed its year end to December 31.   b Jan–Sep.

Table 86

American Motors Corporation: Consolidated Profit and Loss Account, 1975/76–81

	Year ended Sep 30						
	1975/76	1976/77	1977/78	1978/79	1979/80	1980[a]	1981[b]
	('000 units)						
Passenger cars	440	227	214	208	242	58	163
Jeep vehicles		154	181	207	111	20	82
	440	381	395	415	353	78	245
	($ mn)						
Net sales	2,315.5	2,236.9	2,585.4	3,117.1	2,684.0	657.9	1,967.8
Other income	17.3	16.1	21.2	26.8	20.7	5.0	17.7[c]
	2,332.8	2,253.0	2,606.6	3,143.9	2,704.7	662.9	1,985.5[c]
Less							
cost of sales	2,028.2	1,921.4	2,198.5	2,648.5	2,454.1	586.1	1,754.3
selling, general & administration	215.0	211.9	241.3	278.7	300.2	75.4	224.4
depreciation & amortisation	63.2	61.2	63.5	58.4	46.1	12.9	38.7
pensions	37.0	35.4	41.5	41.2	41.4	10.4	34.4
interest paid	17.7	17.3	22.3	20.6	22.1	7.4	24.9
	(28.3)	5.8	39.5	96.5	(159.2)	(29.3)	(91.2)[c]
Less taxation	11.9	3.2	16.1	27.1	(4.1)	0.8	0.2
	(40.2)	2.6	23.4	69.4	(155.1)	(30.1)	(91.4)[c]
Equity income of non-consolidated subsidiaries & affiliates	(6.1)	0.5	0.7	(1.3)	(0.6)	1.1	2.0[c]
	(46.3)	3.1	24.1	68.1	(155.7)	(29.0)	(89.4)
	($ per share)						
Earnings[d]	(1.56)	0.10	0.80	2.24	(4.88)	(0.81)	(1.59)
Dividends	–	–	–	0.075	0.15	–	–

a Oct–Dec; in 1980 the corporation changed its financial year end to December 31.   b Jan–Sep.
c Estimated.   d Based on the average shares of capital stock outstanding.

246

Table 87

American Motors Corporation: Consolidated Profit and Loss Account Per Unit Sold, 1975/76-81

	Year ended Sep 30						
	1975/76	1976/77	1977/78	1978/79	1979/80	1980[a]	1981[b]
('000 units)	440	381	395	415	353	78	245
($ per unit sold)							
Net sales	5,263	5,871	6,545	7,511	7,603	8,435	8,032
Other income	39	42	54	65	59	64[c]	72[c]
	5,302	5,913	6,599	7,576	7,662	8,499	8,104[c]
Less							
cost of sales	4,610	5,043	5,568	6,382	6,952	7,514	7,160
other costs	756	855	931	962	1,161	1,361	1,316
	(64)	15	100	232	(451)	(376)	(372)[c]
Less taxation	27	8	41	65	(12)	10	1
	(91)	7	59	167	(439)	(386)	(373)[c]
Equity income of non-consolidated subsidiaries & affiliates	(14)	1	2	(3)	(2)	14	8[c]
	(105)	8	61	164	(441)	(372)	(365)

a Oct-Dec; in 1980 the corporation changed its financial year end to December 31.   b Jan-Sep.
c Estimated.

Table 88

American Motors Corporation: Source and Application of Funds, 1975/76-81

($ mn)

| | Year ended Sep 30 | | | | | | |
	1975/76	1976/77	1977/78	1978/79	1979/80	1980a	1981b
Source							
Cashflow:							
retained earnings	(46.3)	3.1	24.1	65.9	(160.4)	(29.0)	(105.8)c
tax credit	-	5.2	12.6	15.8	-	-	-
depreciation & amortisation	63.2	61.2	63.5	58.4	46.1	12.9	38.7
	16.9	69.5	100.2	140.1	(114.3)	(16.1)	(67.1)
Capital stock:							
Renault	-	-	-	-	15.0	166.7d	44.9
others	0.7	1.1	0.4	1.2	1.2	-	-
Sale of property (net) etce	-	15.7	(2.5)	-	6.6	-	-
Long term debt	(16.6)	(25.4)	(7.4)	(22.4)	65.4	(13.1)d	166.8
Current liabilities	54.5	(17.9)	1.6	41.1	7.4	(130.9)	(32.1)
Other liabilities	(11.0)	(0.4)	5.5	27.8	(18.3)	1.5	(2.5)
	44.5	42.6	97.8	187.8	(37.0)	8.1	110.0
Application							
Capital expenditure	52.4	46.6	41.3	54.6	84.3	26.6	82.2
Current assets	(14.7)	20.7	50.6	125.0	(133.7)	(19.0)	26.0
Non-consolidated sub-sidiaries & affiliates	9.5	(15.8)	0.1	7.5	(0.2)	0.8	} 1.8
Other assets	(2.7)	(8.9)	5.8	0.7	12.6	(0.3)	}
	44.5	42.6	97.8	187.8	(37.0)	8.1	110.0

a Oct-Dec; in 1980 the corporation changed its financial year end to December 31.   b Jan-Sep.
c After transferring $16.3 mn from retained earnings to current liabilities.   d In the three months to December, 1980, Renault converted its $45 mn 9 per cent convertible note to equity.   e Applied to capital expenditure.

248

CONSOLIDATED PROFIT AND LOSS ACCOUNT

Losses have been a characteristic of recent years

Having recorded a loss in 1975/76, the corporation returned to profitability over the next three years - and, indeed, for 1978/79 reported its highest net income ever. However, even then profits before tax (at $96.5 mn) represented only 3.1 per cent of net sales of $3,117.1 mn. The corporation returned to losses in the June quarter of 1979/80, and has not been profitable since.

The main reason for the losses in the year to September, 1980, was that the corporation was unable to increase the price per unit sold in line with the higher costs incurred; the price per unit moved up by 1.2 per cent over the previous year, while total costs increased by 11.5 per cent. In the last quarter of 1980 the price per unit sold rose by 10.9 per cent over the previous year and costs by 9.4 per cent - thus, losses were reduced.

In the nine months to September 1981, the corporation was forced in the poor market to reduce the price per unit sold by almost 5 per cent. However, costs fell by approximately the same amount - with the result that the loss per unit sold was little changed.

SOURCE AND APPLICATION OF FUNDS

Despite problems, capital expenditure is maintained

Over the four years to September 30, 1979, capital expenditure was more than financed by depreciation and amortisation, and the corporation was able to allocate the balance of retained earnings to current assets. The negative cashflow of 1979/80 was financed through a reduction in current assets, while the record capital expenditure was met mainly through the $45 mn convertible loan from Renault and the new equity from Renault of $15 mn. In the three months to December 31, 1980, new equity from Renault was effectively applied to reducing current liabilities and offsetting the negative cashflow, but capital expenditure was maintained at close to the previous rate mainly through further reduction of current assets. In the nine months to September 1981, the continued trading losses have not prevented capital expenditure proceeding at a continued rate - financed through long term debt and preferred shares issued to Renault.

ASSESSMENT OF CURRENT POSITION

New models are coming -

The management has stated that the centrepiece of the corporation's product plans is a new generation of front wheel drive, fuel efficient, Renault designed passenger cars which will be built in the USA by American Motors for introduction at the beginning of the 1983 model year. The second major plank of the corporation's product plans is a new generation of more fuel efficient Jeep vehicles, also to be introduced in the 1983 model year.

Planned capital expenditure is $800 mn over the four year period ending September, 1984. In the year ended September 1981, $108.8 mn was spent, and the plan calls for $300 mn to be spent in the year to September 1982, and $250 mn in the year to September 1983. The financing for the capital expenditure programme has been planned as follows:

	$ mn
Cashflow	210
Renault	
under the 1979 agreement	140
under the 1980 agreement	200
	550
Borrowings	250
	800

– but financing the capital expenditure programme looks like being a strain

It is clear, though, that the financing of the programme is becoming difficult due to the corporation's trading losses. Since September 1980, Renault has contributed $167.5 mn in the form of capital and preferred shares, and indications are that at least $150 mn of long term debt (either through Renault or borrowings) has been taken up. However, of the total of $317.5 mn or so raised, only $108.8 mn has been used for capital expenditure and the balance has been applied mainly to the reduction of short term debt and offsetting losses. It would appear that the corporation has some $270 mn of its planned borrowings available, and it seems possible on this basis that the projected expenditure of $300 mn can be achieved in the year to September 1982. However, at that stage no more long term borrowings under the original plan will be available, and the $250 mn to be spent in the following twelve months period would need to come from the corporation's cashflow or current liabilities. After deducting depreciation and amortisation, the corporation would need to provide from retained earnings and short term liabilities the sum of $180 mn. Bearing in mind that the corporation's record annual earnings are $68.1 mn, and that in the nine months to September 1981 the loss per unit was $365, earnings at a high enough level to meet this requirement seem unlikely – even given a strong recovery in the market.

In these circumstances it is possible that Renault will have to move to protect its substantial investment. The current poor trading (the corporation announced a 20 per cent cut in production in the latter part of 1981) will surely encourage action sooner rather than later.

Volkswagen of America Incorporated

GROUP STRUCTURE

Car production began in 1978

Volkswagen of America Incorporated is a wholly owned subsidiary of Volkswagen AG. In April 1978, the Volkswagen Manufacturing Corporation of America commenced car production in the USA and, in July of that year, merged with Volkswagen of America Incorporated which was the distributor in the USA of Volkswagen products manufactured in West Germany. The administrative headquarters of the merged group moved to Warren, Michigan, and the group took the name of Volkswagen of America Incorporated.

CONSOLIDATED BALANCE SHEET

Heavy support from the West German parent

No details of the balance sheet are published, but issued capital as at December 31, 1980, was $142 mn. Bearing in mind that capital investment from 1976 to 1980 totalled in excess of $500 mn and that trading losses were reported for 1978 and 1980, it would seem probable that retained earnings from the distributing activities of the former Volkswagen of America would not have been adequate. It is understood that financing has been effected mainly through loans either from – or guaranteed by – the parent company, and the amount made available by end 1980 would probably have been in excess of $400 mn.

CONSOLIDATED SALES

A steady increase since 1976

Taking into account imported products (which will remain a part of the range for the foreseeable future) the number of vehicles sold, and the revenue generated, have increased every year since 1976.

Table 89

Volkswagen of America Incorporated: Consolidated Sales, 1976–80

Year ended Dec 31				
1976	1977	1978	1979	1980
('000 units)				
230[a]	282[a]	299[b]	337[b]	368[b]
($ mn)[c]				
1,298.6	1,760.3	2,150.3	2,676.6	3,186.4

a Imported products only.   b Imported and US manufactured products.   c Converted to dollars from published DM figures.

CONSOLIDATED PROFIT AND LOSS ACCOUNT

The ink has primarily been red

No figures are published. The former Volkswagen of America (that is, the distributing company) was profitable in 1976 and 1977, but the merged group reported a loss in 1978. For 1979 it was reported that "a loss was avoided", but a loss was again reported for 1980.

SOURCE AND APPLICATION OF FUNDS

Source and -

Information is available only on issued capital. It would appear that over the past five years Volkswagen AG has subscribed $97 mn, as laid out in Table 90.

Table 90

Volkswagen of America Incorporated:
Subscriptions to Issued Capital, 1976-80
($ mn)

| | Year ended Dec 31 | | | | |
	1976	1977	1978	1979	1980
Volkswagen Manufacturing	10.5	–	19.5	–	50.0
Volkswagen of America Incorporated[a]	–	17.0	–	–	–
	10.5	17.0	19.5	–	50.0

a The former distributing company.

Note: The above subscriptions total $97 mn. The additional $45 mn of the current total issued capital (of $142 mn) is the issued capital of the former Volkswagen of America prior to 1976.

- application

Information on capital investment is shown in Table 91. The total of $505.4 mn compares with the amount subscribed in the form of equity of $97 mn.

Table 91

Volkswagen of America Incorporated: Capital Investment, 1976-80
($ mn)[a]

| | Year ended Dec 31 | | | | |
	1976	1977	1978	1979	1980
Volkswagen Manufacturing	28.6	142.6			
Volkswagen of America Incorporated[b]	44.9	16.3	115.5	52.4	105.1
	73.5	158.9	115.5	52.4	105.1

a Converted to dollars from published DM figures. b The former distributing company.

ASSESSMENT OF CURRENT POSITION

Expansion plans are delayed

In 1980 it was announced that the company was engaged in equipping a second
assembly plant, by which capacity would increase by some 85 per cent - to around
1,700 vehicles per working day; it is believed that the capital cost of the new plant
will be around $300 mn.   However, this expansion has now been delayed in view of
the difficult market conditions and, while the company's record of achieving higher
unit sales (including imports) up to 1980 would justify confidence, in 1981 production from the existing plant was on a declining trend.   In view of the almost certain
losses of the American company in 1981, the second quarter losses of the Volkswagen group as a whole, the recent resignations of the group chief executive and
the group finance chief, the problems of Triumph-Adler in Europe and group
losses in Brazil, it would have been surprising if finance from Europe for the US
expansion programme was readily forthcoming.   And, it would have been equally
surprising if US banks came forward at this time to finance yet another auto producer.   In these circumstances increased US output was always likely to be delayed,
and Volkswagen of America seems destined to be, at best, a marginal operation -
at least for the next two to three years.

International Harvester Company

GROUP STRUCTURE

A recent restructuring

The company's manufacturing activities are conducted through wholly owned operations
in the USA. plus wholly owned manufacturing and assembly subsidiaries in Canada
and a number of foreign countries.   In the UK the heavy duty truck manufacturer,
Seddon Atkinson, is 100 per cent owned, and elsewhere in Europe the group owns
37.5 per cent of DAF Trucks of the Netherlands, and 35 per cent of Enasa in Spain.

On September 9, 1981, the company announced a new structure through which it
will operate in three groups - manufacturing, truck and equipment (the latter being
the agricultural equipment and construction equipment group).   The company's
27 North American plants are now reporting to the head of the manufacturing group.
The truck and equipment groups are to concentrate on marketing, sales, engineering,
finance and international operations (including international manufacturing).

Based on product lines, as previously published, trucks contributed 45.4 per cent
of the company's sales in the five years to October 31, 1980, agricultural equipment 38.1 per cent, and construction equipment 12.2 per cent.   A fourth product
line, Solar (turbo machinery), contributed 4.3 per cent of sales during the period,
but was sold during 1980/81.

Table 92

International Harvester Company: Consolidated Balance Sheet, 1976–81
($ mn)

| | As at Oct 31 | | | | | |
	1976	1977	1978	1979	1980	1981[a]
Assets						
Property, plant & equipment	710.3	796.3	889.7	1,039.1	1,277.2	1,321.5
Current assets	2,272.8	2,324.2	2,648.7	3,265.8	3,427.4	3,061.7
Non-consolidated subsidiaries	472.2	591.1	675.3	827.1	1,014.3	1,114.9
Other assets	119.5	101.8	102.4	115.5	124.6	147.5
	3,574.8	3,813.4	4,316.1	5,247.5	5,843.5	5,645.6
Liabilities						
Stockholders' equity	1,563.8	1,731.0	1,876.2	2,199.1	1,896.5	1,805.7
Long term debt	922.9	953.1	932.5	948.2	1,327.1	1,098.7
Current liabilities	1,041.6	1,050.7	1,438.9	1,873.3	2,480.2	2,714.5
Other liabilities	46.5	78.6	68.5	226.9	139.7	26.7
	3,574.8	3,813.4	4,316.1	5,247.5	5,843.5	5,645.6

a As at Jul 31.

CONSOLIDATED BALANCE SHEET

A surge in current liabilities

Mainly due to the company's capital expenditure programme and, in part, to increasing inventories - although there was a small reduction in these in 1979/80 - total assets rose by 63.5 per cent from October 31, 1976, to October 31, 1980. However, shareholders' funds, reflecting recent trading losses - and despite additional preference capital - have shown little growth over the period, with the major increase in financing being supplied by current liabilities which were 138.1 per cent higher over the period. On October 31, 1980, current liabilities accounted for 42.4 per cent of all liabilities compared with 29.1 per cent four years previously. In the nine month period to July 31, 1981, capital expenditure has continued, current assets have been reduced (particularly inventories), and current liabilities have risen yet further: on July 31, 1981, current liabilities accounted for 48.1 per cent of all liabilities.

Assets: a steady increase up to 1980/81 -

Current assets. Since 1979 the company has reduced its inventories and, in the opening nine months of 1980/81, managed to increase its cash balance. To a large extent this has been helped by a reduction in accounts receivable.

Table 93

International Harvester Company: Current Assets, 1976-81
($ mn)

| | As at Oct 31 | | | | | |
	1976	1977	1978	1979	1980	1981[a]
Inventories	1,584.4	1,729.5	1,892.9	2,342.9	2,331.7	1,917.4
Cash & cash equivalents	40.0	17.2	27.3	25.2	137.1	510.1
Accounts receivable	603.0	537.7	682.6	796.6	627.1	446.7
Others	45.4	39.8	45.9	101.1	331.5	187.5
	2,272.8	2,324.2	2,648.7	3,265.8	3,427.4	3,061.7

a As at Jul 31.

Non-consolidated subsidiaries. These are mainly sales finance subsidiaries, chiefly International Harvester Credit Corporation (which represented 71.5 per cent of sales finance subsidiaries as at October 31, 1980). On October 31, 1980, the capital stock of the sales finance subsidiaries (including capital in excess of par value) was $299.9 mn compared with $140 mn four years previously - an injection over the period of $159.9 mn.

Table 94

International Harvester Company:
Non-Consolidated Subsidiaries, 1976-81
($ mn)

	As at Oct 31					
	1976	1977	1978	1979	1980	1981[a]
Sales finance	393.2	504.9	583.8	704.9	871.4 ⎞	
Others	79.0	86.2	91.5	122.2	142.9 ⎠	1,114.9
	472.2	591.1	675.3	827.1	1,014.3	1,114.9

a As at Jul 31.

- with trucks the second largest sector

On October 31, 1980, the agricultural equipment division accounted for 30.1 per cent of assets, and trucks for 27.8 per cent. However, over the past three years the greatest growth has been in "financial services" and "general corporate items" which, on October 31, 1980, accounted for 24.5 per cent of assets compared with 17.7 per cent two years previously.

Table 95

International Harvester Company: Assets by Product Group, 1978-80
($ mn)

	As at Oct 31		
	1978	1979	1980
Trucks	1,387	1,778	1,627
Agricultural equipment	1,399	1,565	1,758
Construction equipment	528	664	722
Turbo machinery	240	288	306
Others[a]	762	952	1,430
	4,316	5,247	5,843

a Financial services and general corporate items.

Outside the USA, which accounted for 48.6 per cent of assets as at October 31, 1980, the company's assets are spread thinly over a wide area.

Table 96

International Harvester Company: Assets by Area, 1978-80
($ mn)

| | As at Oct 31 | | |
	1978	1979	1980
USA	2,306	2,805	2,840
Canada	200	269	250
Latin America	39	68	91
Europe, Africa & Middle East	794	889	954
Pacific	215	264	278
Others[a]	762	952	1,430
	4,316	5,247	5,843

a Financial services and general corporate items.

Liabilities: forced into a debt restructuring programme

Stockholders' equity. Stockholders' equity is comprised of 32,317,165 outstanding shares of common stock, and two preferred stocks - 466,667 series A $10 cumulative, and 3,000,000 series C $5.76 cumulative, each convertible into $1\frac{1}{3}$ shares of common stock at $37.50 per share of common stock. The company is required to redeem 33,333 shares at $100 per share annually of the series A preferred stock, and may redeem its series C preferred shares at $55.76 per share in 1981, decreasing annually to $50 per share after 1990. The issued price of the series A preferred stock was $100 per share and of the series C preferred stock $50 per share.

All common stock is registered on the New York and Midwest stock exchanges, while the series C preferred stock is registered on the New York stock exchange.

Assets attributable to common stockholders as at July 31, 1980, were $1,609 mn, equivalent to $49.8 per share, but the recent price of the shares was a mere $8\frac{1}{4}$ - for a capitalisation of only $270 mn. This present low value of the shares reflects the current poor trading conditions, the inability to pay dividends, and the market's scepticism on future prospects.

Long term debt. Since 1976, long term debt - in the form of loans, debentures etc of the company and its subsidiaries - has declined. However, increases in the total of long term debt have been brought about through revolving credit agreements, which accounted for 37.7 per cent of all long term debt on October 31, 1980. The "short term" revolving credit agreements are short term loans, the principal repayments of which the company has deferred.

Current liabilities. In 1978/79 the company increased its short term loans mainly to finance inventories. But trading losses since then, together with the increased capital expenditure, have been financed almost entirely by increased short term debt (together with the short term debt transferred to long term debt). As a result, the amount of debt (on July 31, 1981) at $1,364.6 mn had become unmanageable, and the company was forced into a debt restructuring programme in September 1981. Under this agreement it is envisaged that two year term loans of $1.5 bn are to replace outstanding short term borrowings, at a maximum interest rate of 16 per cent.

Table 97

International Harvester Company: Stockholders' Equity, 1976-81
($ mn)

| | As at Oct 31 | | | | | |
	1976	1977	1978	1979	1980	1981[a]
Preferred stock						
series A $10	50.0	50.0	50.0	50.0	50.0	46.7
series C $5.76	-	-	-	-	150.0	150.0
Common stock (incl capital surplus)	566.1	588.9	614.6	644.3	672.2	684.6
Retained earnings	947.7	1,092.1	1,211.6	1,504.8	1,024.3	924.4
	1,563.8	1,731.0	1,876.2	2,199.1	1,896.5	1,805.7

a As at Jul 31.

Table 98

International Harvester Company: Long Term Debt, 1976-81
($ mn)

| | As at Oct 31 | | | | | |
	1976	1977	1978	1979	1980	1981[a]
Loans, debentures etc	807.0	648.9	614.7	602.2	654.6 ⎱	748.7
Subsidiaries	115.9	154.2	167.8	106.0	172.5 ⎰	
	922.9	803.1	782.5	708.2	827.1	
Revolving credit 1982/85	-	-	-	-	230.0 ⎱	350.0
short term	-	150.0	150.0	240.0	270.0 ⎰	
	922.9	953.1	932.5	948.2	1,327.1	1,098.7

a As At Jul 31.

258

Operating profits outside North America represented 12.3 per cent of net sales in 1978/79 - a sufficient margin to show at least some profit when sales remained largely unchanged in the following year. However, the margin of 9.1 per cent in the USA in 1978/79 was not at all adequate when sales fell by 32.4 per cent, and it was the USA which accounted for all of the company's operating losses in that year.

Table 105

International Harvester Company:
Operating Profits by Area, 1977/78-80/81
($ mn)

	Year ended Oct 31			
	1977/78	1978/79	1979/80	1980/81[a]
USA	430	555	(348)	...
Canada	41	79	49	...
Europe, Africa & Middle East	118	145	3	...
Latin America	3	7	13	...
Pacific area	18	41	21	...
	610	827	(262)	...

a Nov-Jul.

SOURCE AND APPLICATION OF FUNDS

A difficult period since 1979/80

From 1975/76 to 1978/79 cashflow was sufficient to finance capital expenditure and, although current liabilities increased, this was mainly due to accounts payable rather than short term loans. But the negative cashflow of $350.9 mn in 1979/80 coincided with peak capital expenditure of $383.8 mn, and thus the company needed to find $734.7 mn for this alone. A total of $150 mn was raised through new preferred stock and $378.9 mn through increased long term debt (mostly revolving credit), but the majority of new finance was obtained through increasing short term debt by $418.6 mn (the additional funds raised, after meeting the deficit on cashflow and capital expenditure requirements, were needed mainly for working capital). In the nine months to July 31, 1981 - despite revenue from the sale of the Solar group and other assets, and the benefits of inventory reduction - it was necessary to increase still further current liabilities.

Table 106

International Harvester Company: Source and Application of Funds, 1975/76-80/81
($ mn)

| | Year ended Oct 31 | | | | | |
	1975/76	1976/77	1977/78	1978/79	1979/80	1980/81[a]
Source						
Cashflow:						
retained earnings	121.3	142.0	119.5	293.2	(452.8)	(379.6)
discontinued operations	-	2.4	-	-	(27.7)	279.6
depreciation & amortisation	90.1	96.9	110.0	126.8	129.6	111.3
	211.4	241.3	229.5	420.0	(350.9)	11.3
Capital stocks :						
preferred	-	-	-	-	150.0	(3.3)
common	15.6	22.8	25.7	29.8	27.9	12.5
Sale of property (net) etc[b]	8.6	(14.9)	6.8	8.7	16.1	113.2
Long term debt	(15.3)	30.2	(20.6)	15.6	378.9	(228.4)
Current liabilities	(52.2)	9.1	388.2	434.4	606.9	234.3
Other liabilities	12.1	32.0	(10.1)	158.4	(87.2)	(113.0)
	180.2	320.6	619.5	1,066.9	741.7	26.6
Application						
Capital expenditure	168.3	168.0	210.2	284.9	383.8	268.8
Current assets	(35.9)	51.4	324.5	617.1	161.6	(365.7)
Non-consolidated subsidiaries	66.5	118.9	84.2	151.8	187.2	100.6
Other assets	(18.7)	(17.7)	0.6	13.1	9.1	22.9
	180.2	320.6	619.5	1,066.9	741.7	26.6

a Nov-Jul.   b Applied to capital expenditure.

ASSESSMENT OF CURRENT POSITION

An extremely difficult financial position -

There can be no doubt that International Harvester's current financial position is extremely difficult. The balance sheet is weak (long term debt probably already exceeds stockholders' equity), capital expenditure needs to be undertaken, and the company is trading at a loss.

Under the agreement negotiated with the company's bankers, it is planned that $1.5 bn of short term loans are to be converted to two year term loans maturing on December 15, 1983. The maximum interest rate of 16 per cent would be favourable to the company in the short term, but in the event of continued high interest rates the company would issue notes for the difference between interest paid in cash and the higher market for short term funds. These notes would take the form of interest rate deferral notes and subordinated loans with warrants. The warrants will provide rights to purchase common stock at $10 per share up to a maximum of 4.4 mn shares. During the term of the agreement the company would be prevented from paying either common or preferred stock dividends. (Since both preferred stocks are cumulative the company is adding over $20 mn per year to its long term debt.)

- raises a questionmark over the future

Management has emphasised the quality of the company's products, the high market shares obtained, and the cost savings programmes. However, with little indication of a short term recovery in the marketplace, and high front end costs on certain of the moves to reduce costs (such as employee severance pay), there is unlikely to be any clear improvement to the balance sheet in the short term. Indeed, it would seem that in the period to December 1983, assuming a maintained capital expenditure programme, there is little chance that the company will be able to make any significant reduction in the $1.5 bn from trading cashflow. Therefore, it is possible that there will have to be sales of assets (the construction equipment group might be sold if conditions were favourable) and/or further loans - and perhaps another negotiation of the loan structure. Thus, in the longer term, the independent survival of the company in its present form must be questionable.

Mack Trucks Inc.

GROUP STRUCTURE

An important part of Signal Companies Inc

Mack Trucks Inc is 90 per cent owned by the Signal Companies Inc and 10 per cent by Régie Nationale des Usines Renault. Renault also owns subordinated debentures convertible into an additional 10 per cent stock interest in Mack. Over the period from 1976 to 1980, Mack Trucks accounted for 42.1 per cent of the consolidated sales revenue of the Signal Companies Inc.

Mack manufactures and sells its trucks through wholly owned operations in the USA and a separate subsidiary in Canada; the Renault class 6 medium duty truck – for which Mack acts as exclusive distributor in North America and certain Central America and Caribbean countries – was added to the range in 1980. Sales outside North America are usually made through independent distributors. In addition, a number of vehicles in kit form are shipped for assembly in the country of destination, and in some cases Mack holds an equity interest in the company responsible for the assembly operation.

In 1980, the sale of trucks and tractors accounted for approximately 77 per cent of Mack's consolidated net sales, while parts and services represented the balance.

CONSOLIDATED BALANCE SHEET

Assets slipped back in 1980

Details are not published, but total assets rose from $680 mn as at December 31, 1976, to $903 mn in 1979 – only to fall back to $798.9 mn as at December 31, 1980, mainly (it would appear) through a reduction in current assets.

It must be appreciated that the financial policy of a subsidiary company is likely to be determined by group demands, and the increase in recent years of long term debt at the expense of shareholders' funds is not necessarily the pattern which would have emerged if the company had been independent.

Table 107

Mack Trucks Inc: Consolidated Balance Sheet, 1976–80
($ mn)

	As at Dec 31				
	1976	1977	1978	1979	1980
Total assets	680.0	737.7	787.9	903.0	798.9
Shareholders' equity	258.2	358.4	334.8	386.0	361.3
Long term debt	198.4	214.2	271.5	280.8	318.9
Other liabilities	223.4	165.1	181.6	236.2	118.7
	680.0	737.7	787.9	903.0	798.9

Renault paid $50 mn for its shares in May, 1979, valuing Mack Trucks at that date at $500 mn.

CONSOLIDATED SALES

Recession in the US truck market has left its mark

With increasing unit deliveries and higher prices, net sales revenue rose by 78.8 per cent from 1976 to 1979 to a record level of $1,833.8 mn. However, deliveries fell by 26 per cent in 1980 and, despite higher prices, net sales revenue declined by 16 per cent. In the first half of 1981 deliveries were 14.9 per cent lower than in the first half of 1980, and sales revenue fell by 4 per cent.

Table 108

Mack Trucks Inc: Consolidated Sales, 1976-81

Year ended Dec 31					
1976	1977	1978	1979	1980	1981[a]
('000 units)					
25.9	33.1	37.9	38.3	28.4	13.0
($ mn)					
1,025.8	1,331.0	1,640.0	1,833.8	1,536.7	763.5

a Jan-Jun.

In 1980, deliveries to the USA accounted for 74 per cent of net sales, Canada for 10 per cent, and elsewhere for 16 per cent.

CONSOLIDATED PROFIT AND LOSS ACCOUNT

The policy of the parent company affects the outturn

As previously noted, the finances of a subsidiary company are likely to be influenced by parent company considerations, and the earnings of Mack Trucks are affected by its contribution to "general corporate expenses". In 1979, "corporate and net interest expenses" of the Signal Companies Inc, plus group taxation, amounted to $208.5 mn and, with Mack Trucks recording an operating profit of $153.1 mn, its share of "corporate and net interest expenses" was $102.3 mn. In 1980, however, Mack reported an operating loss of $5.1 mn, and its contribution to total "corporate and net interest expenses", plus taxation of $178.7 mn, was only $30.6 mn.

In the first half of 1981 Mack's earnings were $4.9 mn, compared with a loss in the first half of 1980 of $4.9 mn.

Table 109

Mack Trucks Inc: Consolidated Profit and Loss Account, 1976-80

	Year ended Dec 31				
	1976	1977	1978	1979	1980
	('000 units)				
	25.9	33.1	37.9	38.3	28.4
	($ mn)				
Net sales	1,025.8	1,331.0	1,640.0	1,833.8	1,536.7
Less:					
operating costs)	965.3	1,216.7	1,463.2	1,659.6	1,519.2
depreciation)		19.7	19.8	21.1	22.6
general corporate) expenses)					
interest paid)	45.8	67.7	99.9	102.3	30.6
taxation)					
	14.7	26.9	57.1	50.8	(35.7)
Equity in non-consolidated subsidiaries	9.1	10.1	11.7	16.5	17.5
	23.8	37.0	68.8	67.3	(18.2)

"Non-consolidated subsidiaries" cover mainly Mack Financial Corporation, which finances Mack's instalment sales and also provides floor plan financing for the truck inventories of many Mack distributors in the USA and Canada.

Dividend distribution policy has also been influenced by the parent company. In 1978, with earnings amounting to $68.8 mn, dividends paid totalled $92.4 mn. Effectively all earnings were distributed in 1979, and dividends of $6.1 mn were paid in 1980 despite the losses.

SOURCE AND APPLICATION OF FUNDS

Long term debt finances capital expenditure

It has been the policy of the parent company to finance Mack's capital expenditure through long term debt rather than cashflow. In 1980 there was a significant reduction in "other liabilities" matched by a similar reduction in "other assets". It is possible that these changes could have been caused by inter group transactions.

Table 110

Mack Trucks Inc: Source and Application of Funds, 1978-80
($ mn)

| | Year ended Dec 31 | | |
	1978	1979	1980
Source			
Cashflow:			
retained earnings	(23.6)	1.2	(24.7)
depreciation	19.8	21.1	22.6
	(3.8)	22.3	(2.1)
Ordinary shares			
Renault	–	50.0	–
Long term debt	57.3	9.3	38.1
Other liabilities	16.5	54.6	(117.5)
	70.0	136.2	(81.5)
Application			
Capital expenditure	32.7	43.1	29.0
Others	37.3	93.1	(110.5)
	70.0	136.2	(81.5)

ASSESSMENT OF CURRENT POSITION

Several factors inspire confidence in Mack's future

Despite the present difficult market conditions, Mack Trucks is in a relatively strong position. In January 1981, the company closed its Hayward assembly plant (in California) and transferred production to the more modern and efficient plant at Macungie, Pennsylvania. The benefits of this move are apparent from the fact that the company was able to report positive earnings on reduced unit sales in the first half of 1981, compared with losses in 1980.

In addition, Mack must surely benefit progressively from the link up with Renault - not only because of the broadening of the company's range of products, but also because of the funds injected.

Finally, Mack's security and ability to meet capital expenditure is enhanced - for the present at least - by being a member of a group of companies. At the end of 1980 Mack accounted for only 25.5 per cent of Signal's assets, and in the first six months of 1981 for only 29.6 per cent of its sales. Given the group management's belief in the long term prospects, it seems safe to state that Mack Trucks has the strength to overcome short term difficulties.

Paccar Inc.

GROUP STRUCTURE

Heavily involved in the US truck sector

The principal activities of Paccar Inc are located in the USA (85 per cent of 1978-80 consolidated net sales) where the group is organised into unincorporated manufacturing divisions. Outside the USA the group manufactures and sells through wholly owned subsidiary companies in Canada, Australia and the UK (Fodens) and, in the case of Mexico, a 49 per cent owned affiliate. Exports from the USA are principally handled through a wholly owned US subsidiary company.

The group's interests lie in two principal sectors - the manufacture of trucks (under the Kenworth and Peterbilt marques) and related parts, and the manufacture of railroad cars and related equipment. From 1978 to 1980 trucks and related parts accounted for 79.5 per cent of consolidated net sales, railroad cars and related equipment for 11.3 per cent, and others (mainly mining equipment) for 9.2 per cent.

CONSOLIDATED BALANCE SHEET

Strong and healthy

Paccar's balance sheet is strong. Since 1976 assets have risen by 75.3 per cent, and as at September 30, 1981, shareholders' funds supported 70.8 per cent of assets compared with 57.5 per cent as at December 31, 1976. Long term debt on December 31, 1980, at only $17.5 mn, was in fact lower than four years previously when it stood at $23.1 mn.

Table 111

Paccar Inc: Consolidated Balance Sheet, 1976-81
($ mn)

| | As at Dec 31 | | | | | |
	1976	1977	1978	1979	1980	1981[a]
Assets						
Property, plant & equipment	76.0	84.2	92.8	126.9	190.9	194.3
Current assets	346.2	400.8	442.9	523.5	471.3	487.6
Non-consolidated subsidiaries & affiliates	46.1	62.0	68.8	85.2	108.8)	147.4
Other assets	4.9	3.5	8.3	6.5	1.6)	
	473.2	550.5	612.8	742.1	772.6	829.3
Liabilities						
Stockholders' equity	271.9	328.8	393.2	482.9	540.5	587.2
Current liabilities	170.2	192.8	187.5	229.5	196.4	211.8
Long term debt	23.1	19.9	21.4	18.2	17.5)	30.3
Other liabilities	8.0	9.0	10.7	11.5	18.2)	
	473.2	550.5	612.8	742.1	772.6	829.3

a As at Sep 30.

Non-consolidated subsidiaries are mainly finance operations, and the most significant affiliate is Vilpac SA (formerly Kenworth Mexicana SA de CV) which is 49 per cent owned.

Paccar's outstanding capital has remained unchanged since 1976 at 8,244,985 shares. The shares are registered on the over the counter market and, at the recent price of $75½, the group was capitalised at $622.5 mn.

CONSOLIDATED SALES

Impressive growth in the second half of the 1970s -

Group consolidated sales rose impressively from $1,001.4 mn in 1976 to $1,882.7 mn in 1979. They fell back by 11.1 per cent to $1,673.7 mn in 1980, but in the first nine months of 1981 were 3.7 per cent higher than the same period of 1980.

Table 112

Paccar Inc: Consolidated Sales, 1976-81
($ mn)

Year ended Dec 31					
1976	1977	1978	1979	1980	1981[a]
1,001.4	1,419.6	1,551.6	1,882.7	1,673.7	1,321.3

a Jan-Sep.

The decline in group sales in 1980 was entirely due to a 17.9 per cent fall in the value of truck sales.

Table 113

Paccar Inc: Consolidated Sales by Segment, 1976-81
($ mn)

| | Year ended Dec 31 | | | | | |
	1976	1977	1978	1979	1980	1981[a]
Trucks)		1,194.8	1,274.2	1,529.0	1,255.7)	
Railroad)	1,001.4	96.7	141.8	199.5	237.2)	1,321.3
Others)		128.1	135.6	154.2	180.8)	
	1,001.4	1,419.6	1,551.6	1,882.7	1,673.7	1,321.3

a Jan-Sep.

- in North America

Paccar's business outside North America - although of little significance within the context of the whole group at 4.8 per cent of 1980 consolidated sales - continues to expand, and the 1980 fall was attributable to a reversal in the USA and Canada. During the fourth quarter of 1980 Paccar acquired substantially all of the assets of Fodens, the UK truck manufacturer.

Table 114

Paccar Inc: Consolidated Sales by Area, 1976-81
($ mn)

| | Year ended Dec 31 | | | | | |
	1976	1977	1978	1979	1980	1981[a]
USA)		1,223.7	1,340.3	1,603.9	1,419.2)	
Canada)	1,001.4	150.4	157.2	209.8	173.6)	1,321.3
Elsewhere)		45.5	54.1	69.0	80.9)	
	1,001.4	1,419.6	1,551.6	1,882.7	1,673.7	1,321.3

a Jan-Sep.

CONSOLIDATED PROFIT AND LOSS ACCOUNT

Costs have been well constrained

From 1976 to 1979 overall costs rose at a marginally lower rate than net sales. And, with useful increments provided by "other income" and non-consolidated subsidiaries and affiliates (particularly in 1979 by the Mexican affiliate), group net income increased by 137.4 per cent. In 1980, though, Paccar was unable to reduce costs in line with the shortfall in sales revenue, but was still nevertheless able to report net income at approximately the same level as the average of the

Table 115

Paccar Inc: Consolidated Profit and Loss Account, 1976–81

	Year ended Dec 31					
	1976	1977	1978	1979	1980	1981[a]
($ mn)						
Net sales	1,001.4	1,419.6	1,551.6	1,882.7	1,673.7	1,321.3
Other income	4.1	5.3	9.8	15.3	22.4	15.0[b]
	1,005.5	1,424.9	1,561.4	1,898.0	1,696.1	1,336.3[b]
Less:						
cost of sales	837.9	1,183.5	1,293.4	1,571.0	1,432.9	1,245.3[b]
depreciation	7.5	8.5	9.8	10.7	13.5	
selling & administration	66.8	84.7	99.5	116.9	127.3	
interest paid	2.9	3.1	3.2	3.2	4.5	
	90.4	145.1	155.5	196.2	117.9	91.0[b]
Less taxation	42.9	72.0	76.1	91.6	52.4	38.8
	47.5	73.1	79.4	104.6	65.5	52.2[b]
Equity income of non-consolidated subsidiaries & affiliates	3.1	2.4	7.3	15.5	15.6	11.0[b]
	50.6	75.5	86.7	120.1	81.1	63.2
($ per share)						
Earnings	6.14	9.15	10.51	14.57	9.83	7.66
Dividends (paid)	0.85	1.85	2.60	2.95	3.85	3.00

a Jan–Sep.   b Estimated.

previous four years. In the nine months to September 1981, although sales were 3.7 per cent higher than the nine months to September 1980, costs rose at a slightly faster rate, and net income declined by 2.5 per cent.

Trucks contributed 89.6 per cent of group operating profits from 1976 to 1979. But margins fell sharply in 1980, and the contribution to group profits declined to 72.4 per cent.

Table 116

Paccar Inc: Operating Profit by Segment, 1976-80
($ mn)

| | Year ended Dec 31 | | | | |
	1976	1977	1978	1979	1980
Trucks	85.1	147.0	148.9	178.6	85.2
Railroad	3.3	–	7.0	13.8	17.9
Others	9.6	10.2	10.5	10.8	14.5
	98.0	157.2	166.4	203.2	117.6

Although operating profits in the USA dipped sharply in 1980 – and were down by 39 per cent – the fall was sharper in Canada and elsewhere. This reflects the continued profitability of the railroad and "others" segments in the USA.

Table 117

Paccar Inc: Operating Profit by Area, 1976-80
($ mn)

| | Year ended Dec 31 | | | | |
	1976	1977	1978	1979	1980
USA)		140.6	156.0	175.4	106.9
Canada }	98.0	13.9	5.0	21.8	7.1
Elsewhere)		2.7	5.4	6.0	3.6
	98.0	157.2	166.4	203.2	117.6

SOURCE AND APPLICATION OF FUNDS

Cashflow has been adequate for capital expenditure

Cashflow has more than covered capital expenditure. In 1980 the purchase of Fodens was almost covered by cashflow, and the balance needed was met by a reduction in current assets. Despite the fact that cashflow in the first nine months of 1981 was at around the same level as in the equivalent period of 1980, capital expenditure was reduced by some 65 per cent.

Table 118

Paccar Inc: Source and Application of Funds, 1976-80
($ mn)

	Year ended Dec 31				
	1976	1977	1978	1979	1980
Cashflow:					
retained earnings	38.2	56.9	64.4	89.7	57.6
depreciation	7.5	8.5	9.8	10.7	13.5
	45.7	65.4	74.2	100.4	71.1
Sale of property (net) etc[a]	–	5.1	0.9	0.5	1.9
Long term debt	(5.4)	(3.2)	1.5	(3.2)	(0.7)
Current liabilities	70.1	22.6	(5.3)	42.0	(33.1)
Other liabilities	1.8	1.0	1.7	0.8	6.7
	112.2	90.9	73.0	140.5	45.9
Application					
Capital expenditure	8.0	21.8	19.3	45.3	55.0
Purchase of Fodens	–	–	–	–	24.4
	8.0	21.8	19.3	45.3	79.4
Current assets	98.7	54.6	42.1	80.6	(52.2)
Non-consolidated subsidiaries & affiliates	5.3	15.9	6.8	16.4	23.6
Other assets	0.2	(1.4)	4.8	(1.8)	(4.9)
	112.2	90.9	73.0	140.5	45.9

a Applied to capital expenditure.

Over the past four years 73.2 per cent of capital expenditure has been made on the trucks segment.

Table 119

Paccar Inc: Capital Expenditure by Segment, 1976-80
($ mn)

	Year ended Dec 31				
	1976	1977	1978	1979	1980
Trucks)		13.4	12.4	37.4	40.3
Railroad)	8.0	1.7	2.7	3.2	2.4
Other)		6.7	4.2	4.6	12.3
	8.0	21.8	19.3	45.3	55.0

ASSESSMENT OF CURRENT POSITION

Waiting for the upturn with confidence

In the second half of 1981 it is probable that Paccar's truck production was running at about 70 per cent of capacity, while most railroad car output stopped at the end of the second quarter of 1981. Nevertheless, Paccar was able to report profits in 1981's third quarter, and this together with the strong balance sheet (the ratio of long term debt to stockholders' equity was 0.03:1 as at December 31, 1980) should ensure that the company will be in a strong position when market conditions improve.

Under the 1981 tax law, railroad companies have been permitted to write off about $8 bn in rail trucks. Some of this increased cashflow is likely to find its way to Paccar, and the railroad car business could recover substantially.

COMPARATIVE
FINANCIAL ANALYSIS

OVERALL SUMMARY

The companies taken together in terms of -

The tables in Part 4 refer to the five fiscal years, 1976-80, and nine months trading
of the 1981 year for the following companies: General Motors, Ford, Chrysler,
Paccar (all of whose fiscal years end on December 31). American Motors (whose
fiscal year ended on September 30 up to 1979, and thereafter on December 31)
and International Harvester (whose fiscal year ends on October 31). Of the companies reviewed in Part 3, Volkswagen of America and Mack Trucks are excluded
in most tables since neither publishes detailed information.

- a consolidated balance sheet -

Total assets of the combined companies (excluding Volkswagen of America and
Mack Trucks) rose by 25.4 per cent from 1976 to 1978, and during that time there
was little change in the structure of the overall balance sheet. Property, plant
and equipment accounted for 30 per cent of assets at the end of 1976 and for 30.9
per cent two years later, while current assets over the same period moved from
58.9 per cent of all assets to 57.5 per cent. On the other side. stockholders'
equity financed 50.6 per cent of assets at the end of 1976, and 50 per cent two
years later.

But since 1978 there has been a considerable switch in emphasis in the balance
sheet, and a marked deterioration - caused by the heavy capital expenditure and
trading losses. Over the two and three quarter years from 1978 total assets
increased by 13.7 per cent, but during the same period property, plant and equipment increased by 63.2 per cent to reach 44.3 per cent of total assets, compared
with 30.9 per cent two and three quarter years earlier. Compensating for this
exceptional rise in property, plant and equipment, current assets (mainly cash)
fell by $6.8 bn.

At the same time as the structure of assets altered - with capital expenditure to
an extent offset by a reduction in cash - the financing of the assets also changed,
due to the losses of 1980 and 1981. Stockholders' equity fell from $32.8 bn at the
end of 1978 to $28.8 bn at the end of September 1981, and financed 38.7 per cent
of assets compared with 50 per cent two and three quarter years previously.
Current liabilities have risen rather more quickly than the total of liabilities, but
long term debt and other long term liabilities combined have increased in two and
three quarter years by no less than 81.7 per cent.

The decline in current assets together with the rise in current liabilities has meant that combined net current assets have fallen over two and three quarter years from $13.7 bn to a mere $1.3 bn, while the fall in stockholders' equity and the rise in long term debt and other long term liabilities means that the ratio of long term debt and other long term liabilities to stockholders' equity has moved from 0.27:1 to 0.56:1 (long term debt alone from 0.13:1 to 0.29:1).

- consolidated net sales -

Table 121 shows the combined sales of all the manufacturers reviewed, including Volkswagen of America and Mack Trucks (sales figures on these companies are available). The total sales increased every year from 1976 to 1979, but the rate of increase was lower in each succeeding year, and in fiscal 1980 there was a fall of 14.1 per cent.

For the first nine months of fiscal 1981 the manufacturers' sales (excluding Volkswagen and Mack Trucks) totalled $93,013 mn compared with $81,807.4 mn over the equivalent period of the previous year - an increase of 13.7 per cent. However, it seemed unlikely that the total of combined sales in fiscal 1981 would reach the 1978 level.

Table 121

US Vehicle Manufacturers' Combined Net Sales, 1976-80
($ mn)

Fiscal year

1976	1977	1978	1979	1980
102,688	122,233	134,215	139,729	120,090

The companies' interests are predominantly in North America which, in the four fiscal years from 1977 to 1980, accounted for 77.3 per cent of combined sales. However, the decline in revenue during fiscal 1980 was almost entirely due to a fall of 18 per cent in North America, whose share of total revenue fell to 73.3 per cent.

Table 122

US Vehicle Manufacturers' Combined Net Sales by Region, 1977-80
($ mn)

	Fiscal year			
	1977	1978	1979	1980
North America	96,383	107,238	107,299	88,030
Elsewhere	25,850	26,977	32,430	32,060
	122,233	134,215	139,729	120,090

Table 120

US Vehicle Manufacturers' Combined Consolidated Balance Sheet, 1976-81
($ mn)

	As at the end of the fiscal year					
	1976	1977	1978	1979	1980	1981[a]
Property, plant & equipment	15,686.0	17,957.4	20,251.1	24,597.9	29,263.9	33,055.0
Current assets	30,809.7	34,325.4	37,692.1	35,831.4	34,381.1	30,993.2
Non-consolidated subsidiaries & affiliates	4,534.1	5,110.7	5,699.4	6,622.0	6,985.2 }	10,529.2
Other assets	1,294.7	1,495.5	1,961.3	2,455.3	2,561.3 }	
	52,324.5	58,889.0	65,603.9	69,506.6	73,191.5	74,577.4
Stockholders' equity	26,454.6	29,529.0	32,810.0	34,546.9	29,369.7	28,847.5
Long term debt	4,560.8	4,727.5	4,344.7	4,154.2	8,364.6	8,312.2
Current liabilities	18,488.1	21,059.2	23,957.5	25,023.5	29,345.0	29,672.6
Other liabilities	2,821.0	3,573.3	4,491.7	5,782.0	6,112.2	7,745.1
	52,324.5	58,889.0	65,603.9	69,506.6	73,191.5	74,577.4

a After nine months.

278

Table 123

US Vehicle Manufacturers' Combined Gross Margins, 1976–81
($ mn)

	Fiscal year					
	1976	1977	1978	1979	1980	1981[a]
Net sales	100,363.4	119,142.7	130,424.7	135,218.6	115,366.7	93,013.0
Less cost of sales	83,576.2	99,506.0	109,716.0	117,171.6	106,384.2	82,946.6
	16,787.2	19,636.7	20,708.7	18,047.0	8,982.5	10,066.4
Gross margin (%)	16.7	16.5	15.9	13.3	7.8	10.8

a Nine months.

<u>- consolidated profit and loss account -</u>

Table 123 excludes Volkswagen of America and Mack Trucks, for which detailed figures are not available. During the fiscal years 1976 to 1979 the cost of sales increased at a faster rate than net sales, and in fiscal 1980 decreased at a slower rate - with the result that over the five year period gross margins fell from 16.7 per cent to 7.8 per cent. In the first nine months of fiscal 1981, though, costs have been well controlled, and margins have improved to 10.8 per cent.

All costs other than the cost of sales accounted for only 13.2 per cent of total costs in fiscal 1980, but rose from $10 bn in fiscal 1976 to $16.1 bn in fiscal 1980 - an increase of 61.1 per cent (compared with an increase in net sales over the same period of 14.9 per cent and in the cost of sales of 27.3 per cent). In particular, the cost of interest paid rose over the five fiscal years from $0.8 bn to $1.6 bn.

The high rate of increase in "other" costs meant that the gross margin of 7.8 per cent in fiscal 1980 was quite inadequate, and there was a combined loss before taxation in that year of $6.1 bn - compared with peak pretax profits in fiscal 1977 of $9.5 bn. In the first nine months of fiscal 1981 the gross margin of 10.8 per cent was still not enough, and the combined pretax loss was $1.8 bn.

Dividend payments have continued despite the losses - although American Motors, Chrysler and International Harvester have withdrawn from the lists.

<u>- and combined source and application of funds</u>

From fiscal 1976 through fiscal 1978 a rising cashflow was sufficient to meet rising capital expenditure. But when cashflow declined in fiscal 1979 and capital expenditure increased there was a shortfall of $3.2 bn, and in fiscal 1980 the shortfall was no less than $10.8 bn. The situation improved in the first three quarters of fiscal 1981, but there has still nevertheless been a shortfall of $5.7 bn.

The total shortfall of cashflow against capital expenditure since fiscal 1978 has been a staggering $19.7 bn. This money has been found mainly through a reduction in current assets (particularly cash) of $6.7 bn, but current liabilities have risen by $5.7 bn, long term debt by $4 bn, and other long term liabilities by $3.3 bn. In addition, $1.1 bn has been raised through the issue of preference shares.

CONSOLIDATED BALANCE SHEETS

<u>Total assets have shown a steady upward trend</u>

Since fiscal 1976 the assets of two companies - the largest and the smallest, General Motors and Paccar - have shown a consistent upward trend. Ford's assets are virtually unchanged since fiscal 1978, while Chrysler's have dropped in every year since fiscal 1977. International Harvester, having increased its asset base in every year up to fiscal 1980, fell back in 1981 to date. American Motors, thanks to support from Renault, has been the only company (other than General Motors and Paccar) to increase its assets in the first nine months of 1981.

Table 124

US Vehicle Manufacturers' Combined Consolidated Profit and Loss Account, 1976-81
($ mn)

| | Fiscal year | | | | | |
	1976	1977	1978	1979	1980	1981[a]
Net sales	100,363.4	119,142.7	130,424.8	135,218.6	115,366.7	93,013.0
Other income	910.3	761.8	772.9	1,389.8	1,027.5	831.9
	101,273.7	119,904.5	131,197.7	136,608.4	116,394.2	93,844.9
Less:						
cost of sales	83,576.2	99,506.0	109,716.0	117,171.6	106,384.2	82,946.6
selling, general & administration	4,321.5	4,786.4	5,426.3	5,919.8	6,473.6	4,772.1
depreciation & amortisation	3,819.8	4,051.4	4,885.5	5,388.2	6,916.4	5,449.5
pensions, bonus etc	1,042.7	1,262.0	1,287.0	1,277.8	1,117.4	830.5
interest paid	823.5	814.5	868.3	1,062.8	1,615.1	1,663.0
	7,690.0	9,484.2	9,014.6	5,788.2	(6,112.5)	(1,816.8)
Less taxation	3,660.1	4,544.8	4,359.9	2,743.3	(1,119.4)	(90.9)
	4,029.9	4,939.4	4,654.7	3,044.9	(4,993.1)	(1,725.9)
Equity income in non-consolidated subsidiaries & affiliates	387.1	478.3	549.9	487.6	502.4	427.7
Minorities	(25.5)	(3.6)	(14.8)	(10.0)	2.0	5.0
	4,391.5	5,414.1	5,189.8	3,522.5	(4,488.7)	(1,293.2)
($ per share)						
Earnings[b]	8.24	10.15	9.66	6.42	(8.22)	(2.29)
Dividend[b]	3.67	4.60	4.30	3.97	2.42	1.24

a Nine months.   b Based on the combined average number of shares outstanding, and after deducting preference dividends.

Table 125

US Vehicle Manufacturers' Combined Source and Application of Funds, 1976–81
($ mn)

	Fiscal year					
	1976	1977	1978	1979	1980	1981[a]
Source						
Cashflow:						
retained earnings	2,536.8	3,008.3	2,905.0	1,393.4	(5,816.2)	(1,728.2)
depreciation & amortisation	3,819.8	4,051.4	4,885.5	5,388.2	6,916.4	5,349.5
	6,356.6	7,059.7	7,790.5	6,781.6	1,100.2	3,621.3
Sale of property (net) etc[b]	181.5	45.4	868.8	225.1	356.8	164.6
Capital stock:						
common	32.1	66.1	159.0	341.9	487.4	258.8
preference	–	–	217.0	1.7	151.6	945.3
Long term debt	(318.8)	166.7	(382.8)	(190.6)	4,210.4	(52.4)
Current liabilities	2,913.8	2,575.7	2,898.3	1,066.0	4,321.5	327.5
Other liabilities	444.4	747.7	918.4	1,290.3	330.2	1,634.9
	9,609.6	10,661.3	12,469.2	9,516.0	10,958.1	6,900.0
Application						
Capital expenditure	4,015.1	6,368.2	8,048.0	9,960.1	11,939.2	9,305.2
Current assets	5,030.2	3,515.7	3,366.7	(1,860.7)	(1,450.3)	(3,387.9)
Non-consolidated subsidiaries & affiliates	496.5	576.6	588.7	922.6	363.2 }	982.7
Other assets	67.8	200.8	465.8	494.0	106.0 }	
	9,609.6	10,661.3	12,469.2	9,516.0	10,958.1	6,900.0

a Nine months.   b Applied to capital expenditure.

Table 126

US Vehicle Manufacturers' Consolidated Assets, 1976–81

($ mn)

	As at the end of the fiscal year					
	1976	1977	1978	1979	1980	1981[a]
General Motors	24,442.4	26,658.3	30,598.3	32,215.8	34,581.0	36,910.0
Ford	15,768.1	19,241.3	22,101.4	23,524.6	24,347.6	23,752.9
Chrysler	7,074.4	7,668.2	6,981.2	6,653.1	6,617.8	6,339.3
American Motors	991.6	957.3	994.1	1,123.5	1,029.0	1,100.3
International Harvester	3,574.8	3,813.4	4,316.1	5,247.5	5,843.5	5,645.6
Paccar	473.2	550.5	612.8	742.1	772.6	829.3
Total	52,324.5	58,889.0	65,603.9	69,506.6	73,191.5	74,577.4

a After nine months.

Note: Volkswagen of America's assets (for which no detailed figures are available) have grown substantially since 1976, financed by equity and loans from the parent company. Assets of Mack Trucks rose from $680 mn at the end of fiscal 1976 to $903 mn at the end of fiscal 1979, but fell back to $798.9 mn in 1980.

283

Table 127

US Vehicle Manufacturers' Property, Plant and Equipment (Net of Depreciation), 1976-81 ($ mn)

	As at the end of the fiscal year					
	1976	1977	1978	1979	1980	1981[a]
General Motors	6,961.1	8,202.9	9,605.6	11,638.2	14,986.8	18,818.1
Ford	5,579.8	6,207.5	7,418.5	9,227.0	10,025.9	9,979.7
Chrysler	2,087.2	2,425.2	2,022.9	2,348.9	2,520.0	2,434.8
American Motors	271.6	241.3	221.6	217.8	263.1	306.6
International Harvester	710.3	796.3	889.7	1,039.1	1,277.2	1,321.5
Paccar	76.0	84.2	92.8	126.9	190.9	194.3
Total	15,686.0	17,957.4	20,251.1	24,597.9	29,263.9	33,055.0

a After nine months.

<u>Property, plant and equipment.</u> The growth in assets of General Motors and Paccar has been due to continued capital expenditure. From the end of fiscal 1976 to fiscal 1981 after nine months, the value of property, plant and equipment of General Motors rose by 170.3 per cent, and of Paccar by 155.7 per cent - compared with an average for Ford, Chrysler, American Motors and International Harvester of 62.4 per cent.

However, it should be noted that, for all the companies, there has been a strong trend towards property, plant and equipment in the composition of total assets.

Table 128

US Vehicle Manufacturers' Property, Plant and Equipment (Net of Depreciation) as a Percentage of Total Assets, 1976-81
(%)

	As at the end of the fiscal year					
	1976	1977	1978	1979	1980	1981[a]
General Motors	28.5	30.8	31.4	36.1	43.3	51.0
Ford	35.4	32.3	33.6	39.2	41.2	42.0
Chrysler	29.5	31.6	29.0	35.3	38.1	38.4
American Motors	27.4	25.2	22.3	19.4	25.6	27.9
International Harvester	19.9	20.9	20.6	19.8	21.9	23.4
Paccar	16.1	15.3	15.1	17.1	24.7	23.4
Total	30.0	30.5	30.9	35.4	40.0	44.3

a After nine months.

<u>Current assets.</u> Paccar alone has been able to increase current assets every year since 1976. Over the past two and three quarter years the current assets of General Motors have declined by $4.8 bn, of Ford by $1.5 bn and of Chrysler by $0.9 bn.

The main reduction in current assets has been in cash - in particular, a huge reduction by General Motors in the latest nine months. It is mainly because of this that the total cash of the companies reviewed has fallen by $3 bn in the first nine months of fiscal 1981. International Harvester's cash balances were improved in fiscal 1981 by the proceeds from the sale of the Solar division.

The fall in current assets, together with the rise in current liabilities, has led to a substantial decline in net current assets. This was particularly the case with Chrysler in 1979, Ford in 1980 and International Harvester in the first nine months of fiscal 1981. However, by far the largest fall is that of General Motors in the first nine months of 1981; indeed, General Motors now has net current assets in line with those of American Motors, International Harvester and Paccar. This compares with the position at the end of fiscal 1978 when General Motors had net current assets of $7.95 bn - no less than $2.16 bn more than all the other companies combined.

Table 129

US Vehicle Manufacturers' Current Assets, 1976–81
($ mn)

As at the end of the fiscal year

	1976	1977	1978	1979	1980	1981[a]
General Motors	15,472.6	15,957.2	17,999.5	16,556.5	15,421.3	13,235.9
Ford	8,242.5	10,872.4	12,370.6	11,571.3	11,559.0	10,879.0
Chrysler	3,878.3	4,152.8	3,561.8	3,120.7	2,861.2	2,662.1
American Motors	597.3	618.0	668.6	793.6	640.9	666.9
International Harvester	2,272.8	2,324.2	2,648.7	3,265.8	3,427.4	3,061.7
Paccar	346.2	400.8	442.9	523.5	471.3	487.6
Total	30,809.7	34,325.4	37,692.1	35,831.4	34,381.1	30,993.2

a After nine months.

Table 130

US Vehicle Manufacturers' Cash, Deposits and Marketable Securities, 1976–81
($ mn)

As at the end of the fiscal year

	1976	1977	1978	1979	1980	1981[a]
General Motors	4,624.9	3,240.0	4,054.8	2,986.4	3,715.2	649.3
Ford	1,664.3	3,371.5	3,799.0	2,192.6	2,587.2	2,358.2
Chrysler	572.0	408.8	522.8	474.3	297.3	247.8
American Motors	91.3	60.2	75.1	100.1	64.7	71.8
International Harvester	40.0	17.2	27.3	25.2	137.1	510.0
Paccar	7.2	13.0	13.5	14.0	16.8	17.0[b]
Total	6,999.7	7,110.7	8,492.5	5,792.6	6,818.3	3,854.1

a After nine months.   b Estimated.

Table 131

US Vehicle Manufacturers' Net Current Assets, 1976-81
($ mn)

As at the end of the fiscal year

	1976	1977	1978	1979	1980	1981[a]
General Motors	7,556.6	7,630.3	7,948.9	6,688.2	3,148.3	366.9
Ford	2,245.7	2,988.6	3,092.6	2,308.3	487.0	127.6
Chrysler	1,052.4	1,062.9	1,076.0	(110.9)	(27.9)	(61.5)
American Motors	59.7	102.9	151.9	235.8	206.6	264.7
International Harvester	1,231.2	1,273.5	1,209.8	1,392.5	947.2	347.1
Paccar	176.0	208.0	255.4	294.0	274.9	275.8
Total	12,321.6	13,266.2	13,734.6	10,807.9	5,036.1	1,320.6

a After nine months.

Table 132

US Vehicle Manufacturers' Stockholders' Equity, 1976-81
($ mn)

As at the end of the fiscal year

	1976	1977	1978	1979	1980	1981[a]
General Motors	14,385.2	15,766.9	17,569.9	19,179.3	17,814.6	17,710.5
Ford	7,107.0	8,456.9	9,686.3	10,420.7	8,567.5	7,746.5
Chrysler	2,815.3	2,924.6	2,926.5	1,824.1	116.3	624.2
American Motors	311.4	320.8	357.9	440.8	434.3	373.4
International Harvester	1,563.8	1,731.0	1,876.2	2,199.1	1,896.5	1,805.7
Paccar	271.9	328.8	393.2	482.9	540.5	587.2
Total	26,454.6	29,529.0	32,810.0	34,546.9	29,369.7	28,847.5

a After nine months.

Liabilities: stockholders' equity falls as debt rises sharply

Stockholders' equity. Apart from Paccar, all of the companies had lower stock-holders' equity after the opening nine months of fiscal 1981 than a year and three quarters earlier. In the case of Chrysler the deficit on retained earnings had completely eliminated the value of the common stock as at the end of 1980, and all stockholders' equity is now represented by preferred stock - issued in 1978 and 1981. American Motors also had a deficit on retained earnings as at September 30, 1981; of its stockholders' equity of $373.4 mn at that date, $226.6 mn had been subscribed by Renault over the past two years. International Harvester improved its position in fiscal 1980 with the issue of $150 mn preference shares.

Long term debt. In order to maintain the investment in property, plant and equip-ment in 1980 despite the fall in stockholders' equity, the companies were forced to increase long term debt sharply (particularly Chrysler). General Motors has continued to raise more long term debt in 1981, as has American Motors, but Chrysler has achieved a reduction through the issue of preference shares.

As stockholders' equity increased from the end of fiscal 1976 through fiscal 1979 and long term debt fell, the companies' long term debt to stockholders' equity ratio declined. In fiscal 1980, however, due in large measure to Chrysler, the ratio more than doubled and the overall average remained at the higher level in fiscal 1981. Although still having a lower long term debt to shareholders' equity ratio than any company with the exception of Paccar, General Motors now has a ratio almost three times that at the end of 1979.

Short term debt. The financial problems of Chrysler in 1979 and International Harvester more recently have been caused by ever increasing short term debt. Short term debt at Ford almost tripled from 1978 to 1980, but has since declined, while at General Motors the level has more than doubled in the past year and three quarters.

Table 135

US Vehicle Manufacturers' Loans Payable, 1976-81
($ mn)

| | As at the end of the fiscal year | | | | | |
	1976	1977	1978	1979	1980	1981[a]
General Motors	...	793.3	1,115.2	924.1	1,676.5	2,002.1
Ford	614.8	681.1	865.6	1,190.4	2,405.6	2,133.0
Chrysler	241.1	340.7	61.6	876.5	316.7	292.5
American Motors	84.6	83.5	73.8	9.0	54.4	45.8
International Harvester	302.1	294.8	379.7	441.9	860.5	1,364.6
Paccar	8.9	14.9	8.2	10.7	16.1	...
Total	...	2,208.3	2,504.1	3,452.6	5,329.8	...

a After nine months.

288

Table 133

US Vehicle Manufacturers' Long Term Debt, 1976–81
($ mn)

	As at the end of the fiscal year					
	1976	1977	1978	1979	1980	1981[a]
General Motors	1,044.0	1,068.2	978.9	880.0	1,886.0	2,419.7
Ford	1,411.4	1,359.7	1,144.5	1,274.6	2,058.8	2,250.1
Chrysler	1,047.7	1,240.3	1,188.5	976.7	2,966.4	2,251.1
American Motors	111.7	86.3	78.9	56.5	108.8	275.6
International Harvester	922.9	953.1	932.5	948.2	1,327.1	1,098.7
Paccar	23.1	19.9	21.4	18.2	17.5	17.0[b]
Total	4,560.8	4,727.5	4,344.7	4,154.2	8,364.6	8,312.2

a After nine months.   b Estimated.

Table 134

US Vehicle Manufacturers' Ratio of Long Term Debt to Shareholders' Equity, 1976–81

	As at the end of the fiscal year					
	1976	1977	1978	1979	1980	1981[a]
General Motors	0.07:1	0.07:1	0.06:1	0.05:1	0.11:1	0.14:1
Ford	0.20:1	0.16:1	0.12:1	0.12:1	0.24:1	0.29:1
Chrysler	0.37:1	0.42:1	0.41:1	0.54:1	25.51:1	3.61:1
American Motors	0.36:1	0.27:1	0.22:1	0.13:1	0.25:1	0.74:1
International Harvester	0.59:1	0.55:1	0.50:1	0.43:1	0.70:1	0.61:1
Paccar	0.08:1	0.06:1	0.05:1	0.04:1	0.03:1	0.03:1[b]
Total	0.17:1	0.16:1	0.13:1	0.12:1	0.28:1	0.29:1

a After nine months.   b Estimated.

CONSOLIDATED PROFIT AND LOSS ACCOUNT

Consolidated net sales dipped sharply in 1980 –

Excluding Chrysler, the combined sales of all of the other manufacturers reviewed rose by 46.6 per cent from fiscal 1976 through fiscal 1979. Volkswagen of America was outstanding with an increase of 106.1 per cent, while the truck manufacturers Mack and Paccar rose by 78.8 per cent and 88 per cent respectively. International Harvester increased revenue over the period by 52.9 per cent and Ford by 50.9 per cent, but General Motors' sales rose by only 40.5 per cent and American Motors' by 34.6 per cent. In contrast, Chrysler's sales fell by 22.8 per cent; in part, this was due to the sales of the European and certain Latin American operations, but, even excluding sales of these operations from the figure for fiscal 1976, Chrysler's sales still fell by 1.9 per cent.

In fiscal 1980, Volkswagen of America continued its upward trend with an increase of 19 per cent, but the average for all the companies was 14.1 per cent down. International Harvester, affected by a strike, fell by 24.8 per cent, and Chrysler dropped a further 23.1 per cent. All other companies performed approximately in line with the average.

International Harvester has shown the best improvement in the first nine months of 1981 with a rise of 40.7 per cent, but the comparison is invalid since 1981 was strike free. The most remarkable achievement belongs to Chrysler, whose fiscal 1981 sales were 25 per cent up on the same period of 1980, compared with an average for all the companies (excluding Volkswagen of America and Mack Trucks, for which comparable figures are not available) of 13.7 per cent. In fiscal 1981 American Motors (up 3.9 per cent on the equivalent period of 1980) and Paccar (up 3.7 per cent) have lagged.

– and markets outside North America increased their relative importance

Ford, by a considerable distance, has the most significant business outside North America – 45.3 per cent of its own sales in fiscal 1980, and 52.4 per cent of all the sales outside North America of the companies reviewed.

The rise for all companies combined in the percentage of sales outside North America in fiscal 1979 was due to static sales in North America and increased revenue elsewhere. In particular, Ford's sales outside North America rose in 1979 by 29.1 per cent (compared with a fall inside North America of 11.2 per cent). In fiscal 1980, sales outside North America for all of the companies, with the exception of Chrysler (down 22.4 per cent), were little changed, but the share of revenue increased due to the falls in North America.

Table 136

US Vehicle Manufacturers' Consolidated Net Sales, 1976-81
($ mn)

	Fiscal year					
	1976	1977	1978	1979	1980	1981[a]
General Motors	47,181.0	54,961.3	63,221.1	66,311.2	57,728.5	47,149.2
Ford	28,839.6	37,841.5	42,784.1	43,513.7	37,085.5	29,233.5
Chrysler	15,537.8[c]	16,708.3[c]	13,618.3	12,001.9	9,225.3	8,077.5
American Motors	2,315.5	2,236.9	2,585.4	3,117.1	3,341.9[b]	1,967.8
Volkswagen of America	1,298.6	1,760.3	2,150.3	2,676.6	3,186.4	...
International Harvester	5,488.1	5,975.1	6,664.3	8,392.0	6,311.8	5,263.7
Mack Trucks	1,025.8	1,331.0	1,640.0	1,833.8	1,536.7	...
Paccar	1,001.4	1,419.6	1,551.6	1,882.7	1,673.7	1,321.3
Total	102,687.8	122,234.0	134,215.1	139,729.0	120,089.8	...

a Nine months.   b 15 months.   c Not comparable with subsequent years due to the sale of the European and certain Latin American operations.

Table 138

US Vehicle Manufacturers' Consolidated Gross Profit[a], 1976-81
($ mn)

	Fiscal year					
	1976	1977	1978	1979	1980	1981[b]
General Motors	9,705.5	10,870.0	12,159.9	11,022.8	5,977.4	6,014.7
Ford	4,577.5	6,210.0	6,433.6	5,758.4	2,928.0	3,236.1
Chrysler	1,964.2	1,687.2	1,015.5	430.4	150.1	888.6
American Motors	304.6	331.6	408.1	495.4	327.4[c]	231.2
International Harvester	978.1	1,058.3	1,196.6	1,402.8	363.9	316.6
Paccar	167.6	241.4	268.0	327.0	263.2	210.8
Total	17,697.5	20,398.5	21,481.7	19,436.8	10,010.0	10,898.0

a Defined for the purpose of this review as net sales revenue less cost of sales.   b Nine months.
c 15 months.

Table 137

US Vehicle Manufacturers' Percentage
of Consolidated Net Sales Outside North America, 1976-80
(%)

	Fiscal year				
	1976	1977	1978	1979	1980
General Motors	...	15.1	17.1	18.3	20.6
Ford	31.1	29.4	30.3	38.4	45.3
Chrysler	28.3[a]	28.5[a]	10.3	12.4	12.5
American Motors	7.0	7.0	7.0	7.0	9.6[b]
Volkswagen of America[c]	-	-	-	-	-
International Harvester	21.0	20.1	20.0	18.8	25.1
Mack Trucks	23.0	20.0	15.0	12.0	16.0
Paccar	...	3.2	3.5	3.7	4.8
Average	...	21.1	20.1	23.2	26.7

a Not comparable with subsequent years due to the sale of the
European and certain Latin American operations. b 15
months. c Assumed to be 100 per cent in North America.

1981 sees a recovery in consolidated gross profits -

From fiscal 1976 through fiscal 1979, the cost of sales of American Motors,
International Harvester and Paccar rose at approximately the same rate as net
sales revenue, with the result that absolute gross profits improved. On the other
hand, for General Motors and Ford the continued rise in cost at a faster rate than
revenue meant that gross profits fell by approximately 10 per cent in each case
in 1979. The declining sales of Chrysler over the period were not offset by an
equivalent decline in costs.

In fiscal 1980 none of the companies were able to cut costs at the rate that sales
revenue fell. International Harvester, especially badly hit because of the strike,
saw gross profits fall by 74.1 per cent. However, cost cutting programmes in
fiscal 1981 have been such that, in nine months, total gross profits are higher than
for the whole of fiscal 1980. Chrysler has been particularly successful.

Consolidated profit before interest paid. Continued rises in selling and administrative costs, and in depreciation and amortisation, meant that for all companies -
except Paccar - gross profits were entirely eliminated in 1980, although for
Chrysler this position had been reached in 1978. In 1980, Chrysler's losses before interest paid increased, but the decline from 1979 was more severe for
General Motors, Ford, American Motors and International Harvester. In the
first nine months of fiscal 1981, General Motors managed to join Paccar in
recording profits before interest paid, and all the other companies have succeeded
in reducing losses significantly. Indeed, Chrysler is closer to breakeven at this
level than at any time since 1978.

Table 139

US Vehicle Manufacturers' Consolidated Profit Before Interest Paid[a], 1976–81
($ mn)

	Fiscal year					
	1976	1977	1978	1979	1980	1981[b]
General Motors	5,569.9	6,331.3	6,699.4	5,226.2	(837.0)	607.0
Ford	1,819.5	3,044.7	2,814.5	1,610.0	(1,735.2)	(405.3)
Chrysler	700.7	384.0	(171.1)	(829.3)	(1,280.9)	(128.2)[c]
American Motors	(10.6)	23.1	61.8	117.1	(159.0)[d]	(66.3)
International Harvester	340.7	367.4	319.6	527.6	(607.7)	(255.8)
Paccar	93.3	148.2	158.7	199.4	122.4	94.8[c]
Total	8,513.5	10,298.7	9,882.9	6,851.0	(4,497.4)	(153.8)

a Calculated by deducting all costs other than interest paid from gross profit (as defined in footnote to Table 138) and crediting "other income" – but not equity income in non-consolidated subsidiaries and affiliates. b Nine months. c Estimated. d 15 months.

Table 140

US Vehicle Manufacturers' Consolidated Interest Paid, 1976–81
($ mn)

	Fiscal year					
	1976	1977	1978	1979	1980	1981[a]
General Motors	284.0	281.7	355.9	368.4	531.9	608.9
Ford	216.6	192.7	194.8	246.8	432.5	502.1
Chrysler	181.0	202.0	166.2	275.4	332.8	254.5[b]
American Motors	17.7	17.3	22.3	20.6	29.5[c]	24.9
International Harvester	121.3	117.7	125.9	148.4	283.9	268.8
Paccar	2.9	3.1	3.2	3.2	4.5	3.8[b]
Total	823.5	814.5	868.3	1,062.8	1,615.1	1,663.0

a Nine months. b Estimated. c 15 months.

Table 141

US Vehicle Manufacturers' Consolidated Profit Before Tax, 1976–81
($ mn)

	Fiscal year					
	1976	1977	1978	1979	1980	1981[a]
General Motors	5,285.9	6,049.6	6,343.5	4,857.8	(1,368.9)	(1.9)
Ford	1,602.9	2,852.0	2,619.7	1,363.2	(2,167.7)	(907.4)
Chrysler	519.7	182.0	(337.3)	(1,104.7)	(1,613.7)	(382.7)
American Motors	(28.3)	5.8	39.5	96.5	(188.5)[b]	(91.2)[c]
International Harvester	219.4	249.7	193.7	379.2	(891.6)	(524.6)
Paccar	90.4	145.1	155.5	196.2	117.9	91.0[c]
Total	7,690.0	9,484.2	9,014.6	5,788.2	(6,112.5)	(1,816.8)

a Nine months.　b 15 months.　c Estimated.

Note: Both Volkswagen and Mack Trucks reported losses in 1980.

Table 142

US Vehicle Manufacturers' Consolidated Net Income, 1976–81
($ mn)

	Fiscal year					
	1976	1977	1978	1979	1980	1981[a]
General Motors	2,902.8	3,337.5	3,508.0	2,892.7	(762.5)	236.7
Ford	983.1	1,672.8	1,588.9	1,169.3	(1,543.3)	(713.8)
Chrysler	328.2	124.8	(204.6)	(1,097.3)	(1,709.7)	(436.1)
American Motors	(46.3)	3.1	24.1	68.1	(184.7)[b]	(89.4)
International Harvester	173.1	200.4	186.7	369.6	(369.6)	(353.8)
Paccar	50.6	75.5	86.7	120.1	81.1	63.2
Total	4,391.5	5,414.1	5,189.8	3,522.5	(4,488.7)	(1,293.2)

a Nine months.　b 15 months.

<u>Consolidated profit before tax.</u> Interest payments approximately doubled for all
the companies from fiscal 1976 through fiscal 1980, while in the first nine months
of fiscal 1981 both General Motors and Ford paid more than in the whole of 1980.

For all of the companies combined, consolidated profit before tax averaged 90 per
cent of profits before interest paid from fiscal 1976 through fiscal 1979, but in
1980 - when interest paid was approximately double that of 1976 - overall consolidated
losses before tax were 35.9 per cent higher than before interest paid. And in the
first nine months of fiscal 1981 interest paid accounted for all of General Motors
profits, more than doubled the losses of Ford and International Harvester, and
almost tripled the loss of Chrysler.

- but consolidated net income is still in the red

Thanks to tax credits and contributions from non-consolidated subsidiaries losses
at the net level for Chrysler were reduced from losses at the pretax level by
39.3 per cent in 1978, and by a small margin in 1979. However, there have been
no such benefits in 1980 or the first nine months of fiscal 1981.

In 1980, for the same reasons pretax losses of General Motors were reduced by
44.3 per cent, of Ford by 28.8 per cent and of International Harvester by 58.5 per
cent. Losses for Ford and International Harvester have also been reduced in
fiscal 1981, while General Motors has been able to report positive earnings.

General Motors, Ford and Chrysler publish net income by areas. For General
Motors North America accounted for 90 per cent of net income from 1976 to 1979
and, of the losses incurred during 1980, operations outside North America
accounted for 87.5 per cent. Ford's operations in North America started to notch
up losses in 1979, and further losses in 1980; however, operations outside North
America (despite losses in West Germany in 1980) have remained profitable.
From 1978 Chrysler has obtained a small profit from operations outside North
America.

SOURCE AND APPLICATION OF FUNDS

Cashflow has been the prime source of funds until recently -

From fiscal 1976 through fiscal 1979 the prime source of funds for all of the
companies - with the exception of Chrysler - was cashflow. However, in fiscal
1980 American Motors and International Harvester joined Chrysler with a negative
cashflow, while Ford achieved little more than a breakeven position. Cashflow
of General Motors declined by 44.1 per cent in 1980. In the first three quarters of
fiscal 1981 the position has improved, although Chrysler and American Motors
were still negative.

- when long and short term debt has taken over -

In order to supplement cashflow and meet capital expenditure requirements,
Chrysler raised $217 mn in the form of preference shares in 1978, and International
Harvester $150 mn in fiscal 1980. American Motors received $181.7 mn in the

form of common stock from Renault in fiscal 1980 and a further $44.9 mn in the form of preference in the latest nine months. However, the major source of funds in fiscal 1980 and 1981 has been debt - both long term and short term. General Motors raised $1 bn long term debt and $0.8 bn short term debt in 1980, while in total Ford increased long and short term debt by $2 bn, Chrysler by $1.4 bn and International Harvester by $0.8 bn.

In the first nine months of fiscal 1981 General Motors has increased long and short term debt by a further $0.9 bn, and International Harvester by $0.3 bn. American Motors has been forced to raise $0.2 bn long term debt. Ford, on the other hand, has been able to make an overall reduction of $0.1 bn and Chrysler, through its restructuring programme, has reduced long term debt by $0.7 bn.

Table 144

US Vehicle Manufacturers' Changes in Debt, 1976-81
($ mn)

	Fiscal year					
	1976	1977	1978	1979	1980	1981[a]
Long term debt						
General Motors	(153.2)	24.2	(89.3)	(98.9)	1,006.0	533.7
Ford	(122.5)	(51.7)	(215.2)	130.1	784.2	191.3
Chrysler	(5.8)	192.6	(51.8)	(211.8)	1,989.7	(715.3)
American Motors	(16.6)	(25.4)	(7.4)	(22.4)	52.3[b]	166.8
International Harvester	(15.3)	30.2	(20.6)	15.6	378.9	(228.4)
Paccar	(5.4)	(3.2)	1.5	(3.2)	(0.7)	(0.5)
Total	(318.8)	166.7	(382.8)	(190.6)	4,210.4	(52.4)
Loans payable						
General Motors	...	...	321.9	(191.1)	752.4	325.6
Ford	(192.7)	66.3	184.5	324.8	1,215.2	(272.6)
Chrysler	(192.5)	99.6	(279.1)	814.9	(559.8)	(24.2)
American Motors	19.4	(1.1)	(9.7)	(64.8)	45.4[b]	(8.6)
International Harvester	(203.1)	(7.3)	84.9	62.2	418.6	504.1
Paccar	3.4	6.0	(6.7)	2.5	(0.6)	...
Total	...	...	295.8	948.5	1,871.2	...

a Nine months.   b 15 months.

– in order to maintain capital expenditure programmes

Up to fiscal 1979 capital expenditure absorbed virtually all of the cashflow of all of the companies, although Chrysler - in order to maintain expenditure in line - had been forced to issue preference stock and raise short term debt, and Ford had needed to increase debt in 1979. In 1980, despite the severe reductions in cash-flow, only Ford reduced capital expenditure. However, in the first nine months of fiscal 1981 (on a pro rata basis) all companies have cut back except for American Motors (financed by Renault) and General Motors. The increased rate of expenditure by General Motors, bearing in mind the debt that has been raised to finance it, is remarkable. On a pro rata basis, fiscal 1981 expenditure is the equivalent

US Vehicle Manufacturers' Cashflow, 1976–81
($ mn)

	Fiscal year					
	1976	1977	1978	1979	1980	1981[a]
General Motors	3,535.6	3,760.2	4,818.8	4,546.8	2,541.1	3,058.3
Ford	1,740.4	2,426.4	2,486.0	2,306.1	113.3	753.9
Chrysler	806.6	496.9	81.8	(731.8)	(1,144.0)	(193.1)
American Motors	16.9	69.5	100.2	140.1	(130.4)[b]	(67.1)
International Harvester	211.4	241.3	229.5	420.0	(350.9)	11.3
Paccar	45.7	65.4	74.2	100.4	71.1	58.0
Total	6,356.6	7,059.7	7,790.5	6,781.6	1,100.2	3,621.3

a Nine months.   b 15 months.

Table 145

US Vehicle Manufacturers' Capital Expenditure, 1976–81
($ mn)

	Fiscal year					
	1976	1977	1978	1979	1980	1981[a]
General Motors	2,307.3	3,646.7	4,564.5	5,386.8	7,761.5	7,199.3
Ford	1,055.0	1,762.0	2,542.0	3,440.0	2,769.0	1,529.8
Chrysler	424.1	723.1	670.7	748.5	834.6	210.4
American Motors	52.4	46.6	41.3	54.6	110.9[b]	82.2
International Harvester	168.3	168.0	210.2	284.9	383.8	268.8
Paccar	8.0	21.8	19.3	45.3	79.4	14.7[c]
Total	4,015.1	6,368.2	8,048.0	9,960.1	11,939.2	9,305.2

a Nine months.   b 15 months.   c Estimated.

of $9.6 bn – almost as much as what the total industry spent in fiscal 1979. And in six years General Motors has increased its rate of capital expenditure by more than four times.

Through fiscal 1978 it had been possible for all companies, on balance, to add to cash held, but in 1979 General Motors and Ford reduced their holdings by $1.1 bn and $1.6 bn respectively, part of which was replaced in the following year through short term debt. In the first nine months of 1981 General Motors withdrew no less than $3.1 bn, equivalent to 82.5 per cent of its cash balance.

Table 146

US Vehicle Manufacturers' Changes in Balances of Cash, Deposits and Marketable Securities, 1976–81
($ mn)

	Fiscal year					
	1976	1977	1978	1979	1980	1981[a]
General Motors	1,242.1	(1,384.9)	814.8	(1,068.4)	728.8	(3,065.9)
Ford	767.9	1,707.2	427.5	(1,606.4)	394.6	(229.0)
Chrysler	344.3	(163.2)	114.0	(48.5)	(177.0)	(49.5)
American Motors	5.9	(31.1)	14.9	25.0	(35.4)[b]	7.1
International Harvester	(9.5)	(22.8)	10.1	(2.1)	111.9	372.9
Paccar	–	5.8	0.5	0.5	2.8	0.2[c]
Total	2,350.7	111.0	1,381.8	(2,699.9)	1,025.7	(2,964.2)

a Nine months.   b 15 months.   c Estimated.

CONCLUSIONS

A cautious short term outlook –

For three consecutive years since 1978 vehicle sales in the USA have fallen, and the characteristically optimistic industry is now forecasting car sales in 1982 of around 9-9.5 mn units compared with 9 mn units in 1980 and 8.5 mn units in 1981. Furthermore, the industry expects that an upward trend in sales is now unlikely to start before 1982's second half. To an extent this gloomy outlook may be conditioned by the fact that optimism would not be helpful in the 1982 wage negotiations, but the current performance of the US economy as a whole does not indicate that the industry's forecasts are over cautious – indeed, possibly the reverse.

In these circumstances a further deterioration in the balance sheets of all the companies must be expected over the next year – General Motors is now effectively stripped to the bone, with no cash and no earnings. If the corporation's expenditure programme is to be maintained further borrowings will have to be made, and in anticipation of this Moody's has recently cut General Motors' credit rating from triple A to double A. Nevertheless, even in the expected depressed market of 1982. General Motors should at least approximately break even, including servicing any increased debt. And the corporation should be a prime beneficiary of any upturn in the market.

The only other company which on its own merits is in a strong position is the smallest company reviewed – Paccar. Through all the problems of recent months this company has remained profitable, and improved its balance sheet. Mack Trucks is also in a strong position – with new facilities and financial backing from its parent group, and possibly also from Renault.

Ford's position in North America is extremely difficult. Net losses of $2.1 bn in 1980 will have been followed by further losses in 1981, and 1982 will probably be loss making also. Outside North America, profits in 1981 are likely to be lower than in 1980, and the US operations cannot expect significant contributions from the cashflow of foreign subsidiaries. Thus, in a depressed market, Ford's borrowings will increase and overall profits seem unlikely. Nevertheless, bearing in mind its comparative strength with foreign operations – in terms of both finance and products – Ford should be in a position to participate effectively in a revived US market – even if, before the revival, US manufacturing operations have been severely curtailed.

Chrysler, International Harvester, American Motors and Volkswagen of America exist now only because those who have money in them are at present prepared to take the view that the long term returns will be better than what short term returns would be if the companies were wound up. To the question as to whether any of these companies will survive, the answer is that since losses can be expected in 1982, they will do so only if their present creditors are prepared to follow their previous investments with further good money. The fact that the European companies have not established a firm footing in the USA earlier is somewhat surprising - but it would be even more surprising if Renault and Volkswagen - having come this far - were to back out at this stage. For American Motors the result could be absorption by Renault and the withdrawal from the market of a large proportion of its traditional products, while for Volkswagen of America there could be a long delay in pursuing its expansion plans. Nevertheless, by the mid 1980s it is likely that these two companies will still be active manufacturers of modern cars in the USA.

- will cause problems for the weakest companies

Thus, the two largest manufacturers, General Motors and Ford, appear to have the muscle to maintain their positions, as do the two smallest, Mack and Paccar, while the European backed ventures, American Motors and Volkswagen of America, are likely to stay. In addition, Japanese imports are unlikely to fall, and within the next few years Honda and Nissan at least will be US manufacturers. The productive capability of these sources combined would probably be sufficient for a US market perhaps 25 per cent larger than it was in 1981. But unless the US market revives strongly in 1982, or Chrysler and International Harvester can suddenly significantly boost their shares of the market - both of which seem unlikely events - it is possible that both companies will be faced with widespread closures followed by absorption by their competitors.

Part Three:
Short Term Prospects for the Japanese Motor Industry

Short Term Prospects for the Japanese Motor Industry

INTRODUCTION

A background of huge capital investment and a dedicated workforce, coupled with
an intensive and aggressive export offensive, has made the Japanese motor
industry the most effective and successful in the world. And, thanks to the US
recession, in 1980 it was also the largest. It is possible, though, that this success
contains the seeds of its own destruction and that the industry has already reached
its zenith - at least as far as passenger cars are concerned. Motor Business forecasts that passenger car output will contract somewhat in 1981 - despite being
ahead up to the end of May - and that a further fall will occur in 1982, despite
the likelihood of the beginnings of economic recovery in the Western world. The
reason for this can be expressed quite simply as politics. The depth of feeling
within North America and Western Europe regarding the success of the Japanese
motor industry should not be underestimated, and no government - of whatever
political colour - will remain unmoved for long by the pleadings of its own domestic
motor sector in the face of increasing Japanese penetration. Some governments
will play it rougher than others - but all will take action if necessary. Reasonably
conclusive evidence of this is provided by recent developments in the USA and
West Germany.

By necessity, therefore, any Japanese producer wishing to further its market
presence in the mature markets of the West will increasingly have to resort to
joint ventures, licensing agreements or a local presence. The first moves in
this direction have already been made, and many more can be expected in the first
half of the 1980s. It is also probable that this is the method they will need to adopt
more and more in other regions.

Due to the unknown impact of the various moves taking place to restrict Japanese
vehicle shipments, this period is particularly difficult for forecasting. It is
assumed that production schedules for passenger cars will be trimmed in the
second half of 1981 and for much of 1982 - not only because of uncertainties on
the export front but also because of weaker conditions in the domestic market.
In the commercial vehicle sector it is forecast that the industry will at least be
able to maintain its output volume, and perhaps improve upon it slightly. But
the years of heady growth seem over.

Our analysis of the Japanese motor industry begins with a review of the passenger
car sector.

PASSENGER CARS

Production rises markedly to over 7 mn in 1980 –

Even by the Japanese motor industry's own sparkling standards, 1980 was a remarkably successful year. Output of passenger cars increased by 14 per cent to top 7 mn for the first time. This is all the more amazing when it is remembered that 1980 was the year in which the current global recession took a grip on the worldwide motor industry.

Table 1

Japanese Production of Passenger Cars by Engine Size Group

Cubic capacity	1979	1980	% change 1980/79	1981 (Jan–May)
Up to 550	175,100	195,923	11.9	80,776
551–2,000	5,588,115	6,438,847	15.2	2,658,670
Over 2,000	412,556	403,338	-2.2	178,408
Total	6,175,771	7,038,108	14.0	2,917,854
(of which diesel)	(75,514)	(174,901)	131.6	...

Source: Japan Automobile Manufacturers' Association (Jama).

Examining production by engine size group it can be seen that the only category to suffer a reversal was the over 2,000 cc sector. Interestingly, after being on the decline since 1977, the up to 550 cc group bounced back significantly in 1980 to record a near 12 per cent gain.

Another interesting feature is the growing volume of diesel engined cars produced, with a 131.6 per cent gain in 1980 over 1979. In terms of penetration, diesel engined cars are still insignificant, yet they grew from 1.2 per cent of total output in 1979 to 2.5 per cent in 1980.

During the opening five months of 1981 further gains have been notched up by the industry. At just over 2.9 mn units, output has risen by 2.3 per cent. The pattern of production in 1981 has confirmed the trends noted last year, with an increase in the two smaller engine size categories and a further decline above 2,000 cc.

– and all manufacturers share in these gains

Table 2 shows that the good times of 1980 were enjoyed by all manufacturers.

Table 2

Japanese Passenger Car Production by Manufacturer

	1979	1980	% change 1980/79	1981 (Jan-May)
Toyota	2,111,302	2,303,284	9.1	968,523
Nissan	1,738,946	1,940,615	11.6	749,786
Honda	706,375	845,514	19.7	364,573
Toyo Kogyo	647,001	736,544	13.8	342,736
Mitsubishi	528,555	659,622	24.8	257,621
Fuji	153,841	202,038	31.3	75,950
Daihatsu	133,556	155,604	16.5	69,031
Isuzu	86,397	107,057	23.9	51,631
Suzuki	69,798	87,830	25.8	38,003
Total	6,175,771	7,038,108	14.0	2,917,854

Source: Jama.

In 1979 Jama reclassified the vehicle production and export statistics to exclude production and export of non-countable KD (knocked down) sets which have a content less than 60 per cent of the complete vehicle by factory sales value. The production of non-countable KD car sets by manufacturer in 1979 and 1980 is shown in Table 3.

Table 3

Japanese Production of Non-Countable KD Passenger Car Sets

	1979	1980	% change 1980/79
Nissan	135,966	141,410	4.0
Toyota	62,900	66,840	6.3
Mitsubishi	56,304	55,584	-1.3
Toyo Kogyo	36,100	42,400	17.5
Honda	8,000	5,200	-35.0
Fuji	800	-	-100.0
Total	300,070	311,434	3.8

Source: Jama.

Apart from Toyota, the percentage increase for all companies was in double figures. As a general guide the smaller producers scored the biggest percentage gains, and the two largest producers - Toyota and Nissan - achieved relatively modest advances of 9.1 per cent and 11.6 per cent respectively. The largest percentage gain was made by Fuji, with a 31.3 per cent rise to 202,038 units. But it should be remembered that Toyota's absolute gain - of 191,982 units - was approximately the equivalent of the combined 1980 output of the two smallest producers, Isuzu and Suzuki.

Production of non-countable KD passenger car kits showed a more restrained advance of 3.8 per cent, with individual company fortunes more mixed. It is worth making the point that the number two producer (Nissan) is far more active than the number one (Toyota) in assembly operations overseas, as is evident from Table 3.

New registrations slip back -

The Japanese market for passenger cars retreated in 1980 in sympathy with the slowing down of the economy. At 2,854,185 units, sales were 6 per cent below 1979's level. The only engine size group to maintain its volume was the up to 550 cc sector which recorded a 2.2 per cent gain. The middle group (551-2,000 cc) fell by about the average, while above 2,000 cc there was a sharp fall of 15.1 per cent. These developments indicate that the Japanese motorist is becoming increasingly conscious about fuel economy.

In the first five months of 1981 the market has continued to weaken slightly, by 2.8 per cent to 1,166,071 units.

Table 4

New Registrations of Passenger Cars in Japan by Engine Size Group

Cubic capacity	1979	1980	% change 1980/79	1981 (Jan-May)
Up to 550	170,250	174,039	2.2	72,357
551-2,000	2,781,888	2,608,215	-6.2	1,064,176
Over 2,000	84,721	71,931	-15.1	29,538
Total	3,036,859	2,854,185	-6.0	1,166,071

Source: Japan Automobile Dealers' Association.

Apart from Suzuki and Isuzu all domestic manufacturers experienced a setback. Imports fell back by a disappointing 25.4 per cent, at which level they account for a paltry 1.6 per cent of the market (2 per cent in 1979).

Table 5

New Registrations of Passenger Cars by Make in Japan

	1979	1980	% change 1980/1979	1981 (Jan-May)
Toyota	1,142,293	1,064,172	-6.8	446,607
Nissan	890,427	828,158	-7.0	326,603
Mitsubishi	266,780	250,706	-6.0	105,960
Toyo Kogyo	203,133	196,560	-3.2	89,848
Honda	175,919	166,975	-5.1	69,143
Daihatsu	99,934	91,181	-8.8	35,549
Fuji	82,197	77,192	-6.1	24,593
Suzuki	65,554	71,555	9.2	25,593
Isuzu	50,474	62,806	24.4	25,552
Imports	60,161	44,871	-25.4	16,623
Total	3,036,872	2,854,176	-6.0	1,166,071

Source: Japan Automobile Dealers' Association.

Further details of imports by country of origin and supplier are provided in Table 6.

Table 6

Passenger Car Imports by Make and Size Group

	1979			1980		
	Small	Large	Total	Small	Large	Total
West Germany						
Volkswagen/Audi	19,344	1,842	21,186	16,677	1,128	17,805
Daimler–Benz	–	5,341	5,341	–	3,887	3,887
BMW	2,556	1,514	4,070	1,946	1,241	3,187
Others	1,839	679	2,518	670	489	1,159
Total	23,739	9,376	33,115	19,293	6,745	26,038
USA						
General Motors	4	8,671	8,675	80	5,889	5,979
Ford	–	6,895	6,895	3	4,443	4,446
Others	511	658	1,169	290	353	633
Total	515	16,224	16,739	373	10,685	11,058
UK						
BL	2,216	898	3,114	2,375	757	3,132
Others	880	132	1,012	436	105	541
Total	3,096	1,030	4,126	2,811	862	3,673
Italy						
Fiat	1,168	–	1,168	714	–	714
Others	1,286	99	1,385	897	73	970
Total	2,454	99	2,553	1,611	73	1,684
Sweden						
Volvo	–	1,712	1,712	–	1,243	1,243
Saab	124	–	124	102	–	102
Total	124	1,712	1,836	102	1,243	1,345
France						
Peugeot Citroën	1,040	448	1,488	568	251	819
Renault	303	–	303	253	–	253
Others	1	–	1	–	–	–
Total	1,344	448	1,792	821	251	1,072
Others	–	–	–	1	–	1
Grand total	31,272	28,889	60,161	25,012	19,859	44,871
Total new registrations (over 550 cc)	2,781,888	84,721	2,866,609	2,608,215	71,931	2,680,146
Market penetration (%)	1.1	34.1	2.1	1.0	27.6	1.7

Note: The definition of small and large cars is according to Japanese number plate classifications. Small cars have five figure plates and are 4.7 m or less in length, 1.7 m or less in width and have an engine capacity of 2,000 cc or less, but excluding cars under 550 cc. Large cars have three figure plates.

Source: Japan Automobile Importers' Association.

- but exports surge ahead

The reason for the Japanese motor industry's impressive production performance
in 1980 rests solely on higher exports. A 27.2 per cent increase propelled shipments
to an all time record 3,947,160 units. Some measure of the nature of this achievement can be gained from the fact that the increase in exports amounted to almost
0.85 mn units. It also means that Japanese passenger car exports have more than
doubled in five years.

Table 7

Japanese Passenger Car Exports by Engine Size Group

Cubic capacity	1979	1980	% change 1980/79	1981 (Jan-May)
Up to 550	11,690	21,124	80.7	12,695
551-2,000	2,735,309	3,580,623	30.9	1,626,602
Over 2,000	354,991	345,413	-2.7	154,866
Total	3,101,990	3,947,160	27.2	1,794,163

Source: Jama.

The increase in the up to 550 cc category was especially impressive, but the industry
must have been disappointed that exports of the (higher value) over 2,000 cc models
recorded a slight decline. This is probably more a reflection of difficult market
conditions in the more affluent Western countries than a failure on the part of the
Japanese producers to make acceptable models in that sector.

Given prevailing economic conditions worldwide, it is perhaps surprising that export
volume has made further progress in 1981. Up to the end of May shipments were
10 per cent up on the corresponding level of 1980 at 1,794,163 units.

Examining exports by region reveals that notable gains were secured everywhere
except Africa, where a modest 6.3 per cent advance occurred. Activity was especially
marked in Latin America - an area of potentially significant growth. In the increasingly
sensitive markets of North America and Western Europe the Japanese suppliers
recorded a slightly below average expansion rate, but even so exports moved ahead
appreciably. North America remained easily the most important market, taking
50.1 per cent of total shipments in 1980. Europe was the next most important market
with 25.5 per cent of shipments. An interesting feature of Japan's marketing thrust
into Europe in 1980 was the 50.2 per cent rise in exports to non-EEC markets.
This is of great concern to the EEC vehicle makers because these are exactly the
markets which have traditionally been the preserve of companies such as Fiat,
Renault, Volkswagen, Ford etc. And they are markets where governments are less
likely to take action against Japanese imports.

The following four tables provide details of various aspects of Japan's export efforts
in 1980. Table 10 shows that all manufacturers boosted their exports in 1980.

Table 8

Japanese Passenger Car Exports by Region

	1979	1980	% change 1980/79	1981 (1st Qtr)
North America[a]	1,607,644	1,977,467	23.0	503,157
Europe	808,792	1,007,532	24.6	286,270
of which:				
EEC	(645,934)	(762,850)	18.1	(221,850)
non-EEC	(162,858)	(244,682)	50.2	(64,420)
South East Asia	162,782	233,544	43.5	69,554
Middle East	179,908	241,452	34.2	55,693
Central & South America	113,158	211,998	87.3	66,195
Africa	80,036	85,040	6.3	37,718
Oceania	149,499	189,861	27.0	53,276
Domestic exports	171	266	55.6	1,966
Total	3,101,990	3,947,160	27.2	1,073,829

a USA and Canada.

Source: Jama.

Table 9

Japanese Exports of Non-Countable KD Passenger Car Sets

	1979	1980	% change 1980/79
Australia	118,132	105,072	-11.1
South Africa	63,008	103,260	63.9
Mexico	38,600	43,204	11.9
Taiwan	44,486	37,800	-15.0
South Korea	16,800	8,400	-50.0
Total	281,026	297,736	5.9

Source: Jama.

311

Table 10

Japanese Passenger Car Exports by Manufacturer

	1979	1980	% change 1980/79	1981 (Jan-May)
Toyota	905,392	1,149,420	27.0	489,656
Nissan	836,680	1,041,113	24.4	440,827
Honda	539,231	651,142	20.8	306,344
Toyo Kogyo	434,662	500,348	15.1	269,839
Mitsubishi	243,720	360,242	47.8	155,105
Fuji	71,551	126,281	76.5	54,985
Daihatsu	30,931	57,590	86.2	35,152
Isuzu	36,008	44,909	24.7	26,877
Suzuki	3,815	16,115	322.4	15,378
Total	3,101,990	3,947,160	27.2	1,794,163

Source: Jama.

Table 11

Japanese Exports of Non-Countable KD Car Sets by Manufacturer

	1979	1980	% change 1980/79
Nissan	140,126	135,684	-3.2
Toyota	63,880	67,800	6.1
Mitsubishi	36,720	43,872	19.5
Toyo Kogyo	34,100	43,380	27.2
Honda	5,400	7,000	29.6
Fuji	800	–	-100.0
Total	281,026	297,736	5.9

Source: Jama.

The prospects for 1982

Table 12 provides details of our forecasts of new registrations, exports and production in 1982. Following slacker conditions in the domestic market during 1981 it is anticipated that cautious recovery will occur in 1982 as the Western economies begin their much heralded (and hoped for) recovery. It is doubtful, though, whether the upturn will be other than modest, and therefore we are predicting a return to the level of 1980 which was itself almost 0.2 mn units below the record sales of 1979. It is difficult to become excited about the prospects for the importers, although a slight boost could occur in 1982 - as much as anything to recover the ground lost in the last couple of years. The Japanese market, however, is likely to remain the almost exclusive property of the domestic suppliers. In any case, when recovery comes the Americans and Europeans will turn their attention to supplying their own booming markets - and those of their near neighbours - rather than the exceptionally difficult Japanese market on the other side of the world.

On the question of exports the position is a good deal more hazy. The most important development recently was the undertaking by the Japanese to limit their shipments to the USA in 1981 to 1.68 mn units (compared with 1.82 mn in 1980). This is not a quota and has not been imposed by the US government. But there is the clear inference that if the Japanese cannot restrain themselves someone will do it for them - and in a way which will hurt a lot more. Initially it was felt that extra shipments would be diverted to Europe to make up the shortfall, but the Europeans too have been applying muscle. For 1981 it is probable that exports will slightly exceed 1980's outturn - but only because they made such a good start to the year. Indeed, our forecast in Table 12 implies a marked slowdown in the second half of the year, a slowdown which continues into 1982.

The implications for production is a fall of about 4.8 per cent in 1981 over 1980 to 6.7 mn units, and a further slip in 1982 to 6.5 mn units. Thus, there could be the unusual spectacle of Japanese output falling at a time of general recovery elsewhere. If they keep to their agreements with the USA and Europe it is difficult at the moment to visualise any other outcome.

Table 12

Forecasts of Passenger Car Sales and Production in Japan

	1979	1980	1981 forecast	1982 forecast	% change 1982/80
New registrations	3,036,872	2,854,176	2,750,000	2,850,000	-0.1
domestic	2,976,711	2,809,305	2,710,000	2,800,000	-0.3
imports	60,161	44,871	40,000	50,000	11.4
Exports	3,101,990	3,947,160	3,990,000	3,700,000	-6.3
Production	6,175,771	7,038,108	6,700,000	6,500,000	-7.7

Source: EIU forecasts.

COMMERCIAL VEHICLES

A new record level of production

As with the passenger car sector, a new record level of output was achieved in the commercial vehicle sector in 1980. Production, at just over 4 mn units, was 15.8 per cent ahead of 1979's outturn. The only major area of weakness occurred at the heavier end of the goods vehicle range; trucks of over 8 tons carrying capacity fell by 27 per cent, while articulated units expanded by only 2 per cent. In contrast, there was a giant leap in output of goods vehicles of 4 to 6 tons carrying capacity and an even bigger increase in the case of small buses (of up to 30 passengers). Table 13 provides the details.

Table 13

Japanese Commercial Vehicle Production by Type

	1979	1980	% change 1980/79	1981 (Jan-May)
Light trucks up to 2 tons loading capacity				
Midget (up to 550 cc)	733,762	914,679	24.7	434,328
Other light trucks	1,892,696	2,113,311	11.7	853,768
Total light trucks	2,626,458	3,027,990	15.3	1,288,096
Trucks over 2 tons loading capacity				
3-4 tons	629,286	745,263	18.4	...
4-6 tons	34,851	50,359	44.5	...
6-8 tons	15,776	18,139	15.0	...
8 tons & over	75,638	55,246	-27.0	...
Articulated units	10,226	10,428	2.0	...
Special purpose vehicles	4,979	5,763	15.7	...
Total trucks over 2 tons	770,756	885,198	14.8	376,813
Buses				
Up to 30 passengers	47,011	75,118	59.8	43,079
Over 30 passengers	15,550	16,470	5.9	7,310
Total buses	62,561	91,588	46.4	50,389
Total commercial vehicles	3,459,775	4,004,776	15.8	1,715,298

Source: Jama.

Tables 14 and 15 provide details of goods vehicle and bus production by manufacturer respectively.

With the exception of Hino, all Japanese producers of goods vehicles increased their output in 1980. Toyota remained the undisputed leader, accounting for 24.4 per cent of total production. The sector's momentum continued into the early months of 1981; up to the end of May the industry had produced 1,664,909 units, a 4.1 per cent gain over the corresponding period of 1980.

There were some spectacular gains in the bus sector, with Nissan, Toyo Kogyo and Daihatsu each more than doubling their output over the previous year. More modest gains were made by the other companies - except for Mitsubishi which was the only company to suffer a decline. Bus production has made an excellent start to 1981, with output up by 40.6 per cent to 50,389 to the end of May. As was the case last year, the higher output arises chiefly from the buoyancy of the small bus category.

For the record, Table 16 provides details of production of non-countable KD commercial vehicle sets by manufacturer.

Table 14

Japanese Goods Vehicle Production by Manufacturer

	1979	1980	% change 1980/79	1981 (Jan-May)
Toyota	858,094	954,200	11.2	408,419
Nissan	587,441	678,646	15.5	276,980
Mitsubishi	402,110	438,063	8.9	179,569
Suzuki	275,137	380,853	38.4	180,066
Toyo Kogyo	322,482	379,517	17.7	139,923
Isuzu	331,286	356,342	7.6	136,972
Daihatsu	232,171	274,981	18.4	132,804
Fuji	180,449	223,595	23.9	107,266
Honda	95,494	111,388	16.6	60,070
Hino	71,248	69,003	-3.2	26,139
Nissan Diesel	40,908	45,788	11.9	16,382
Others	394	812	106.1	319
Total trucks	3,397,214	3,913,188	15.2	1,664,909

Source: Jama.

Table 15

Japanese Bus Production by Manufacturer

	1979	1980	% change 1980/79	1981 (Jan-May)
Toyota	26,829	35,860	33.7	18,696
Nissan	11,434	24,791	116.8	17,772
Isuzu	7,105	8,728	22.8	3,122
Mitsubishi	7,852	7,245	-7.7	3,485
Hino	5,260	5,887	11.9	3,098
Toyo Kogyo	1,938	4,955	155.7	2,437
Nissan Diesel	1,525	2,333	53.0	1,024
Daihatsu	618	1,789	189.5	755
Total buses	62,561	91,588	46.4	50,389

Source: Jama.

Table 16

Japanese Production of Non-Countable
KD Commercial Vehicle Sets by Manufacturer

	1979			1980		
	Trucks	Buses	Total	Trucks	Buses	Total
Nissan	38,320	–	38,320	46,928	–	46,928
Toyo Kogyo	26,560	–	26,560	31,160	–	31,160
Toyota	14,060	–	14,060	19,810	–	19,810
Mitsubishi	10,110	–	10,110	19,218	252	19,470
Fuji	12,900	–	12,900	9,500	–	9,500
Nissan Diesel	–	450	450	–	380	380
Total	101,950	450	102,400	126,616	632	127,248

Source: Jama.

The domestic market: a notable weakness in the medium and heavy sectors

The slowdown of the Japanese economy took its toll in the domestic market for
trucks of over 2 tons loading capacity. Sales fell by a hefty 16.8 per cent to 154,472
units. This reflected the more cautious approach to business investment in the light
of economic uncertainty. The light truck sector managed to secure a modest gain
(of 4 per cent to 1,983,446 units) but only because of an extremely buoyant demand
for midget units of up to 550 cc. Other light trucks fell back by 6.3 per cent. The
bus market too was dull, total sales being down by 2.5 per cent to 23,387 units,
with the fall spread more or less evenly between small and large buses. The
overall result of these changes left the total market 2.1 per cent down at 2,161,305
units.

In broad terms this pattern has continued into 1981. Figures for the first five
months show that new registrations of trucks of over 2 tons carrying capacity fell
back by a further 23 per cent, while midget units rose by 24.9 per cent. New
registrations of buses were down by 2.3 per cent.

Table 17

New Registrations of Commercial Vehicles by Type in Japan

	1979	1980	% change 1980/79	1981 (Jan–May)
Light trucks up to 2 tons loading capacity				
Midget (up to 550 cc)	686,494	839,279	22.3	396,933
Other light trucks	1,220,668	1,144,167	–6.3	477,136
Total light trucks	1,907,162	1,983,446	4.0	874,069
Trucks over 2 tons loading capacity	185,732	154,472	–16.8	56,903
Buses				
Up to 30 passengers	14,396	13,973	–2.9	6,311
Over 30 passengers	9,589	9,414	–1.8	4,694
Total buses	23,985	23,387	–2.5	11,005
Total commercial vehicles	2,116,879	2,161,305	2.1	941,977

Source: Japanese Automobile Dealers' Association.

Tables 18 and 19 provide details of new registrations by manufacturer for goods vehicles and buses respectively.

Table 18

New Registrations of Goods Vehicles by Manufacturer in Japan

	1979	1980	% change 1980/79	1981 (Jan-May)
Toyota	463,713	424,963	-8.4	177,213
Nissan	340,278	335,040	-1.5	149,250
Suzuki	229,345	301,415	31.4	135,955
Mitsubishi	274,383	271,049	-1.2	113,832
Daihatsu	186,859	196,338	5.1	91,231
Toyo Kogyo	200,918	195,279	-2.8	72,323
Isuzu	145,738	127,379	-12.6	53,907
Fuji	81,653	114,023	39.6	56,479
Honda	86,946	103,952	19.6	56,313
Hino	54,467	43,873	-19.5	15,890
Nissan Diesel	28,594	24,607	-13.9	8,579
Imports	-	-	-	-
Total trucks	2,092,894	2,137,918	2.2	930,972

Source: Japanese Automobile Dealers' Association.

Table 19

New Registrations of Buses by Manufacturer in Japan

	1979	1980	% change 1980/79	1981 (Jan-May)
Mitsubishi	5,893	5,673	-3.7	2,718
Toyota	5,040	5,216	3.5	2,304
Isuzu	4,486	4,659	3.9	2,235
Hino	3,341	3,307	-1.0	1,538
Nissan	3,947	3,241	-17.9	1,517
Nissan Diesel	1,024	1,081	5.6	599
Toyo Kogyo	254	210	-17.3	94
Total buses	23,985	23,387	-2.5	11,005

Source: Japanese Automobile Dealers' Association.

Exports advanced significantly in 1980

Exports of Japanese commercial vehicles in 1980 totalled 2,019,801 units, a 38.3 per cent rise on 1979. All sectors shared in these bright conditions, as can be seen from Table 20. Moreover, further gains have been achieved in the first five months of 1981. During this period truck shipments have increased by 11.4 per cent, gains of 10.9 per cent and 14.2 per cent being recorded in the under 2 tons class and over 2 tons class respectively. Bus exports have increased even more remarkably, by 79.4 per cent to 40,790 units.

Table 20

Japanese Commercial Vehicle Exports by Type

	1979	1980	% change 1980/79	1981 (Jan-May)
Light trucks up to 2 tons loading capacity				
Midget (up to 550 cc)	40,613	73,177	80.2	41,575
Other light trucks	1,107,420	1,548,251	39.8	663,791
Total light trucks	1,148,033	1,621,428	41.2	705,366
Trucks over 2 tons loading capacity	275,897	332,257	20.4	142,665
Buses				
Up to 30 passengers	30,778	58,500	90.1	37,091
Over 30 passengers	6,083	7,616	25.2	3,699
Total buses	36,861	66,116	79.4	40,790
Total commercial vehicles	1,460,791	2,019,801	38.3	888,821

Source: Jama.

Table 21 shows that increased shipments were the order of the day for all regions during 1980. North America came off relatively lightly with a "mere" 14.2 per cent increase, but elsewhere some enormous gains were seen. Of particular worry to the Europeans must be the 92 per cent gain to "other European" markets - let alone the 34.1 per cent rise to EEC countries. Friction has been caused in various markets following the sales success of Japanese light van models. In the UK, for example, an attempt has been made to make them subject to the same restrictions as applied to cars.

Table 21

Exports of Japanese Commercial Vehicles by Region

	1979	1980	% change 1980/79
North America	538,622	615,110	14.2
EEC	112,425	150,788	34.1
Other Europe	35,748	68,634	92.0
South East Asia	233,357	347,572	48.9
Middle East	209,189	301,503	44.1
Central & South America	93,541	170,233	82.0
Africa	153,734	237,289	54.4
Oceania	82,979	127,004	53.1
Domestic exports	1,196	1,668	39.5
Total exports	1,460,791	2,019,801	38.3

Source: Jama.

Details of goods vehicle and bus exports by manufacturer are given in the following two tables. No manufacturer failed to increase its exports in 1980.

Table 22

Japanese Exports of Goods Vehicles by Manufacturer

	1979	1980	% change 1980/79	1981 (Jan-May)
Toyota	458,120	604,673	32.0	269,103
Nissan	289,526	405,085	39.9	173,600
Isuzu	173,600	222,853	28.4	81,728
Mitsubishi	127,485	208,815	63.8	93,443
Toyo Kogyo	144,603	194,518	34.5	75,157
Fuji	103,100	105,898	2.7	51,601
Daihatsu	47,117	83,047	76.3	36,519
Suzuki	45,205	79,965	76.9	45,435
Hino	16,302	22,625	38.8	9,038
Nissan Diesel	11,153	18,362	64.6	9,389
Honda	7,719	7,844	1.6	3,018
Total	1,423,930	1,953,685	37.2	848,031

Source: Jama.

Table 23

Japanese Exports of Buses by Manufacturer

	1979	1980	% change 1980/79	1981 (Jan-May)
Toyota	20,136	31,352	55.7	15,476
Nissan	7,985	19,629	145.8	16,775
Toyo Kogyo	1,702	4,541	166.8	3,466
Isuzu	2,204	3,650	65.6	941
Hino	1,860	2,689	44.6	1,723
Daihatsu	774	1,687	118.0	829
Mitsubishi	1,496	1,639	9.6	1,075
Nissan Diesel	704	929	32.0	505
Total	36,861	66,116	79.4	40,790

Source: Jama.

The outlook for 1982

The dull conditions currently apparent in the domestic market are forecast to continue into 1982, resulting in a further slight decline in new registrations. However, it is possible that exports will be able more than to meet this shortfall in output for the domestic market with the result that the overall production level will harden slightly.

Table 24

Forecasts of Japanese Commercial Vehicle Sales and Production

	1979	1980	1981 (estimate)	1982 (forecast)	% change 1982/80
Light trucks up to 2 tons loading capacity					
Midget (up to 550 cc)					
Domestic registrations	686,494	839,279	850,000	875,000	4.3
Exports	40,613	73,177	100,000	125,000	70.8
Production	733,762	914,679	1,050,000	1,100,000	20.3
Other light trucks[a]					
Domestic registrations	1,220,668	1,144,167	1,000,000	925,000	-19.2
Exports	1,107,420	1,548,251	1,575,000	1,600,000	3.3
Production	1,892,696	2,113,311	2,050,000	2,000,000	-5.4
Total light trucks					
Domestic registrations	1,907,162	1,983,446	1,950,000	1,800,000	-9.2
Exports	1,148,033	1,621,428	1,675,000	1,725,000	6.4
Production	2,626,458	3,027,990	3,100,000	3,100,000	2.4
Trucks 2 tons loading capacity & over[a]					
Domestic registrations	185,732	154,472	150,000	150,000	-2.9
Exports	275,897	332,257	325,000	325,000	-2.2
Production	770,756	885,198	900,000	900,000	1.7
Buses					
Domestic registrations	23,985	23,387	23,000	23,000	-1.7
Exports	36,861	66,116	87,000	97,000	46.7
Production	62,561	91,558	110,000	120,000	31.1
Total commercial vehicles					
Domestic registrations	2,116,879	2,161,305	2,023,000	1,973,000	-8.7
Exports	1,460,791	2,019,801	2,087,000	2,147,000	6.3
Production	3,459,775	4,004,746	4,110,000	4,120,000	2.9

a The definition of light trucks and trucks is different for sales and production.

Source: EIU forecasts.